REGIONAL SECURITY IN THE THIRD WORLD

Regional Security in the Third World

CASE STUDIES FROM SOUTHEAST ASIA AND
THE MIDDLE EAST

Edited by Mohammed Ayoob

WESTVIEW PRESS
Boulder, Colorado

Published in 1986 in the United States of America by Westview Press, Inc., 5500 Central Avenue, Boulder, Colorado 80301; Frederick A. Praeger, Publisher

Published in 1986 in Great Britain by Croom Helm, Ltd., Provident House, Burrell Row, Beckenham, Kent, BR3 1AT

ISBN 0-8133-0375-3

Library of Congress Card Number: 85-52325

Printed and bound in Great Britain

CONTENTS

Preface

Part 1: Regional Security, the Third World and World Order

Part 2: Intra-state Dimensions of Regional Security

Part 3: Inter-state Dimensions of Regional Security

PREFACE

This volume is the outcome of a workshop on Problems of Regional Security in the Middle East and Southeast Asia held in June 1984 in Singapore. The workshop was jointly organized by the Institute of Southeast Asian Studies, Singapore, and the Al-Ahram Centre for Political and Strategic Studies, Cairo.

The workshop, which brought together a number of scholars from Southeast Asia, the Middle East, India and the UK, generated a lively discussion on problems of regional security in a comparative framework.

The papers, which were written from diverse regional and political perspectives, were revised by the authors in the light of their discussions and comments at the three-day workshop.

While the different papers, now the various chapters in this book, retain their individuality, they have all attempted to address certain basic themes and issues which were raised in the working document on 'Regional Security and the Third World', now Chapter 1 of the book, which was circulated to workshop participants well ahead of the meeting. This helped to move the discussion and the papers themselves towards a comparative assessment of regional security issues and also to generate certain general hypotheses which could be tested in the Southeast Asian and the Middle Eastern contexts, as well as in the larger Third World arena.

As the editor, I have not tampered with the substantive propositions and analyses in the various papers, which, therefore, retain their individual flavour. This would, in any case, have been a futile attempt given the diversity of perspectives and the calibre of the workshop participants. All I have tried to do is to impose some order on the issues discussed by presenting the chapters in a sequence that appears logical and makes the transition from one subject to another smooth and relatively easy for the reader. My own views on the general theme are spelt out in the first chapter of the volume.

I would like to thank Professor K. S. Sandhu, Director of the Institute of Southeast Asian Studies, Singapore, for his unfailing and enthusiastic support for this venture which I undertook initially with a certain amount of trepidation. Thanks are also due to the Al-Ahram Centre for Political and Strategic Studies, Cairo, for agreeing to act as joint organizers of the workshop, and especially to Dr El Sayed Yassin, Director of the Centre, for his warm response to my proposal that such a workshop be held. The institutional support and infrastructure provided by the administrative staff of ISEAS, led by its able Executive Secretary, Mrs Y. L. Lee, both for the workshop and in the production of this book was most invaluable and my gratitude to them cannot be adequately expressed in a sentence or two.

I am grateful to the Ford Foundation, and particularly its representative in Southeast Asia, Dr Tom Kessinger, for financial support for the workshop. Dr Ann Lesch of the Ford Foundation office in Cairo also rendered invaluable help both by her intellectual support in the planning stages of the workshop and by gracefully accepting the role of conduit for transmission of messages, between Singapore and Cairo. Miss Shanti Nair, Research Associate in the ISEAS's Regional Security Programme, was extremely helpful in the preparation of this volume, for which I am grateful. Without her assistance the chore would have been much prolonged. Finally, I would like to thank all participants in the workshop, especially the authors of the papers and the commentators, without whom there could have been no workshop and, therefore, this publication could not have seen the light of the day.

Mohammed Ayoob

REGIONAL SECURITY IN THE THIRD WORLD

PART 1: REGIONAL SECURITY, THE THIRD WORLD AND WORLD ORDER

1 REGIONAL SECURITY AND THE THIRD WORLD

Mohammed Ayoob

I

The main purpose of this chapter is not to deal with substantive issues of regional security in either Southeast Asia or the Middle East. It attempts to deal with certain conceptual issues relating to 'regional security' in the Third World in order to raise pertinent questions some of which have been addressed in this volume. It is but a modest attempt to chart certain lines of enquiry which if pursued could perhaps lead to more systematic analysis ('theorizing' is a far too ambitious word) of regional security issues in the Third World in general, and in Southeast Asia and the Middle East in particular.

The concept of regional security has become increasingly popular in recent years in the international relations literature dealing with the Third World. It is often used by political practitioners in the developing countries as well as by journalists and academics in both the Third World and the West to denote an ideal type of regional order where members of a particular regional sub-system are somehow able to attain a form of political *nirvana* by either finding acceptable solutions to their regional problems or by sweeping them so firmly under the carpet that they are not able to re-emerge to haunt them for at least the next few decades.

The term regional security makes three assumptions: (1) that external powers with interests in the region (and these interests can be subdivided into those which are region-specific and those which are offshoots or by-products of the major powers' global interests) would either willingly desist from interfering in regional issues and problems or would be effectively deterred from doing so as a result of regional cohesion and solidarity; (2) that the regional states would have succeeded in successfully managing, if not totally eliminating, problems that create frictions and antagonisms of ethnic, communal, sub-national or socio-economic character within these states themselves, thereby eliminating intra-state tensions as likely sources of inter-state conflict between or among regional states; and (3) that inter-state tensions within specific regions are at a low level (and, therefore, manageable) if not totally non-existent, and further that institutional mechanisms are available which can be used to find acceptable solutions to inter-state problems and conflicts within the region.

If one looks closely at these assumptions, particularly the latter two, underlying the concept of regional security, one would come to the conclusion that the term has been borrowed from a European or western experience which is itself the product of a decades-old process of regional integration, which in turn is based on a centuries-old process of state formation and legitimation of state structures. It is no wonder, therefore, that American political scientists like Ernst Haas[1] and Karl Deutsch[2] have influenced, if only by remote control, the ideas of those academics involved in the study of regional security in the Third World. In fact, even in the case of Europe, regional consolidation and/or security did not reach maturity until the iron-curtain had been put securely in place after the Second World War and Western and Eastern Europe were prodded towards integration, sometimes rather brazenly, by their superpower patrons.

The historical experience in the Third World — both under colonial rule and after political decolonization — has been very different. In fact, it is the differences in the two historical experiences which are related not merely to the process of regional integration but, more importantly, to the process of state formation, that make the substantive problems underlying the issue of regional security in the Third World so different from the European model from which the term has been borrowed.

It is as a result of these major differences that quite often the term 'regional order' (which is closely linked to the term regional security) in relation to Third World regions is used both by political practitioners and academics not in its 'ideal' or normative sense but as a description of a particular status quo. Others skirt the definition of the concept altogether.[3] In order to understand these differences it is imperative that we try to analyse the fundamental concept of security in the context of the Third World and compare its application therein with the way it has been traditionally applied in the developed, industrialized part of the globe.

II*

In the western and western-influenced literature on international relations, the term security has been traditionally defined to mean immunity (to varying degrees) of a state or nation to threats emanating from outside its boundaries. In the words of Walter Lippmann, 'a nation is secure to the extent to which it is not in danger of having to sacrifice core values, if it wishes to avoid war, and is able, if challenged, to maintain them by victory in such a war'.[4] According to Arnold Wolfers, Lippmann's definition 'implies that security rises and falls with the ability of a nation to deter an attack, or to defeat it. This is in accord with the common usage of the term'.[5] Expanding on the concept of security as protection of core values, in the context of small Third World states, Talukder Maniruzzaman has stated that 'By security we mean the protection and preservation of the minimum core values of any nation: political independence and territorial integrity'.[6] This position is one which we can readily identify as the *realist* position in the literature on international relations.

However, within the western tradition there have been authors who have differed significantly from this exclusively state-centric realist perspective. They have viewed the problem of security from the perspective of the international system and have focused on what has, of late, come to be called international security. By adopting this system-centred perspective they have tried to mitigate some of the more Hobbesian characteristics of the realist position. They have taken their cue from views such as those expressed by Martin Wight, who had argued that 'if there is an international society, then there is an order of some kind to be maintained, or even developed. It is not fallacious to speak of a collective interest, and security acquires a broad meaning: it can be enjoyed or pursued in common. Foreign policy will take some account of the common interest. It becomes possible to transfer to international politics some of the categories of constitutionalism.'[7]

The system-oriented approaches to security have taken the society of states ('anarchical' though it may be to use Hedley Bull's phrase[8]) as the relevant object of security. They have argued that the security of the parts of the system are inextricably intertwined

---

* Sections II to V of this paper draw heavily upon my article 'Security in the Third World: The Worm about to Turn?' *International Affairs*, vol. 60, no. 1, Winter (1983–4), pp. 41–51.

with that of the whole. The earliest of the modern systemic analysts of security — namely the idealists of the inter-war period — in fact refused to distinguish the security of the parts from that of the whole system. The post-Second World War breed of system-centred scholars has been more discriminating than its predecessors. They have argued from the assumption that the various segments of the international system were so interlinked that they were, what they called, 'interdependent'.[9] While much of the initial impetus for this line of argument came from the increasingly awesome concentration of weaponry (particularly nuclear weaponry) in the hands of the two superpowers, the economic problems facing the western industrialized countries from the early 1970s onward and the contribution of the 'oil factor' to the exacerbation of these problems concentrated western minds on interdependence as they had never done before.

However, what is most interesting for our purpose is the fact that all these contending schools of thought tended to define the concept of security in external or outward-directed terms — that is, external to the commonly accepted unit of analysis in international relations, namely the state. This definition and the process by which it was reached were both understandable as well as ethno-centric in character. They were understandable because they were the products of a particular intellectual tradition which faithfully reflected a particular process of historical and political development which could be traced back at least to the Peace of Westphalia if not to an earlier period. Moreover, between 1648 and 1945 the natural development of the 'system of states' symbolized by, if not established at, Westphalia and its interaction with the domestic political processes of the major European powers led to the legitimation both of the system and of the individual participants therein. Both these processes — of interaction among sovereign states on the one hand and greater identification of individuals with their respective states on the other, the latter helped along tremendously by the increasing correspondence between national and state boundaries and by the increasingly representative character of governments concerned — strengthened each other and in doing so firmly laid the foundations of the intellectual tradition in which, at least in terms of political analysis, the security of individuals came to be totally subsumed within the category of state security. Therefore, while there has been much debate about the compatible or incompatible nature of state security with the security of the international system and on the measures that could be taken to reconcile the two demands for security, the security of units below the level of the state has rarely, if ever, been an important point at issue in most western discussions and analyses of the concept of security.

Post-Second World War developments have strengthened these western notions of what security is all about. By dividing the western world into two halves and by stabilizing that division by means of a balance of terror, the Cold War (and its latter-day manifestation called *détente*) has frozen the predominant western connotation of 'security' in a bi-polar mould. The concept of 'alliance security' — whether of the Atlantic alliance or of the Warsaw Treaty Organization — has been, therefore, superimposed on the concept of national or state security, but its essential externally-directed thrust remains unchanged. Moreover, by making the security of the major western states — whether capitalist or socialist — the central concern of the security of the international system as a whole (by the Mutual Assured Destruction doctrine and because the security of their European allies is considered both by the US and the USSR as indispensable to their own security) the dominant strand in western strategic thinking has increasingly obliterated even the distinction between the realist (state-centric) and idealist (system-centric) approaches to the study of international security, indeed to the study of international relations as a whole.[10]

III

When we turn to the Third World, however, we find a different situation altogether.[11] The three major characteristics of the concept of state or national security in western states — its external orientation, its strong linkage with system security and its virtually indistinguishable nature from the security of the two major alliance blocs — are, in the Third World, if not totally absent, so thoroughly diluted as to be hardly recognizable when compared to their counterparts in the West.

To take the first and, in a way, the fundamental attribute of the concept of security in the West (in the sense that it is a corollary of the doctrine of state sovereignty in its pure and pristine form), that is its external directedness, one can immediately see that, despite the rhetoric of many Third World leaders, the sense of insecurity that these states — and, more particularly, their regimes — suffer from emanate to a substantial extent from within their boundaries rather than from outside. This does not mean that external threats are totally absent, for they are not. But the 'mix' of internal and external sources of threat to these state structures, and particularly to their regimes, is quite often heavily weighted in favour of internal sources. Moreover, external threats quite often augment the problems of insecurity that exist within state boundaries and, in many cases, would be quite ineffective if internal threats and domestic fissures did not exist within Third World societies.

Any perceptive observer of the South Asian scene in 1970–1 would have realized that the Indian 'threat' to Pakistan was very secondary to the one posed by East Bengali nationalists; also, that the Indo-Pakistani War of 1971 would either not have been fought or, if fought, have had a very different outcome if the bulk of the East Bengali population had not been disenchanted with the then existing structure of the Pakistani state.[12] Similarly, Iran's ideological and political 'threat' to Iraq after the Islamic Revolution of 1979, which led Saddam Hussein to launch his invasion of Iran, would not have reached the proportions it did in the Iraqi regime's perception had the government in Baghdad been more representative of the majority of its population and had it not been as narrowly based as it is today. Its invasion of Iran was, among other things, an attempt to pre-empt an anticipated popular movement against it from within — a movement that would have owed much to the demonstration effect of the success of the Iranian Revolution.[13] In Southeast Asia, one could view the Indonesian policy of 'confrontation' with Malaysia (1963–5) at least partially as a reflection of the Sukarno regime's internal problems and the lack of domestic consensus on fundamental political and economic issues.[14]

Sometimes, internal threats are 'externalized' by regimes which are the targets of such threats. They do so in order both to portray these threats as 'illegitimate' (in the sense that they emanate from abroad and violate the norm of state sovereignty and its corollary of non-intervention by other states) and to portray their repressive actions as 'legitimate'. By turning a political — and quite often a social and economic — problem into a military one and by presenting the military threat as coming from external sources, regimes in the Third World quite often try to choose an arena of confrontation with domestic dissidents that is favourable to themselves, namely, the military arena. While this strategy might work well in the initial stages of such confrontations, it usually leads to much bigger conflagrations within a decade or two of the initial, usually unorganized, outbursts of political dissent. Accumulation of sophisticated instruments of repression should not, therefore, necessarily be equated with strong state structures; in fact, quite often there is a strong negative correlation between the two phenomena.

IV

This characterization of the problem of 'security' faced by many Third World states, and its differences from the pattern of security issues faced by developed western states, has dealt so far only with what one can call, the 'symptomatic' level of this issue. The above mentioned differences are the symptoms of a much deeper divergence in the experiences of the western and Third World states. These differences are related to two major variables:

(a) the history of state formation in the Third World as compared to its counterpart in the West, and
(b) the pattern of elite recruitment and regime establishment and maintenance in the Third World as compared to the same processes in the developed states.

It is essentially the differences in these two broad interrelated areas between the western and Third World states — differences not so much in absolute and culture-based terms as in relative and time-based ones — that determine the differences in the primary security orientations of the two sets of states.

As a result of a centuries-old process of development, modern states in the industrialized western world have reached a position which can be referred to as one of 'unconditional legitimacy'.[15] Moreover, not only are the prevailing state structures in the European world (which includes North America and Australasia) legitimate, they are also strong and cohesive. In fact, the two attributes complement each other. Western states are, therefore, *strong states* (although all of them may not be strong powers they are strong in terms of their state structures). By contrast, state structures in the Third World in their present form do not enjoy unconditional legitimacy and are *weak as states* (once again, one must be careful to distinguish the term weak states from weak powers).[16]

There are many reasons for this major difference in the respective strengths of state structures of the two sets of states. The first is related to the time factor. Most states in the Third World are recent participants in the modern 'system of states' which is European in origin and in its defining characteristics. Until a few decades ago they were mere 'objects' rather than 'subjects' of international relations. Moreover, many of these states have been primarily defined by boundaries drawn by colonial powers for the sake of administrative convenience or as some form of trade-off with colonial competitors. As such, they have not developed the capacity to ensure the habitual identification of their inhabitants with the post-colonial structures that have emerged within colonially-dictated boundaries. Again, as a result of the enormous time gap between the development of *modern* state structures in the Third World and the development of the same structures in Europe, their capacity to act effectively in a system which is defined primarily by its state-centric character is low. The economic gulf between the developed and developing states, with limited and partial exceptions, adds to their ineffectiveness as participants in the system. One can, therefore, even in the 1980s speak with some justification of two types of actors in the international system — the *primary* actors (the original European members of the system and their offshoots in North America and Australasia) and the *secondary* actors (the latecomers, the bulk of the Third World).

The latter's problem is enormously compounded when one looks at the level of consensus on fundamental social and political issues within Third World societies. Western societies reached the current high level of consensus on fundamental issues of social and political organization after centuries of conflict and upheaval within them (witness the Cromwellian episode and the French Revolution as two glaring examples). Having gone through these turmoils, and having had the luxury of doing so over centuries, the present high level of consensus has been attained. For, despite the (sometimes extreme) rhetoric of the various political groupings in the West, their positions on vital political and social issues vary only marginally from each other.

However, with certain limited exceptions, this is a norm that does not prevail in the Third World. Since fundamental issues of political, social and economic organization are involved in political contests they become, literally, life and death issues for the contestants concerned. With so much at stake the ferocity of their attitudes towards one another also becomes understandable.[17] But, from the point of view of the security of Third World societies this has extremely negative consequences. The divisions within these societies — both vertical and horizontal — are exacerbated and the level and intensity of internal threats to state structures (which are identified with the ruling groups) escalates. This is one of the major reasons why in most Third World societies open political contests are not tolerated by their ruling elites.

This brings us to another major difference between western and Third World states. In the absence of a consensus on fundamental issues and in the absence of open political debate and contest, many of these states are ruled by regimes with narrow support bases — both politically and socially — which usually come to power by means of a *coup d'état* and which hang on so tenaciously to office that they have to be, more often than not, physically liquidated to pave the way for any form of political transition.[18] Since it is these regimes, and their bureaucratic and intellectual hangers-on, who define the threats to the security of their respective states, it is no wonder that they define it primarily in terms of regime security rather than the security of the society as a whole. Security, as stated above, has been traditionally defined as the protection and preservation of core values. However, in the case of many Third World states, the core values of the regime — with self-preservation at the very core of this core — are often at extreme variance with the core values cherished by large segments of the population over whom they rule.[19] Once again, given these discrepancies in the definition of core values and, indeed, of security itself, it is no wonder that major threats to the security of these regimes emanate from within their own societies.

Uneven economic development, great, growing and glaring disparities in wealth and income, communal and ethnic tensions, all contribute both to the lack of societal consensus on fundamental issues and to the unrepresentative and repressive character of most Third World states and, therefore, to the internal threats to their security and to the security of the state structures over which they preside. One cannot deny that some of these schisms exist in developed societies as well, for example, racial tensions in the US, denominational antagonisms in Northern Ireland, uneven economic development as between northern and southern Italy, Basque separatism in Spain, ethno-linguistic differences in Canada, etc. However, the scale and intensity of these fissures when compared to the overall identification of a state's population with the concept of that particular state and its unconditional acceptance of the legitimacy of the particular government in power is minimal — and certainly manageable. This is a state of affairs that does not prevail in most Third World states and, therefore, the proportions — in terms of scale and intensity — of the problem are different.

In addition to the sources of friction and conflict that exist within Third World states, the economic and social dimensions of nation-building have been made far too difficult by the workings of an international economy (which is reflected in the operation of national economies in the Third World) which increases economic disparities in both absolute and relative terms between the developed and underdeveloped states and between the rich and the poor within Third World states.[20] This makes the issue of elite-mass identification within Third World countries a near impossible task to achieve and correspondingly increases the alienation of large segments of society both from their ruling elites and quite often from the state structures over which these elites preside.

This, in turn, creates a double source of insecurity for those who claim to represent states in the Third World — for both their legitimacy and the legitimacy of state structures are open to challenge. The dimensions of the security problem — and, therefore, definitions of the concept of security itself — in the Third World are, therefore, very different from the ones applied to, and common in the literature of, the developed West.

V

This, however, is not the end of the story. There is also a remarkable divergence in the way in which the security concerns of Third World states relate to the security and stability of the international system as a whole, as compared to the relationship between the security concerns of the developed countries on the one hand and the security of the international system on the other. What is more, this divergence has grave adverse effects on Third World states as far as the systemic inputs into their security problems are concerned. I have argued earlier that the developed states' security concerns are so firmly interlinked with systemic security concerns as to make them virtually indistinguishable. Any major threat to the security of a developed state immediately takes on the character of a crisis for the whole system, particularly since it has the potential to destabilize the dominant global balance of power between the two superpowers — a balance which in turn forms the underpinning of the stability and security of the international system as it is currently organized.

This is far from the case when one considers the security problems — external or internal — of Third World states (with the possible exception of some of the major oil exporters, though even in their case the linkages between their security concerns and those of the system or of the dominant powers appear to be of an ephemeral and very limited character. There is no commitment in the developed world to the security of these states *as states*: the only commitment seems to be to the security of access to their oil resources). Even in the case of the most important and the largest countries of the Third World the link between their security and that of the system as a whole (a link that is defined, by the dominant powers in the system) is very fragile, if not totally non-existent.

This means that conflicts — whether internal or intra-regional, or even, sometimes, cross-regional — within and among states in the Third World are considered permissible by the dominant powers, *as long as they do not threaten to draw the latter into direct confrontation with each other*. The only conflict in the Third World with this sort of potential is the Arab-Israeli conflict, particularly if the balance of power in the Middle East changes dramatically to Israel's disadvantage. But this is not a typical Third World conflict, for the simple reason that Israel is — in terms of its ideological origins, its pattern of colonization in Palestine, the organization of its society and polity, the composition of its elite, its links with strong and important European and American constituencies (both Jewish and Gentile) and the intensity of one superpower's commitment to its external security (some would argue its expansion) — a European state. Israel may be physically located *in* the Third World but it is not *of* the Third World. Therefore, Israeli security is linked directly to issues of systemic security which is not the case with any other country in Asia and Africa, with the possible exception of South Africa, again for many reasons that are similar to those in Israel's case.

Thus, while setting limits to Third World conflicts (the limits being determined by the superpowers' refusal to enter into a direct confrontation over what are considered peripheral issues), the stability of the central balance not only permits local conflicts in large parts of the Third World — of an intra-state or inter-state character — but, may in fact, even encourage the eruption of such conflicts, partially as a way of letting off steam which helps to cool the temperature around the core issues which are directly relevant and considered vital to the central balance and, therefore, to the international system.[21]

The fragility of the political institutions and state structures in the Third World permit such encouragement, because they allow internal issues to take on international dimensions. Fragile polities, by definition, are easily permeable. Therefore, internal issues in Third World societies not only get transformed into inter-state issues quite readily, they also lend themselves easily to intervention by the superpowers. Traditionally inter-state rivalries, compounded by the complex disputes introduced as a result of colonially imposed boundaries, when added to internal political fragilities of Third World states provide very fertile ground for the superpower rivalry to be played out in the relatively 'safe' areas of the globe without the imminent threat of a direct confrontation between Washington and Moscow. In the process, however, they exacerbate the problem of security — no matter whether you define it in maximalist or in minimalist terms — of vast parts of the Third World.[22]

Superpower policies — and, therefore, the systemic variables as a whole — thus impinge upon the security of Third World states in a fashion extremely deleterious to those states. This is exactly the reverse of what the systemic factors achieve in the case of developed polities where they then tend to augment the security of individual states by making it virtually indivisible from the security of the whole system. In the case of Third World states, the systemic inputs add to the already destabilizing internal dynamics of Third World polities, to render these states and their regimes extremely insecure. The two processes, in fact, feed upon each other to create a vicious cycle of insecurity which has become nearly impossible to break.

VI

The foregoing discussion has made it amply clear that the very connotation of the term security in the context of the Third World is qualitatively different from what the concept connotes in the context of the developed world. When one comes to speak specifically about regional security the difference becomes much sharper. This is related to the fact that issues of regional security in the developed world are defined primarily in cold war terms (NATO versus Warsaw Pact, etc.) and are, therefore, largely indivisible from issues of systemic security. We have already referred to this relationship earlier in our discussion of alliance security.

On the other hand, most of the salient regional security issues in the Third World have a life of their own independent of superpower rivalry, although as has been stated earlier the latter, more often than not, exacerbates regional problems. This is as true of inter-state as of intra-state disputes and conflicts. Even the regional conflict which is most capable of becoming enmeshed with systemic security concerns — the Arab-Israeli conflict — is neither the product nor merely an adjunct of superpower rivalry. (It should not be forgotten that both the superpowers voted in November 1947 in the UN General Assembly for the partition of Palestine and the creation of Israel.) As a result, the regional actors are not susceptible to total, or even substantial, control on the part of the superpowers, whose actions are expected to be largely determined by systemic security concerns. In fact, as the symbiotic relationship between the US and Israel demonstrates, quite often it is the regional client that dictates the contours of the superpower's policies in the Middle East and not vice versa. On the Arab side (or sides) the autonomy of Arab aspirations — both on the part of the Palestinians and other Arabs — from superpower interests is clearly — if anything even more clearly — visible. Even the PLO, as a respected Israeli academic has very convincingly demonstrated, is in no way an unconditional ally — let alone a stooge — of the Soviet Union.[23] Recent events within the PLO and in intra-Arab politics have augmented the validity of this conclusion. Similarly, in Southeast Asia, the Vietnamese capacity for independent action either in Kampuchea or *vis-à-vis* ASEAN should not be underestimated. Hanoi does not merely, or even primarily, reflect Moscow's concerns. In fact, it is largely the other way round with Soviet policy in Southeast Asia substantially reflecting Hanoi's interests and concerns.

Therefore, we have the paradoxical situation of Third World actors being, on the one hand, easily permeable by the superpowers because of their internal fragility, but, on the other, retaining their autonomy of initiative regarding conflicts and issues that are central to regional security concerns.

Furthermore, as has already been stated in the context of our discussion of the concept of security in the Third World, there is a very thin line which divides the inter-state dimension of regional conflict from its intra-state dimension. As a result, internal fissures within Third World societies can be relatively easily transformed into international disputes susceptible to great power intervention. Again, while some of these internal cleavages within Third World societies are the result of ethnic, religious or linguistic factors, others arise out of the process of, what has been called, 'economic development'. Since, more often than not, this process is distorted in favour of certain social classes[24] and regions,[25] while at the same time being perceived by some parts of the traditionally privileged classes as being inimical to their interests,[26] it tends to create further divisions based on class and regional criteria. When these new cleavages are added to those already existing within state structures as bequeathed by the colonial powers, explosive situations quite often result.

Given the overlap between populations of neighbouring countries in terms of ethnic and religious criteria or the impossibility of preventing the mobility of populations across borders (which in many cases are not accepted as legitimate by populations living close to the colonially-imposed boundaries), other regional states either willingly or by compulsion get drawn into conflicts which in their initial stages might be confined within a single state's boundaries. The influx of refugees from East Pakistan into India (1971), from Ethiopia into Somalia (1977), from Kampuchea into Thailand (1979 onward) and from Afghanistan into Pakistan (1980 onward), have all invariably contributed towards raising the level of regional tensions.

In the light of all these considerations a number of things become clear: first, that regional security in the Third World is not a function of systemic security and that, in turn, systemic security is not dependent upon regional security or, as it is sometimes assumed, is not the sum total of regional securities. For there are regions and regions; and as far as Third World regions are concerned, with certain partial and limited exceptions, they are peripheral to the central systemic security concerns. Regional insecurities in the Third World can exist, in fact proliferate, side by side with systemic security which is determined by the stability of the central balance and the management of intra- and inter-alliance relationships in the developed world.[27]

Second, given the fragilities of most state structures in the Third World and the lack of legitimacy of many regimes that preside over these structures, attempts at creating or imposing regional security arrangements are likely to be extremely difficult, based as these attempts would be on the assumption of strong state structures and enduring and viable regimes — models borrowed from the European experience.

Third, and this has been just hinted at so far, one cannot meaningfully talk of regional security in parts of the Third World where one finds states that have emerged during the course of the twentieth century which, by almost unanimous consent within the region, are considered alien and perceived to have been imposed on these regions as a result of the European domination of the Third World. In this context the two instances that immediately come to mind are those of South Africa and Israel — both 'pariah' states embedded in the heart of possibly the two most strategically important regions, in terms of resources and geographic location, in the Third World. The great disparities in power between these two states and their neighbours further augments the perception of the two states as being alien to the respective regions in which they are geographically located. For these disparities are viewed as a function of the 'European' character of the two states concerned, both in terms of race and technology.

The capacity of the two pariah states to call upon external, particularly US, support and sustenance (potential in the case of South Africa and highly visible in the case of Israel) further heightens the regional perception of their alien, that is western, character. If successful plans for regional security are to be devised for the Middle East or southern Africa, it would be essential for the two pariah states to be integrated into their respective regions both in terms of ethos and technology. In order for this integration to take place there must be a drastic reduction in their power *vis-à-vis* their neighbours as well as a conscious dilution of their racial characteristics.

This is a necessary, though by no means sufficient, condition for regional security in the Middle East and southern Africa. Israel and South Africa, while the most important contributory factors to the insecurities in their respective regions, are not the only reasons for lack of regional security in the Middle East or southern Africa. One cannot, therefore, assert that their 'nativization' would immediately result in bright prospects for the success of regional security ventures in the two regions. As any student of Arab or African affairs would testify, there are far too many other factors — intrastate, inter-state and externally-influenced — that would still continue to obstruct the process of regional security in both the Middle East and southern Africa. However, without such nativization of the pariah states even the minimum condition for regional security would not have been met. It is in this context that statements, such as those made by former US Secretary of State, Alexander Haig, regarding the evolution of a 'strategic consensus' in the Middle East encompassing both Israel and the 'moderate' Arab states appear puerile.

One last point needs to be mentioned: the use of regional organizations as bases for regional security in the Third World. The experiences of the three major region-wide organizations, the Arab League, the Organization of American States (OAS) and the Organization of African Unity (OAU), demonstrate that two of them have by and large failed to perform regional security functions. The disarray within the Arab World and Africa which are reflected in the Arab League and the OAU are adequate testimony to this assertion. The OAS may appear to have done marginally better, but its qualified success owes a great deal to the presence of the US among its members. In this sense it has become in many ways an adjunct of one superpower's strategy towards its backyard and this has given the OAS a sense of direction in security terms that the other two organizations have lacked.

Sub-regional groupings like ASEAN and the Gulf Co-operation Council (GCC) have fared better when compared to the more ambitious organizations encompassing entire regions. However, since both organizations are to some extent themselves the products of intra-regional polarizations, their very success seems to have exacerbated further these polarizations — ASEAN v. Indo-China in Southeast Asia, the GCC v. Iran in the Gulf — for the security concerns shared by members of GCC or ASEAN are in the final analysis, shared by only a section of the regional states. Therefore, while such organizations may be considered positive developments as far as sub-regional security is concerned, one is sceptical about their function in, or contribution towards, security of whole regions. Moreover, once the currently dominant security concerns recede in importance, the future of these groupings might begin to look less optimistic than it does now. This scepticism is increased once such sub-regional organizations become attached to, or are perceived as being attached to, one of the two superpowers.

VII

Regional security in the Third World is like a chimera. There are so many problems and pitfalls on the way to the realization of this idea that like *nirvana* it has remained either unattainable or, at least, its attainment remains unverified in terms of recent political experience. Why then are analysts and policy-makers both in the Third World and within the superpowers so concerned with, if not obsessed by, this idea?

The following seem to be the major reasons: first, superpower policy-makers and their intellectual apologists view this term as a convenient one with which to clothe their own interests in and strategies towards Third World regions, particularly those regions which are of great strategic importance to Moscow and Washington.[28] It is worth remembering that attempts were made to sell both the Baghdad Pact (later renamed CENTO) and SEATO to Third World public opinion in the guise of regional or collective security plans. Similarly, in the late 1960s, Brezhnev put forward his Asian Collective Security Plan to legitimize Soviet strategies in Asia aimed primarily at China and secondarily against the United States. Therefore, quite often in the rhetoric emanating from Washington and Moscow the term regional security is used as a euphemism for secure spheres of influence in important Third World regions.

Secondly, many analysts in the West, particularly of the liberal persuasion, tend to look upon the concept as a substitute for, or the first step towards genuine regional integration — an approximation to the West European model. Some of these analysts, following the intellectual footsteps of the pre-war idealists, have even ventured to view efforts aimed at regional security/integration as preliminary steps towards a more highly institutionalized world order — one approaching their goal of world government. Idealists and liberals, often with an inadequate sense of realpolitik, have, therefore, allowed themselves to become apologists for schemes of regional security that usually emanate from outside the region concerned and add very little, if anything at all, to the security of Third World regions. In fact, quite often they tend to work in a contrary direction.

As for the Third World itself, a major reason why the term regional security attracts many policy-makers and members of the intelligentsia is related to the high level of conflict and insecurity — both within and among states — in the regions comprising the Third World. Regional security is perceived as an antidote for intra- and inter-state conflicts, especially since the two sets of conflicts in the Third World are quite often interlinked. The major fallacy with this proposition is that it ignores, or tries to dispense all too lightly with, the genuine issues of ethnic as well as socio-economic character that provide the basis for regional conflicts in the Third World. It is an attempt to delude oneself that state formation and consolidation of regional identities in the Third World can occur painlessly — a hypothesis invalidated by the experience of Europe when it was at a corresponding stage in its own history when political identities were in the process of crystallization.

In addition, narrowly-based and insecure Third World regimes, particularly those under increasing challenge domestically and regionally, use the idea of regional security to form co-operative arrangements with similar regimes in their regions to defend themselves as well as to justify their strategic and political links with external powers whose interests converge with the interests of these regimes. In this process of assuring the security of these regimes, however, they add little to regional security; in fact, they often contribute to regional polarization.

Therefore, to conclude, one cannot realistically begin to talk of genuine regional security until the 'security' of Third World states in general — a problem addressed in the first half of this chapter — becomes far less fragile than it is today. This is related to the legitimation of state structures and regimes in the Third World on the one hand, and the nature of linkages with systemic security on the other. Furthermore, the deleterious effects of superpower competition on the security of Third World states and regions would have to diminish drastically if regional security is to be enhanced. The question as to how does one succeed in delinking Third World regions from superpower rivalry and competition while at the same time strengthening their linkages with systemic security is crucial and one to which there is no easy and immediate answer. It is only the hardening of state structures within the Third World — in other words, the acceptance of their unconditional legitimacy on the part of the states' populations — and the increasingly representative and responsive, therefore, legitimate, character of their regimes, which together could provide Third World regions the autonomy from global powers and the capacity for independent influence within the international system that could make these apparently contradictory goals simultaneously attainable. But, this is sure to be a long drawn out process; until then the Third World must resign itself to live in regionally — as in many other ways — insecure conditions.

Notes

1. Ernst B. Haas, *The Uniting of Europe* (Stanford University Press, Stanford, California, 1958).
2. Karl Deutsch *et al.*, *Political Community and the North Atlantic Area* (Princeton University Press, Princeton, 1957).
3. For example, Michael Leifer, *Conflict and Regional Order in Southeast Asia*, Adelphi Papers, no. 162 (IISS, London, 1980).
4. Walter Lippmann, *US Foreign Policy: Shield of the Republic* (Little Brown, Boston, 1943). p. 51.
5. Arnold Wolfers, *Discord and Collaboration: Essays on International Politics* (Johns Hopkins Press, Baltimore, 1962), p. 150.
6. Talukder Maniruzzaman, *The Security of Small States in the Third World*, Canberra Papers on Strategy and Defence, no. 25, Strategic and Defence Studies Centre (Australian National University, Canberra, 1982), p. 15.
7. Martin Wight, 'Western Values in International Relations' in Herbert Butterfield and Martin Wight (eds) *Diplomatic Investigations* (George Allen & Unwin, London, 1966), p. 103.
8. Hedley Bull, *The Anarchical Society* (Macmillan, London, 1977).
9. For example, see Robert O. Keohane and Joseph S. Nye, *Power and Interdependence* (Little Brown, Boston, 1977).
10. The coincidence of the two approaches is probably best reflected in Leonard Beaton, *The Reform of Power: A Proposal for an International Security System* (Chatto & Windus, London, 1972).
11. The term 'Third World' is used in this paper in a generic sense and deliberately so. It is undoubtedly true that there are diverse elements that constitute the Third World; it is also true that there are intra-mural problems, conflicts and antagonistic relations prevalent within the Third World. However, the Third World countries share enough in terms of their colonial past and their unequal encounter with the European powers following the Industrial Revolution to set them apart from the European states which have traditionally formed the 'core' of the modern system of states. They also share attributes of economic underdevelopment and social dislocation, which are at least partially attributable to their encounter with the West (and which have continued even after the formal process of decolonization

has been completed). They are still inadequately linked to the issue-areas which dominate the international system as it is constituted today, despite all the rhetoric that surrounds such debates as those regarding the New International Economic Order (NIEO). They are, as I have argued later in the paper, still, to a substantial extent, the *objects* rather than the *subjects* of international relations. This makes all the difference in the way they influence and are influenced by the international system and the dominant actors therein. Some of these arguments are foreshadowed in my chapter, 'Autonomy and Intervention: Super Powers and the Third World', in Robert O'Neill and D. M. Horner (eds), *New Directions in Strategic Thinking* (George Allen & Unwin, London, 1981), pp. 104–16.

12. For a systematic account of growing East Bengali disenchantment with the concept of Pakistan, see Rounaq Jahan, *Pakistan: Failure in National Integration* (Columbia University Press, New York, 1972).

13. I have argued this at some length and related it to the history of state formation and the pattern of elite recruitment in both Iraq and Iran, in my chapter 'Perspectives from the Gulf: Regime Security or Regional Security?' in Donald H. Macmillen, *Asian Perspectives on International Security* (Macmillan, London, 1984), pp. 92–116.

14. For various explanatory theories of Indonesian behaviour during its 'confrontation' see J. A. C. Mackie, *Konfrontasi: The Indonesian-Malaysian Dispute 1963–1966* (Oxford University Press, Kuala Lumpur, 1974), pp. 326–33. The explanation mentioned in the text is most strongly argued in Donald Hindley, 'Indonesia's Confrontation with Malaysia: A Search for Motives', *Asian Survey*, vol. 4, no. 6, June (1964), pp. 904–13.

15. For a most valuable account of the origins and growth, both in geographical and chronological terms, of the modern system of states centred on the European states, see Martin Wight, *Systems of States* (Leicester University Press, 1977), Chapters 4 and 5. Also, from different perspectives, see Joseph R. Strayer, *On the Medieval Origins of the Modern State* (Princeton University Press, Princeton, NJ, 1970); Leonard Tivey (ed.), *The Nation-State: The Formation of Modern Politics* (Martin Robertson, Oxford, 1981); and Ralph Pettman, *State and Class* (Croom Helm, London, 1979).

16. For a discussion of the concepts of weak and strong states as against weak and strong powers, see Barry Buzan, *People, States and Fear* (Wheatsheaf Books, Brighton, Sussex, 1983), pp. 65–9.

17. Indonesia, Pakistan, Nigeria, Cyprus, Iran, Nicaragua, El-Salvador, Guatemala, all testify to this pattern.

18. Again, the examples are galore, stretching from Iraq under the Hashemites to Nicaragua under Somoza.

19. Sometimes even the maintenance of existing state boundaries is not considered a core value by important segments of a state's population.

20. Among other sources on this subject, see the two reports published by the Brandt Commission: *North-South: A Programme for Survival* (Pan Books, London and Sydney, 1980), and *Common Crisis, North-South: Cooperation for World Recovery* (Pan Books, London and Sydney, 1983).

21. This argument has been developed in Sisir Gupta, 'Great Power Relations, World Order and the Third World', *Foreign Affairs Reports*, vol. 17, nos. 7–8, July/August (1978).

22. For details of this argument and case studies demonstrating its validity, see Mohammed Ayoob (ed.), *Conflict and Intervention in the Third World* (Croom Helm, London, 1980).

23. See Galia Golan, *The Soviet Union and the Palestine Liberation Organization: An Uneasy Alliance* (Praeger, New York, 1980).

24. For example, the 'comprador bourgeoisie', for the lack of a better word, in Egypt, under Sadat's policy of *infitah* (opening towards the West).

25. For example, West Pakistan in the case of united Pakistan during the 1950s and 1960s.

26. For example, the *bazaris* (the traditional merchant class) in Iran under the Shah during the 1960s and the 1970s.

27. I have developed this theme further in my paper 'The Role of the Third World in the East-West Relationship' in *The Conduct of East-West Relations in the 1980s, Part III, Adelphi Papers* (IISS, London), no. 191, pp. 43–9.

28. For one example, see Michael Nacht, 'Toward an American Conception of Regional Security', *Daedalus*, Winter (1981), pp. 1–22.

COMMENTS

Chandran Jeshurun

It is only right and proper that any serious discussion of the security problems of two strategically important regions such as the Middle East and Southeast Asia should begin with a meaningful survey of the past record of the scholarly work that has been done on the subject. The thought-provoking and stimulating paper by Mohammed Ayoob is, admittedly, a useful way of looking at one of the possible conceptualizations of the whole problem of conflict situations in both these regions. It is difficult to imagine how the problem of regional security can be understood without some idea to begin with of the concept itself. After all, the end of the Second World War clearly signalled the renewal of hostilities in a variety of forms, and the vast majority of such armed conflicts have indeed taken place in those parts of the Third World such as the two regions under study. The difficulty, however, arises not so much over the acceptance of the fact of such conflict-prone situations as from the very definition of the concept of regional security itself. Ayoob has offered us a singularly challenging interpretation which has, indeed, been something of a vogue with many Third World students of the subject, more particularly amongst those from the Indian sub-continent. His cogent analysis, however, needs to be treated with some caution when it is applied to the peculiar evolution of regional security in the Middle East and in Southeast Asia.

In the Southeast Asian context in particular it can be safely said that the problem of regional security is not historically a new phenomenon. On the contrary, the recent political history of the region has clearly shown how states of varying degrees of national independence have sought to manage their individual security needs through a process which in the sum total of their efforts did indeed approximate to the ideas of what might conceptually be accepted as a form of regional security rationalizations. How else would one be able to explain the complex system of interlocking relationships between large external empires, sprawling indigenous kingdoms and a plethora of semi-independent vassal or tributary states that appears to have worked so well in the international relations of the region for some three hundred years before the present century?

24

It is certainly worth considering to what extent, if at all, those political and strategic realities of the past in Southeast Asia have indeed changed albeit in a vastly different technological and military context.

Ayoob has gone to some trouble to detect the likely distortions in the definition of the concept of regional security that are, understandably, bound to occur as a result of an over-dependence on the European origins of the very feeling of insecurity among small and medium nations in vitally important strategic regions. Here, it is pertinent to remember that some of those European nations were themselves at one time, and a few are even to this day, very much party to the regional security apparatus that prevailed both in the Middle East and in Southeast Asia. Undoubtedly, the systemic conditions of international security in the modern world have a direct bearing on the nature of regional security problems of both regions, but there are also, as Ayoob admits, certain domestic or internal factors which need to be better understood and evaluated. Such factors can conceivably be subsumed under the rubric of 'core values' which, even in a specific regional environment such as Southeast Asia, do not lend themselves to any simplistic definition. Moreover, there is the further consideration of unpredictable change in the order of priority of such values which further complicates the problem. Quite clearly, therefore, the internal dynamics of the individual states of both regions require close attention if one is to make anything of the extent to which 'core values' contribute to a better understanding of the concept of regional security.

At some point during the course of any discussion of the problem of regional security in the Middle East and in Southeast Asia one will inevitably be faced with the dilemma of making allowances for the peculiar nature of conflict that usually characterizes most Third World post-colonial societies. The difficulty arises from the variety of forms that such conflicts tend to take from sporadic clashes between relatively small guerrilla-type forces to fairly prolonged civil war-type disruptions. Indeed, it is in view of these methodological disadvantages in the study of regional security in the Third World that it has been suggested, as a sort of temporary *modus operandi*, to differentiate between a variety of conflicts according to their nature, their motivations and their scope of involvement. Notwithstanding these caveats regarding the scholarly approach to the understanding of regional security problems in the Third

World, it has to be borne in mind that ultimately the impact of most of these local clashes on the prevailing state of international security is a primary source of concern at the global level that involves both major powers as well as international organizations.

Without appearing to concentrate too heavily on the purely negative aspects of regional security, it is perhaps appropriate to consider briefly the prospects for achieving greater stability and a relative state of peace and co-operation through the practice of institutionalized conflict resolution. To be sure this is not very often the stated goal of most efforts at what is euphemistically described as regional co-operation. Or, one can, on the other hand adopt some of Ayoob's preferred terminology and speak instead of shared and common security interests among a number of regional states. The increasing attention that the subject itself is beginning to receive from scholars would suggest that here again is another growth industry. However, the feasibility of seemingly collective or common or shared interests being meaningfully dealt with in an inter-communal fashion may in the end turn out to be somewhat chimerical. This is no way to be regarded as a denial of the undoubted success of such regional bodies as ASEAN; but bearing in mind that regional security has been traditionally dealt with in terms of military pacts it would certainly be too sanguine to conclude at this particular point in time that the pursuit of collective interests can be fruitfully conducted through the means of regional organizations. The very definition of those collective interests could invariably be the proverbial straw which could break the camel's back.

There is something to be said for the argument that in the Third World insecurity may be taken to be a given factor for the ever-increasing level of military preparedness of most regional states and not merely in the Middle East and Southeast Asia. This certainly seems to reflect some sort of stoic pragmatism about their lack of security. The military aspects of regional security problems can even be said to be as deserving of attention as others, for one hears ever so often that regional 'arms races' and the suggestive patterns of arms transfers from the developed to the Third World can serve as a timely indicator of the state of affairs in the regional security of certain parts of the world today. Significantly, it is in Southeast Asia where regional co-operation in the management of stability and security is generally believed to have been most successful that one finds, as graphically described in the chapter by Paribatra and

Samudavanija, an overwhelming and implacable expansion in military hardware as well as in numerical strength over the past decade or so. What do these developments suggest, therefore, for the better understanding of regional security?

Having attempted to review some of the many conceptual issues raised in Ayoob's paper, albeit in a somewhat unfairly truncated form, it must be admitted that the appeal for a reappraisal of the term regional security and its definition in the Third World context is indeed persuasive. There can be no denying that the external sources of regional conflict should not deter one from recognizing the inherent dynamism within such regions as the Middle East and Southeast Asia which have generally been ignored in the past by western scholars. Without delving any further into that controversy, one other observation that may deserve more than passing attention has to do with the attitudes and perceptions of policymakers and professionals in the field of regional security and its maintenance. The fear, in this case, is that scholars are apt to ignore or overlook the very real and often determining role that these groups of individuals play in shaping the parameters of many regional security problems. How true would it be, then, to conclude that, stripped of all their theoretical and environmental dimensions, regional security problems in the final analysis will continue to be defined and addressed by these practitioners of diplomacy and defence in sheer military terms? By its very nature that purely military approach to regional security is severely limited and even relatively prosperous and well-endowed regions such as the Middle East and Southeast Asia have no choice but to assess correctly the alternative approaches to regional security problems.

COMMENTS

S. D. Muni

Mohammed Ayoob in his well-researched paper has done a commendable job of focusing attention on a vital aspect of security in the Third World which has so far remained only scarcely explored. Some of the recent writings of Shahram Chubin, S. N. Macfarlane, Mehnaz Ispahani and Jonathan Alford have drawn attention to the internal sources of insecurity in Third World countries, but none have gone into the clinical details of nation- and state-building processes and the involvement of regimes into these processes which promotes insecurity, as Ayoob has done.

The concept of state is central to the discussion in the paper. The question of the weak and fragmented nature of the state is rather complex. In most of the cases, where Third World countries have undergone a colonial experience, the state inherited by the nationalist rulers at the time of independence was in fact a colonial creation equipped adequately to perpetuate exploitation of labour and expropriation of resources. This state apparatus was extremely powerful in its coercive strength. However, this was also a state which was alienated from its own people and, to that extent, it had a very narrow social base. The widening of this social base in the post-independence period depended upon the nature of the polity and the style of rulership. Here the nature of the transfer of power — through polite negotiations, a freedom struggle or a fiercely fought war of liberation — has played a key role in shaping the post-colonial state.

However, in most cases, the state in the Third World has remained generally alienated from its people. Externally, the colonial state was weak and vulnerable in relation to the metropolitan centre. In the post-independence period also, it has continued to remain so *vis-à-vis* the great powers that include most of the former colonial/imperial masters. Even those Third World states that did not formally come under imperial/colonial rule remained internally strong, coercive and alienated and externally weak and vulnerable. The Iranian state under the Shah and the Thai state may be mentioned as ready instances. Thus the character of the state in the Third World has to be understood in its full

28

complexity in order to comprehend its subsequent development. In this context, state-building is not quite the same as nation-building. The concept of popular legitimacy seems to be inherent in Ayoob's analysis of the state-building process. In fact, this concept is more relevant with regard to nation building than state building. The Shah of Iran did build an extremely powerful state without troubling about popular legitimacy. The Shah's regime collapsed but the Iranian state has survived.

There is also another underlying assumption in Ayoob's paper that state- and nation-building processes in the Third World are autonomous exercises wherein the failures or successes are the doings of the domestic regimes alone. This is not really so. These processes in the Third World invariably involve exogenous factors in more than incidental ways. The role of these external factors is more often than not decisive in shaping, conditioning and constraining the state- and nation-building processes in the Third World. It is here that the Third World experience is strikingly different from the similar experience in Europe. The European countries had their respective conflicts and convulsions but these could be sorted out within the parameters of European civilizational dynamics. There was neither any extra-regional great power nor any over-arching influence of global political, economic and strategic systems to interfere with the historical evolution of European states and societies.

In the case of Third World, even after the formal withdrawal of colonialism, the legacies of colonial rule in various walks of life continued to be relevant and powerfully influential. In addition to this, the impact of the post-Second World War global system in economic, ideological, cultural, technological and military-strategic fields, has been all too pervasive and decisive. Mostly, the global system, including the great powers and international economic forces, has intervened subtly through aid, ideological propaganda and informational and technological linkages, to influence developmental processes in the Third World. Institutions like the International Monetary Fund (IMF) and the World Bank prescribe social and economic policies for the aid-receiving countries. These policies have direct implications for political processes and systems. Money and influence from the great powers also penetrate political processes in Third World countries through many subtle and covert channels, thus vitiating and disorienting them.

The intensity and extent of the great powers' intervention through multifaceted channels in the Third World countries vary depending upon the nature of the intervening powers' stakes and objectives. Such stakes may be either *intrinsic* or *derivative*. *Intrinsic* stakes are in the form of assuring the supply of vital raw materials (including oil and strategic minerals), protection of markets and investment, flow of commercial traffic and the establishment, expansion and preservation of strategic bases or facilities. *Derivative* stakes are of secondary importance and may be limited to the objective of containing or reducing the presence and influence of a rival power. Accordingly, in all such Third World countries or regions where an external power's stakes are intrinsic, that power's involvement and intervention would naturally be deep and extensive. The US presence in Central America and the Gulf, the Chinese approach towards South and Southeast Asia and the Soviet involvement in the Middle East and Afghanistan are obvious examples. The point which needs to be stressed here is that domestic insecurity and conflict in the Third World instead of being only internal developments are the product of the interaction between these developments and external influences. And since the so-called internal state- and nation-building processes are not wholly internal, the insecurity resulting from them also has to have an external dimension.

In explaining the conflict and insecurity resulting from the state- and nation-building processes within Third World countries, Ayoob has rightly emphasized the role of diversity in the Third World. This diversity is the result of numerous cleavages, such as ethnic, religious, linguistic, regional, economic, ideological and political. These cleavages precipitate conflict and insecurity, but not always and necessarily on their own. The cleavages are intensified and exploited so as to yield conflict by external as well as internal vested interests. As for the internal vested interests, there are several examples of Third World regimes as well as their adversaries encouraging and allowing a certain level of social and political conflict by exploiting domestic cleavages in pursuance of their power rivalries and economic interests. It is, however, a different matter that at times the regimes may not succeed in manipulating and regulating social conflicts according to their designs and may even become victims of the conflicts generated by themselves.

This bears a close resemblance to the machinations of the great powers at the global level. This similarity between the Third World internal political order and the global political order is incidental but important. The two political orders and the violence created by them are closely interlinked in many cases. In both instances low levels of conflict are consiously engineered or allowed to disturb the status quo and justify deviant behaviour — repression and authoritarianism in a Third World society and intervention and hegemonism by the great powers.

Thus the systemic linkages run through national, regional and global levels of insecurity and it may not be possible to isolate internal sources from regional or global sources of insecurity except for analytical purposes. Ayoob is acutely aware of this when he discusses the systemic concept of world security. It is only, perhaps, for analytical purposes that he takes a swing towards highlighting the 'internal' aspects of Third World security and tends to view it differently from the security of the western states in its external orientation and linkages with systemic security. The global integration brought about by the communication revolution, the extensive reach and the stakes of the great powers and implications of nuclear weapons make it unrealistic to compartmentalize or even regionalize security problems.

Ayoob's paper is concerned mainly with the internal sources of insecurity in the Third World. He has not dealt with the forms, patterns and consequences of this insecurity for a given country and its external environment (global and regional). Ayoob has also wisely refrained from prescribing ways and means to ensure security except for a mention, in passing, of regional organizations. While discussing regional organizations and their role in ensuring regional security, particularly of the Gulf Co-operation Council (GCC) and ASEAN with which this workshop is concerned, an important aspect is often ignored. In a way, the regional organizations approach to regional security reflects a kind of strategic division of labour between the great powers and the regional influentials. Both GCC and ASEAN are under the strategic umbrella of the western powers in general and the US in particular. They seem to be concrete manifestations of the Nixon and Carter doctrines augmented by President Reagan's assertive stances. The regions concerned are of intrinsic value to the West and the lineage of the regional organizations can be traced to military alliances and pacts of the cold war phase. The new cold war and the complexities of changed security situations have obviously dictated the forms and functions of these organizations. This explains their avowed economic objectives but pronounced security functions. In fact the performances of both GCC and ASEAN on the economic front have been disappointing. On the strategic front, both these organizations have facilitated the consolidation of US presence in the region and led to the sharpening of intra-regional conflicts in the Gulf (between Iran and the Arab states of the Gulf) and Southeast Asia (between Indochina and ASEAN). It is debatable if security prospects for the member countries would have been worse without these organizations than they are today. As for the state- and nation-building processes within the member countries, the organizations have not even made an effort to make them viable. The objective of collective security through regional organizations can be achieved only if the organization is designed to seek greater independence and autonomy of action as well as being a long-term basis for economic development and socio-political stability.

2 REGIONAL SECURITY AND WORLD ORDER IN THE 1980s

Robert O'Neill

The theme of this chapter is modelled in the perspective that dominant powers exist, but they are the more significant because of their setting and they depend on its stability. International security is discussed all too often simply in terms of the Soviet-American rivalry. But, thanks to other views that are being articulated, not least through the institutes sponsoring this conference, analysis of international security issues is now encompassing a widening range of actors and points of view.

The foundation of regional security is the nation state, 'the basic unit of international politics' as J. D. B. Miller has characterized it in his book *The World of States*. The world, he reminds us, is made up of all kinds of actors, from individuals at one end of the scale through to the United Nations at the other, but international politics is conducted essentially through national governments or, in short, states. Sub-national groups and international organizations all have roles to play but are not fundamental elements in the same way that states are. The sort of international politics that students of strategy and international security are concerned with is almost wholly that of inter-state relations, because essentially it is states which control the means of enforcing or threatening to enforce their will. There are of course exceptions in the form of national groupings which do not control their own territory, such as the PLO, the Khmer Rouge and the Afghan rebel groups on the one hand, and multinational peace-keeping forces on the other, but these are more temporary phenomena. The PLO and the Kampuchean and Afghan rebels as we now know them are state-oriented in that they are fighting to gain or regain sovereign statehood; and peace-keeping forces may be withdrawn or broken asunder at the behest of the states contributing the constituent national elements.

Those who analyze the security problems of developing countries have many concerns about state viability. Their attention is frequently focused on internal questions because it is from discontent and injustice, greed and fear, opportunism and lawlessness within the national culture that most of their security problems

33

come. But we must also recognize that despite internal instability, individual states as we know them today are proving to be a remarkably durable set of organizations. When Africa was decolonized in the late 1950s and early 1960s it was composed of some 40 states. Twenty years later that continent has still essentially the same state system. Tribal groups have fought with each other, military and civil revolutions have come and gone but the state structure scarcely has been altered. Experience such as that of Uganda leads to the conclusion that stability is not a necessary condition for the existence of a state. The situation in other parts of the developing world is little different.

The essential conditions for the existence of a state are, first, a form of sovereign national government which can, for at least some of the time, make its writ run through most of its territory and for most of its population, and, second, recognition (either open or tacit) of its national borders by other states. In the mid-1980s we can say with confidence that the present set of states, including those which are most poorly developed, seems likely to continue in effect, with very little change, for a very long time. Forms of state governments may change dramatically, as shown by a host of relatively recent examples such as Bangladesh, Ghana and Thailand. International alignments can swing from pro-US to pro-Soviet or vice versa, as shown by Somalia, Egypt and Ethiopia, but these national entities themselves continue and throughout it all display remarkable continuity of character and interests. Dependence relationships can reduce sovereignty, but they do not obliterate it, leaving open the possibility of national reassertion when external circumstances permit.

Turbulent states are, almost *ipso facto*, insecure ones. Liberal democracies alone have learned how to change political complexion regularly without bloodshed or severe curtailment of rights of political expression. Other forms of government, be they dictatorial or semi-closed systems, require repeated internal use of police, military or other force in order to change or preserve governments. All forms of state are, however, subject to the threat of turbulence, and many fear instability itself. As we take stock of our world, what can we distinguish by way of criteria for the development of sound intra-state security?

Criteria for Intra-state Security

Most importantly there seems to be a slowly growing number of states which recognize that their internal security depends upon their accommodation to and positive acceptance of pressures for change. The numbers of dyed-in-the-wool, traditional, absolutist rulers are waning. Even in states where the headship of the executive government is a hereditary office, such as amongst some of the Arab states of the Gulf, processes of devolution are underway. Indeed, perhaps the only states where devolution of authority from a single individual cannot be detected are those where the leader of a revolution still holds power tightly in his own hands, such as in North Korea, Cuba or several African states recently subject to revolution. In most others the structure of authority is complex, combining elements of liberal pluralism and authoritarianism in varying degrees over a wide spectrum.

Closed societies are governed by elites of various kinds (military, religious, or civilian) and ideologies, from left to right, but mostly on the extremes of the scale. Their common element is intolerance of any thought which differs significantly from that of the head of government, and in essence they are dictatorships of one kind or another, be it the rule of a single dominant individual, or that of a small group of leaders. Analysis of the security of such societies is difficult, partly because the necessary information is hard to obtain and partly because their operational codes are often poorly regulated, and highly dependent on personal factors. Some are narrowly authoritarian while others allow a degree of free thinking within the ranks of the ruling party or other form of oligarchy so that the ruler has at least a selection of views from which to choose. None the less it is possible to adduce certain characteristics to these types of state: they are unpleasant to their neighbours; their economies do not work very well (although a few of them, such as Libya, are rich through oil or other scarce resources); their intellectuals command little respect abroad (except in the cases of dissidents); and they are relatively highly militarized. They pay dearly for security through diversion of resources from the productive to the non-productive sectors of their economies and the national humour is exhibited through jokes revealing frustration, disillusionment and individual withdrawal.

Individually these states represent time-bombs for their citizens and neighbours. Sooner or later they will blow up, unless someone defuses them first. It should be said in passing that the defusing operation is usually a delicate one, to which foreign states, and especially great powers, are poorly suited. It is inevitably a dangerous mission for internal operators but, curiously, human nature is such that there are usually people who are willing to run the necessary risks so that changes in closed states are due, more often than not, to internal action, although a little secondary foreign support is a frequent accompaniment. Examples that come more readily to mind of this kind of state are Libya, Chile, Albania and Kampuchea under Pol Pot. Nobody in their right mind considers these as security paradigms.

States of the semi-closed variety are much more numerous. Circumstances such as tradition, prevailing philosophy, lack of infrastructure, etc. rule out full liberal democracy as a preferred option for most developing countries, and the defects of the essentially closed state are all too obvious to make that course desirable. The semi-closed states are characterized by a high degree of political orthodoxy, perhaps to the extent of being a one-party state. Sometimes, although not always, they make a distinction between security of the state and security of tenure of a particular leader. More often the connection is made between that of a particular group (the regime) and that of the state, enabling some regulated means of changing the leadership at the highest level. Public participation in the choices open regarding changes of government may be extremely limited. But generally these states are more secure than those of the first group which suffer the double jeopardy of a leader whose whims cannot be contradicted and for the sake of whose security all kinds of diverse activities by his subjects cannot be tolerated, even though those activities might bear no direct relationship to the stability of his seat but rather promote the strength and well-being of the nation at large.

Other characteristics of the semi-closed state include a substantial degree of political authority for the military, often accompanied by a high level of defence expenditure, a mixed economic performance, reasonable in a few regards but poor in many others, censorship of the mass media, a high rate of emigration of really able people, limited performance of their universities and other institutes of higher learning, particularly in the social sciences, a high degree of state involvement in the economy and strictly regulated access by foreigners, at least in so far as these foreigners accept the confines of legality.

The presence of these characteristics alone is enough to cause insecurity, but frequently they are combined with others including the presence of ethnic and religious minorities, irredentist problems with neighbours, former colonial boundaries which do not match local political and ethnic divisions, economic dependence on the export of one or two commodities whose prices are subject to severe fluctuation, usually downwards and acute inefficiency of government.

Obviously states in this category have serious internal security concerns. Repressed or frustrated popular sentiment is a breeding ground for those who seek change by violent means. The economic, ethnic, religious and other problems all go to compound the feelings of insecurity of the regime in power. Some have sufficient means of coercion ready to hand to keep their states relatively stable; others suffer instability in varying degrees; yet others preserve stability by internal dynamism and flexibility, moving towards accommodation of popular desires and general improvement in all of the three major indices of state performance, while still retaining authoritarianism in key areas. Not all of the semi-closed category of states are able to accommodate pressures for change in this way, of course, and some that are capable of so doing give up the practice after a while and rely on demagoguery, mixed with mild repression to manipulate public opinion to the degree necessary to ensure relatively comfortable regime survival.

The third group of states to which I have referred, namely those with a relatively open structure, practising constitutional democracy, has all too few members amongst the ranks of developing countries. Perhaps the outstanding example is India, a state which has many internal security problems but which is essentially firm and stable as a total political entity, accommodating conflicting ideas and change within broad limits, relying on the ballot box rather than the military to determine the fates of governments. There are other examples in Latin America such as Argentina since the fall of the Junta, and in Southeast Asia and the Southwest Pacific. These states generally are characterized by a high degree of confidence and unity, and their internal security problems, while still formidable in several cases, are solved at less cost to the nation at large than those of the closed or semi-closed category.

The lesson of this overview is not obscure: efficient, durable state security is related ultimately to the degree of openness of a nation. Open states make best use of human initiative. Not all open societies are secure, of course. Those which are performing weakly, particularly in economic and administrative terms, may be prey to upheavals, even reversion to a semi-closed situation. But if the tradition of openness is well founded, sooner or later most national communities will find their way back to it, as we have seen with Greece, Portugal and Spain in the past decade.

It is also true that not all closed or semi-closed societies are in the immediate grip of insecurity. But the security of these exceptional states is transitory and bought at a high price in terms of rate of national development, social harmony, repression of creative minds and maintenance of coercive forces. Other costs include loss of standing in the eyes of the international community, particularly neighbours who are the hardest to deceive. They also tend to be non-participants in the continuing global evolution (or is it more of a revolution?) made possible by the free transfer of ideas, political, economic, social and technological, amongst vigorous, talented people whose receptivity is unshackled by fear that contact with these ideas, and advocacy of them if they seem sensible, will lead to loss of position and even freedoms in their own societies.

This is, of course, an old message but it can bear repetition in the mid-1980s, particularly in the current situation where there is a tendency, at least amongst the great powers, to measure security very largely in military terms. The process of transition from the more closed to the more open type of society is fraught with risks, but whatever the challenges, the ultimate benefits of the stronger, more open type of society makes these risks worth running. They are, of course, an acid test of leadership, perceptiveness and moral principal at many levels. Not everyone succeeds in this process. But those who do not attempt it will be worse off in the long run.

Regional Viability

Now let me pass from problems of state viability to regional viability. We have before us many examples of different kinds of regional relationships. They span the range from near anarchy, such as we have in the Middle East in the group of states which consists of Israel, Lebanon, Syria and Jordan, through various forms of limited conflict such as is taking place in Central America, to more loosely co-ordinated co-operation, as in the front-line states against South Africa, the Arab League and the South Pacific

Forum, and finally to formally structured, closely co-ordinated co-operation such as we have in the case of the Gulf Co-operation Council. ASEAN, although not a security organization in the formal sense, must not be left out of consideration because it fulfils none the less several security purposes.

There are other examples of regional co-operation that are often left out of consideration in these comparisons, but which are salutary to keep in mind, such as the North Atlantic Alliance, the Warsaw Pact and the European Community. One could perhaps add Comecon, but as it includes Vietnam it goes beyond the limits of what is normally defined to be a regional organization.

But these others are worth remembering not only to remind ourselves that they are regional, and have important security lessons for other regions to ponder, but also to note that they involve the superpowers intimately. Most other forms of regional organization do not involve the superpowers directly, unless one includes the Organization of American States, the four American trans-Pacific alliances and the Antarctic Treaty. None the less there are few, if any, forms of regional co-operation which lack some form of connection with either of the superpowers. More usually the United States is the active partner but sometimes, as in the cases of Indochina, Cuba, Nicaragua, Ethiopia and Yemen, it is the Soviet Union.

Superpower involvement raises questions of dependence, hegemony and conflict of interests. The more intimately a superpower is committed to supporting a regional security grouping, the more dependent upon it the regional powers tend to become. In some cases, particularly if they are located in close proximity to a superpower, regional states may slide under their partner's hegemony, thereby surrendering a substantial portion of their freedom of action. Furthermore, they all too easily become pawns in the great power rivalry, taking on security concerns and responsibilities of which they are free when not linked to so powerful an ally. Sometimes circumstances leave no other choice to a regional state than to depend on a superpower for support, particularly in the case of an exposed, militarily weak state like Japan. In these situations, proper consultation arrangements, treaty provisions and good political judgement on both sides can obviate the issue of dependence. Similarly, alliance partners do not have to be hegemonized, particularly if the more dependent partner can compete with its protector in other ways. Admittedly security obligations may be incurred which relate to the protecting power's interests than to those of the protected when viewed in a narrow sense, but when viewed in the wider sense of the outcome of a competition between rival systems, the interests of the protected state are often closely involved.

Hence another dimension of our analysis has to be to ask whether special circumstances exist which make the close involvement of a superpower in regional security arrangements desirable or undesirable. Bearing this in mind, I shall return to the discussion of types of regional relationships and their relevance to the security and viability of a region as a whole.

One problem to be faced in any such analysis is that the world does not divide neatly into regions which include all states unambiguously. Pakistan belongs both to Southwest Asia and to South Asia. Indonesia, while being primarily Southeast Asian, borders on Papua New Guinea and hence on the Southwest Pacific. Egypt has both African and Middle Eastern concerns. And there are some, such as South Africa, Libya or Cuba, and probably India, which are so different from their neighbours that they defy attempts to include them in regional security arrangements that would be acceptable to other potential partners. Hence the regional approach is no complete solution for every state's security problems. Furthermore, different regional groupings may gang up on each other once they become established as viable entities.

But let us set our goals more modestly and consider simply those parts of the world where there already exist significant regional security arrangements. They include Southeast Asia, the Gulf, western and southern Africa, the Southwest Pacific and the eastern Caribbean. For the purposes of this analysis, however, I shall focus on the two more obvious candidates, ASEAN and the GCC.

In the case of the former we have a well-formed regional organization but for political, economic and social co-operation rather than directly security-related or military purposes. The latter is much more specifically a security organization, but not solely so. In each region, the major security problem is presented by two other regional powers or forces at war with each other: Vietnam against the Khmer Rouge and allied groups, and Iran against Iraq. Hence there is already a severe split in each region tending to polarize the contending parties and the prosepects are for sub-regional rather than full regional co-operation.

ASEAN

ASEAN is now out of its juvenile years and well into adolescence, making good progress and increasing everybody's confidence in the future prospects of the six members, notwithstanding concern about the internal political difficulties of the Philippines. This severely stressed state clearly has major problems ahead of it, but as I have already indicated my view on the direction in which a true solution of those problems might be found, I will not dwell further on the issue, than to say that it is one for the Filipinos themselves to handle.

From the outset there has been a danger that ASEAN might have been dominated by its biggest member, Indonesia, but in practice this problem has been overcome to the satisfaction of most. Certainly there has not been imposition of Indonesia's views on discussions of how to handle the Indochina problem, but rather a positive affirmation of the approach that strength lies in diversity. In dealing with a difficult neighbour, Vietnam, which is dangerous to at least one member, Thailand, but which is also faced with severe internal and external difficulties itself, ASEAN's 'unity in diversity' approach is well suited, both to offer united condemnation if Vietnam goes too far and to show a little warmth if she seeks a more moderate approach. What makes this approach convincing by ASEAN, where in other groupings such as Contadora it is not, is the solid community of political and other interests that the six members share, supported by the organization's track record.

It is important to continue to nurture these interests through consultation and avoidance of internal policies which would be regionally divisive. Viability of a regional organization requires mutual respect for other members' sensitivities. It is reassuring, for example, to see new evidence of co-operation between Malaysia and Singapore, not least in defence arrangements.

The question as to whether or not ASEAN should add formal military security co-operation to its functions is not new, but still it is frequently put. The arguments against it doing so, namely the essentially internal nature of the security problems of member states, and their relative inability to contribute very much to help each other, are strong. It remains counter-productive for ASEAN to take on any formal military role.

But it would be perhaps a little coy of ASEAN to deny that, in the broader sense, the Association has a security role. In helping to promote political contact and economic and social well-being, it is both laying important foundations for regional security and reducing tensions between members as they arise. ASEAN manages to do all this without placing intolerable shackles on the diplomacy of its constituent states. A formal alliance would probably not be so flexible and resilient, leading to the growth of divisive issues. Furthermore, it may well present the wrong face to the rest of the world, particularly to its troublesome neighbours.

None of these considerations rule out a degree of bilateral military co-operation, such as standardization of equipment and procedure, exchanges of views and information and joint training and exercises. Such activities might, from time to time, be carried out more effectively on a multilateral basis, but ASEAN should not be the vehicle for them, at least unless the security situation in Southeast Asia as a whole should deteriorate sharply. For handling the present type of security problems in the region, ASEAN is best left as it is.

The question of co-operation with external powers is bound to be contentious from time to time. For several reasons, including the nature of internal Communist threats and the degree of Soviet support for Vietnam, there is a natural tendency for ASEAN members to look to the West for what security support they might need. It is one thing to look and another to receive a response. Although the Five Power Defence Arrangements still exist, British interest in and capacity to contribute to their support is becoming increasingly limited. Other European powers, such as France, the Netherlands and Italy, might be glad to expand their defence equipment market amongst ASEAN members but not to do more. Other pro-western regional powers, particularly Australia and New Zealand, remain actively committed to the security of the region, but with relatively limited military resources themselves, even by comparison with those of several ASEAN members, they are in a better position to contribute information, advice and expertise rather than man-power, firepower and logistic support.

Hence despite the strong preference of Malaysia and Indonesia, at least, for more open non-alignment, some connection with the United States for equipment, information exchanges and specialized training cannot be avoided. Indeed the long standing relationship of the Philippines and Thailand with the US shows that for at least two out of the six, active trans-Pacific co-operation is viewed very positively, although not unambiguously so, particularly when it comes time to renegotiate payment for access to base facilities.

None the less it is important, both for ASEAN members and for the US, that they do not slide into an extensive arrangement involving clear American guarantees. The situation is not so bad as to require it; regional polarization would be increased, possibly in the form of a stronger Soviet presence in Vietnam's regional aspirations for non-alignment, and respect by other non-aligned states would be sacrificed, again to the cost of all; and it must be recognized that the US has many higher priority areas for which to preserve its strength. Thus although access to equipment order books, training and a flow of information should be provided by Washington, that is going far enough in the present situation. For further strengthening of their joint security, due care should be taken to see that security co-operation amongst ASEAN members should be essentially directed indigenously rather than fostered externally.

The Gulf Co-operation Council

The Gulf Co-operation Council is at a much more tender state of development, yet it is pursuing what seems to be a more ambitious set of aims than ASEAN. Now some 4 years old, the organization has at least passed successfully through the trials of infancy. The GCC had the advantage, by comparison with ASEAN, of being initiated by a group of more 'like-minded' states, enabling a faster rate of consolidation. Despite differences in viewpoint between them, ranging from the Kuwaiti preference for avoiding close alignment with the West to the Omani willingness to foster such co-operation, and internal and external challenges, the GCC has increased in cohesiveness and credibility. Unfortunately (or perhaps fortunately?) it has not been spared, as was ASEAN in its early years, a major and direct regional security challenge. Although the Vietnam War was raging for the first seven years of ASEAN's existence, the active involvement of the United States, plus what were generally believed to be the limited aims of North Vietnam and the associated Communist guerrilla forces operating in Indochina, combined to mollify fears that the external security of the ASEAN states was under serious threat. This is not the case with the GCC, as Iran and Iraq continue to batter each other, and show signs of willingness to widen their conflict to include other

Gulf states. This escalation is threatened in two forms: direct attacks on shipping, ports, oil production, storage and transport facilities and other sensitive targets; and internal revolt or terrorism designed to put pressure on, or even to topple, Gulf rulers through unleashing religious turmoil. The plight of the Gulf states is made more difficult because of their support for Iraq. This support has become something of an embarrassment and GCC members have played down other than economic aspects of their co-operation with Iraq. The GCC's position *vis-à-vis* Iraq is all the more difficult because the latter opposed the Council's creation, arguing that it would undermine the Arab League and other forms of Arab co-operation. Iran has been openly contemptuous of the GCC, claiming that no Gulf organization which omitted her, the most powerful Gulf state, could have any credibility.

GCC members have achieved a reasonable record in overcoming the political differences which exist between themselves. They have taken action to strengthen individual response capabilities against internal threats, looking in the process to ASEAN for some guidance. They still have a long way to go before they can be said to have developed individually the strengths that ASEAN members have achieved in this regard.

Their task is complicated by the additional dimension of co-operation that the GCC has openly undertaken: joint action to improve security against external attack. The fact that the task is complicated, however, does not render it impossible. Indeed, in the existing circumstances, one can ask whether it would be possible for the GCC to refrain from formal external security co-operation and still remain a useful organization.

None the less the challenges it faces are formidable: great care and determination will have to be applied by member states if it is to come through the trying year or two ahead. Internally GCC members are bearing a heavy burden through economic support for Iraq. The money given to Saddam Hussein could well be used to improve infrastructures in the donor states. It may well prove in later years that their internal problems are more serious than the external threat posed by Iran, thus overturning the argument deployed by Saddam to sustain the flow of aid. Indeed, more than his argument might be overturned. Externally the GCC has to face several difficult choices regarding co-operation with each other and with non-member nations, especially the United States and Egypt.

Military co-operation amongst GCC members is moving ahead

steadily in the form of joint exercises and exchanges of information. But whether political differences and apprehensions between members can be reduced sufficiently for a real joint effort remains to be seen. Also uncertain is the degree to which the smaller states are willing to leave decision-making power and operational responsibility principally in the hands of Saudi Arabia. Indicators at present are not totally pessimistic on these counts, but much remains to be done, particularly in terms of rationalizing procurement plans so that the large sums to be spent (reported to be US \$35 billion over the next three years) will be used most effectively. Efforts are also called for to standardize operating procedures. Unfortunately standardization of air defence systems will be extremely difficult to achieve because the Saudis have bought theirs from the US while other GCC members operate Western European equipment.

The degree of co-operation which should exist between GCC members and the United States is a more controversial question. Because of the perceived importance of Gulf oil to the West generally, the United States senses a vital interest at stake and its involvement is not quite as optional in the case of GCC members as it is in the case of ASEAN. While GCC states can withhold co-operation from the US, they have to reckon with a different order of American priorities regarding regional intervention than do the ASEAN states. Furthermore, they have to think about a more narrowly-based and higher level of economic dependence on the West in general than do the ASEAN states. Also they know that the US can sustain a major naval and naval-air presence in the Arabian Sea and the Gulf itself, irrespective of co-operation with GCC members. Even more importantly, GCC states may have no other major source of assistance available to deal with an aggressive Iran. Hence there are many incentives for extensive co-operation.

There are also disincentives, however. The United States may, through intervention, make an already delicate situation worse and then prove unable to restore it. The Soviets may be simulated to play a greater role, either *vis-à-vis* Iran and Iraq or the Gulf states themselves (indirectly rather than directly). There may be internal reactions of disapproval following any close co-operation with the US, such as giving access to base facilities. Clearly the choices before the GCC states are difficult, although more of a consensus seems to be developing in favour of co-operation as the Iran-Iraq conflict worsens.

In so doing, GCC states can minimize their risks by being judicious regarding forms and extent of co-operation. They can ask for consultation regarding US contingency planning, offering advice in cases where Washington or the US armed forces do not appear to have thought sufficiently about the consequences of certain actions. Perhaps most importantly they can keep the threshold for direct US intervention relatively high by strengthening the security effectiveness of GCC members themselves, both individually and collectively. Thus while the external and internal situations of the Gulf states are very different from those of ASEAN members, there are none the less many common concerns and areas in which the GCC can learn from the other organization's experience. Perhaps there will also be ways in which ASEAN can gain from close observation of the way in which the GCC states tackle some of their problems.

Each organization has potential for growth. The six ASEAN states could conceivably add to their members immediate neighbours such as Burma and Papua New Guinea. Other more distant states such as Australia and New Zealand have, in times now long past, expressed interest in some formal linkage with ASEAN. The present six members, however, do not appear eager to enlarge their number. There are problems enough in maintaining close working relationships amongst themselves, and further members could cause more trouble than their worth to the organization. There is a great deal that the present six have in common, but others, being very different culturally and with relatively little to contribute which might be of political, economic or security benefit to the six, would be seen as more likely to weaken cohesion than to strengthen it.

The growth prospects for the GCC are somewhat similar in nature. The two missing Gulf states amongst the Council's membership, Iraq and Iran, would scarcely be welcomed to its circle, particularly Iran with its critical attitude towards the GCC. Even though GCC members support Iraq, they are not seeking closer involvement in its conflict with Iran. Other candidates suggest themselves, such as Jordan and North Yemen, particularly the former which already has close co-operative links with GCC states. The present members may balk, however, at adding another which lacks a Gulf coastline, although given territorial contiguity with Saudi Arabia, the commonality of Arabic culture, Islamic religion, political structure and security interests, it would be the easiest addition to make. But again the calculus of costs and benefits must be made, and a system of states under pressure may well choose to err on the side of caution in any decision regarding future member-ship, at least until that pressure ceases to be felt so acutely.

Co-operation between GCC members and Egypt is likely to become a more salient question in coming years. Gradually Egypt is being re-admitted to the Islamic fold, not least because President Mubarak's provision of assistance to Iraq has led to the latter's successful support for the Egyptian cause in the Islamic Conference and to further efforts aimed at achieving Egypt's return to the Arab League. GCC states appear to require further persuasion, however, withholding return to full diplomatic relations and discreetly limiting other contacts with Egypt. The extent of what Egypt has to offer to the GCC states is clearly limited. Yet she may help to keep high the threshold for that degree of direct US intervention which requires access to Gulf states' facilities. Clearly it is an issue which will come under more discussion amongst GCC members in the next year or two.

Conclusion

In conclusion it is worth emphasizing that both ASEAN and the GCC offer important examples to states in other parts of the world in terms of what it takes to make a regional association viable. Neither is immune to failure, of course, although ASEAN has survived long enough and with sufficient effectiveness to have high credibility as a regional force for the coming decade. Each sprang out of spontaneous common concern amongst neighbouring states that their region was in for a testing time, together with their belief that political and other differences within each organization could be handled successfully and gradually reduced. Each organization has internal problems to deal with such as latent potential for asser-tion of local hegemony by one of its members. Each has to handle questions of relations with major external powers which have capacity for intervention in the region. Each has its own approach to the issue of how openly dedicated it should be to formal security co-operation.

What states in other regions should make of these examples for their own consideration is difficult to prescribe. Not all states have a significant opportunity to join a regional organization and not all regions have what is necessary to make a viable grouping. But potential exists in Africa, Central America and the South Pacific, and hence prospects exist for a more orderly world based on stronger building units. The time span within which such developments will occur is likely to be relatively long in terms of the dimensions normally involved in international political analysis, that is a generation or two. None the less every little consolidation helps in moving towards a world in which regional security crises will be less destabilizing for the whole system than in the 1960s and early 1970s. There are still many areas of turbulence in Latin America, Asia and Africa which can flare and spread with serious consequences for world order generally. We still, of course, have many problems to settle at the level of the global East-West confrontation, some of which, such as potential for technological destabilization of the military-strategic relationship, will become worse in the absence of significant arms control agreements. But at least the prospect of a wider East-West clash being caused by weak, insecure, crisis-prone regions may be decreased by better regional co-operation. What we now have to do is to maintain the progress of the past few years in this field and continue to urge the great powers and alliance blocs to make stronger, more intelligent, efforts to control their rivalry, and limit the arms competition through a new series of agreements. Each of these two endeavours is important and neither can be entirely successful without the other.

COMMENTS

S. D. Muni

Robert O'Neill has raised very vital and pertinent issues involved in the relationship between regional security in the Third World and world order. This relationship is not easy to grasp in its entirety because it is enormous and highly complex. His paper has tackled this difficult theme competently and has offered very valuable insight on the subject by lucidly and succinctly analyzing its major dimensions.

None can dispute O'Neill's contention that international security cannot be simply discussed 'in terms of the Soviet-American rivalry'. Each superpower has direct basic and specific interests in many of the Third World countries and regions that transcend the rivalry between them, notwithstanding the rhetoric and the public explanations usually extended. Guy Pauker in his Rand Report on projections about 'Possible World Order Crisis in the 1980s' described the resource conflict within the North-South context as one such area. Even strategically the Soviet intervention in Afghanistan, Britain's Falklands War and the recent US intervention in Grenada cannot be understood in the framework of East-West conflict alone. Not only this, many inter-state and regional conflicts in the Third World may be exploited and intensified by the superpowers to serve their interests but they are not usually initiated or controlled and resolved by the considerations of their mutual rivalry. The 5-year-old war between Iran and Iraq is a unique example of the autonomy of Third World conflicts and insecurities.

The state as an entity and principle actor has come to stay in world politics. But this state is not like a billiard ball. There are many dynamic forces operating and competing with each other in its confines involving regimes, governments and people. The paper has also identified many non-state actors like the PLO, the Kampuchean and Afghan rebels but described them, rightly, as 'temporary phenomena' and also as being state-oriented, struggling to 'gain or regain sovereign statehood'. In addition to these transitory non-state actors, there are also more permanent non-state actors like the multinational corporations, that play no insignificant

49

role in giving substance to present-day politics. There are reasons to believe that these actors will grow in their power and influence.

In analyzing the problem of intra-state security, O'Neill has done well to divide the Third World states into three categories, namely, closed, semi-closed and open social structures. Thus the viability or otherwise of the state is linked to the nature of social processes and political structures. The dividing lines among these three categories are fairly thin and ambiguous but one does get an idea as to what the author means. About the states of closed societies O'Neill says that 'sooner or later they will blow up'. By the expression blow up he is not suggesting the collapse of the state because that would contradict his earlier assertion that the 'state has come to stay'. He is, perhaps, trying to highlight the vulnerability and internal security potential of closed states. This becomes clear when he says that 'durable state security is related ultimately to the degree of openness of a nation'. Therefore, he goes further to recommend that transition from 'more closed' to 'more open' societies should be induced and encouraged. This, of course, is easier said than done. Besides other things, one wonders if the managers of international politics are indeed looking for a totally conflict- and insecurity-free world.

Coming to the question of regional security through co-operative groupings, there are four aspects of this problem; namely, the criteria for a regional grouping, its objectives, the role of the super-powers and its performance and growth prospects. I have said in my comments on Ayoob's paper that a significant aspect of regional co-operation framework like GCC and ASEAN is that, notwithstanding their stated objectives and functions, they represent a sort of strategic division of labour between one of the superpowers (the US in this case) and the regional actors. Because of this, the factor of strategic harmony has been a key criterion and that is why GCC and ASEAN do not encompass all the regional actors. Another criterion can be developmental wherein the strategic differences in a given region will have to be given a back seat. An example of this type is taking shape in the form of South Asian Regional Co-operation (SARC) where, notwithstanding strategic divergences and schisms among the member countries, a common and co-ordinated approach to developmental issues is being developed. Pakistan's swing towards Southwest Asia is limited only to the strategic aspect, as a consequence of its security preoccupation with India, which has often received impetus and encouragement from extra-regional vested interests. But in terms of socio-cultural, economic and geographical reality, Pakistan belongs only to South Asia. Pakistan's Islam which is portrayed as an identity factor to club it with Southwest Asia is sub-continental rather than Arab or Persian.

The security objective of regional organizations has two components that are so closely interlinked that one affects the other. Both GCC and ASEAN have shown excessive preoccupation with the internal component of security. They have been concerned about domestic stability as well as intra-regional stability (ASEAN versus Indochina states and GCC versus Iran). Their approach towards both those concerns has been heavily biased in favour of military solutions. The lack of capabilities and confidence to achieve desired results has led these states to welcome external involvement, which has in turn vitiated their external security dimension, intensified internal cleavages and distorted developmental priorities. The result is that prospects of insecurity continue to haunt the regional actors in spite of these regional organizations. A more viable approach should have been to grapple with the issues of development and institutional changes so as to reduce, if not to eliminate, the sources and potentialities of internal insecurity on a long-term basis. It is amazing that neither GCC nor ASEAN has paid any attention to this aspect. This is where the prospects of O'Neill's recommendation of transforming 'more closed' societies into 'more open' societies for greater intra-state security seem discouraging.

Regarding the role of superpowers, O'Neill makes a very candid assertion that the 'US involvement is not quite optional in GCC'. This raises the question of the autonomy of regional organizations. Further, it clearly underlines the fact that GCC will have to co-ordinate and synchronise its overall strategic perspective with the US in order to function properly. Then what would be the implication of developments like Kuwait's purchase of arms from the Soviet Union? In the case of ASEAN, the lesser extent of US involvement as compared to GCC is a difference more of degree rather than of substance; because, in ASEAN, the US seems to have worked out an unwritten and unspecified arrangement with China regarding the sharing of strategic obligations. Any reference to the threat posed by China is conspicuous in O'Neill's paper by its absence. China is a major factor in the ASEAN states' threat perceptions, which is responsible for the undercurrent of strategic divergence between Thailand and Singapore on the one hand and Malaysia, Indonesia and the Philippines on the other.

In fact, it may not be an exaggeration to say that ASEAN does not have a deeply shared and viable regional security perception, notwithstanding its declaratory position on the Vietnam-Kampuchea issue. All that it has in common is a broad, loosely defined global strategic view, that gravitates towards the US. The tendency of the ASEAN members to look to the West existed much before the recent Kampuchean crisis and the grant of facilities by Vietnam to the Soviet Union in Cam Rahn Bay and Da Nang. O'Neill describes this ASEAN tendency as 'natural' but does not explain why this is so. He also indirectly hints that if the security situation deteriorates for ASEAN, more extensive arrangements 'involving clear American guarantees' cannot be ruled out. There seems to be an attempt in the paper to explain and even justify the ASEAN members' security links with the US. In any such attempt the charge that the US-ASEAN connection has been responsible for perpetuating ASEAN-Indochina tensions should also have been dealt with.

Both the Gulf and ASEAN regions are inherently unstable. A pertinent question that arises here is what would be the form of a blown-up security crisis, particularly in the Gulf, in the coming years? What would be the consequences of such a crisis not only for regional actors but also for world order? The US which is sufficiently deeply involved in the Gulf may have to intervene directly in any such crisis; more so during Reagan's second term, because controlled and orchestrated response may lead to greater domestic pressures as was the case in the Carter years. Action in Grenada, in a way diverted attention from its fiasco in Lebanon. Such diversions may not be available in future. Some of the possible scenarios emerging out of the questions raised above could have been discussed in the paper.

There is a whole range of other issues that is relevant to the subject of the paper but has not been analyzed. These issues pertain to the ways and means through which the global economic, technological, strategic and ideological systems impinge upon Third World security. These systems have been undergoing significant changes continuously, affecting the security situation in the Third World in one way or another. The transition from cold war to détente to the second cold war has added to the numbers, duration and intensity of inter-state and regional conflicts in the Third World. The breakdown of the North-South dialogue and the increasing economic burden in the form of debts on many Third World countries have made their internal stability precarious. What will be the shape of things to come on this front? Moreover, arms purchases in the Third World are increasing. How are these increases related to the production of newer and more sophisticated weapons in the developed countries? What will be the future security implication if this nexus between arms production and arms purchases continues to expand and consolidate itself notwithstanding all the peace, disarmament and development rhetoric? These and many such questions will confront human intelligence and innovativeness in the coming years. The two regions under discussion at the workshop could be sensitized to these questions.

PART 2: INTRA-STATE DIMENSIONS OF REGIONAL SECURITY

3 INTERNAL DIMENSIONS OF REGIONAL SECURITY IN SOUTHEAST ASIA

Sukhumbhand Paribatra and
Chai-Anan Samudavanija

Regional security in a broad sense can be taken to mean the degree to which relationships among states of a previously defined region as well as between those states and extra-regional actors are free from violence or threats of violence stemming directly or indirectly from a number of possible geostrategic, political, socio-economic and psychological sources both external and internal to that region.

It is not the purpose of this chapter to break new ground with compelling evidence from detailed research or apocalyptic new theories. Rather, this paper seeks to provide, on the basis of existing achievements of scholarship, what is hoped to be a 'fresh' and thought-provoking analysis of the nexus between domestic factors and regional security.

More specifically, this chapter aims first to identify what are understood to be the salient internal dimensions which are more or less common to Southeast Asian countries; secondly to analyze how and how far these internal dimensions may become 'externalized' or, to put it another way, may induce certain conditions or types of action and behaviour which (a) directly cause violence, (b) make violence more likely, or (c) exacerbate already existing violence, with consequences on regional security as previously defined; and thirdly to examine briefly the overall implications of these linkages.

Before the discussion begins, however, a number of caveats and explanations are in order. First of all, in a paper of this nature generalizations with their attendant pitfalls and inaccuracies are inevitable and it needs to be stressed that although here the emphasis is on commonality, the existence of differences and divergences within the region is fully acknowledged and taken into consideration. Secondly, much of the discussion that follows involves propositions which are not susceptible to scientific proofs, and indeed a search for such may prove to be both fruitless and counter-productive given the nature of the task at hand. Thirdly, while the focus is on 'instability', 'conflict', 'violence' and so on,

Table 3.1

Country	Role(s)	Output	Consequences/Implications
1. Indonesia	1.1 Leader of anti-colonialism 1.2 Leader of Malay world 1.3 Regional leader	Takeover West Irian 1962–3 Konfrontasi with Malaysia 1963–6 'Liberation' of East Timor 1975–6	Force used Tension/Conflict with neighbours especially Malaysia, Australia and Papua New Guinea
	1.4 Active-independent 1.5 Regional sub-system collaborator 1.6 Conciliator	Multidirectional diplomacy, especially in the regional, sub-regional contest Bridge-building *vis-à-vis* Communist Indochinese states	Development of ASEAN as sub-regional organization Development of ties with Vietnam Low-level but growing conflict with Thailand over Kampuchea issue (?)
2. Malaysia	2.1 Active-independent 2.2 Regional sub-system collaborator 2.3 Ideals promotor 2.4 Conciliator	Multidirectional diplomacy, especially in the regional, sub-regional context Bridge-building *vis-à-vis* Communist Indochinese states	Development of ASA as sub-regional organization Development of ASEAN as sub-regional organization Development of ZOPFAN concept Development of ties with Vietnam Possible conflict with Thailand over Kampuchea?
	2.5 Islamic world representative	Some groups in Kelantan and Sabah giving aid to armed Moslem separatist movements in Thailand and Sabah respectively	Mitigation of internal communal conflict Conflict with Thailand and Phillippines
3. Singapore	3.1 Active anti-Communist	Promotion of anti-Communist coalition Hardline policies against Communist states Armed preparedness ('Poisoned Shrimp' concept)	Tension/Conflict with Communist states Tendency towards arms accumulation in region Reaffirmation of US role in the region
	3.2 Regional sub-system collaborator	Active diplomacy in sub-regional context	Development of ASEAN as sub-regional organization Mitigation of intra-regional ethnic conflict

	3.3 Progressive economic centre	Multidirectional economic relationships competition with other countries	Economic relations forged with Indo-chinese states but conflict with Thailand and ASEAN partners
4. Thailand	4.1 Anti-Communist front-line state 4.2 Faithful ally	Promotion of anti-Communist coalition Hardline policies against Communist states, especially Vietnam Close alliance with US	Tension/Conflict with Communist states Reaffirmation of US role in region Development of ASEAN as an anti-Communist sub-regional organization Low-level but growing conflict with Indonesia and Malaysia over Kampuchea(?) Conflict with Malaysia over Moslem minority National security state with military established as predominate political force Tendency towards arms accumulation in region
	4.3 'Big Brother' (to Laos and Kampuchea)	Interventions, subversion, negative sanctions for 'bad behaviour'	Force used Long-standing conflict especially on Mekong river By extension, conflict with Vietnam
5. Vietnam	5.1 Leader of Indochina 5.2 Champion of anti-imperialist forces 5.3 Champion of revolution	Assertion of domination over Laos and Kampuchea by all means necessary Hardline policies toward anti-Communist and 'uncommunist' countries Support of revolutionary activities in other countries Special relationships with extra-regional Communist powers, first PRC, then USSR	Force used Conflict with anti-Communist countries Conflict with PRC (after 1975) Conflict with Thailand and by extension supporters of Thailand's position Presence of USSR in region Tendency towards arms accumulation in region

it must be pointed out here that although unrest, armed rebellions, revolutions and wars there certainly have been in post-independence Southeast Asia, the region *as a whole* has not been without a certain degree of tranquillity, security, and well-being. Outside Indochina no armed rebellion or revolution has succeeded in completely and comprehensively overturning an existing system of government and politics; there have only been three major revisions of the map of Southeast Asia by actual or threatened use of force (West Irian, 1963; Vietnam and East Timor, 1975–6); armed conflicts between regional states have been infrequent and, with the exception of Vietnam, Southeast Asians do not have mighty war machines poised to wage mighty wars upon one another; and despite a rapid population growth and much ill-advised exploitation of its natural endowments, the region remains a relatively rich one, possessing a balanced array of vital resources. Thus, when referring to instability, conflict, violence and such in Southeast Asia, one is not dealing in absolutes but, as is often the case in sciences dealing with human and social dimensions, in nuances, degrees and relativity.

The Problem of Legitimacy

The first, and perhaps the most crucial, internal dimension of Southeast Asian countries taken as a whole, is the lack of what has been aptly termed 'unconditional legitimacy'.[1] Although, as pointed out above, the post-independence map of Southeast Asia has not been much revised and outside of Indochina no major revolutionary transformation has successfully taken place, there exist challenges, both armed and unarmed, to the prevailing state boundaries as just and definitive lines of political, social and economic division; to the ruling regimes as appropriate orders of distributive justice; and to governments as fair and effective instruments of security and progress. Table 3.2 lists the major armed rebellions which have taken place or are still taking place in post-independence Southeast Asia.

One set of explanations for this lack of unconditional legitimacy may be termed 'structural'. As has been pointed out,[2] one meaning or component encompassed by the Weberian concept of legitimacy is a *common belief* in a given political and social order. For a number of reasons this common belief has been absent or weak from the time of independence.

Table 3.2: Major Armed Rebellions in Post-Independence Southeast Asia

Country	Armed Rebellion (dates of rebellion)	Objective of challenging State[1]	Regime[2]
Burma	1. Burma Communist Party (1948–)		x
	2. Ethnically-related armed rebellions (1948–)[3]	x	
Cambodia	1. Khmer Rouge (1970–5)		x
	2. Khmer Rouge/Khmer People's National Liberation Front/Moulinaka (1979–)		x
Indonesia	1. Madium Communist rebellion (1948)		x
	2. Darul Islam (1948–62)		x
	3. PRRI Permesta (1958–61)	x	
	4. Organisasi Papua Merdeka (1963–)	x	
	5. PKI (1965)		x
	6. Aceh Merdeka (1976–9)	x	
	7. Fretilin (1976–)	x	
Laos	1. Pathet Lao (1951–75)		x
	2. Le Lique de Résistance Meo (1946–75)	x(?)	x
Malaysia	1. Communist Party of Malaya (1948–)		x
	2. North Kalimantan Communist Party (1950s–)		x
Philippines	1. Huks (1946–54)		x
	2. New People's Army (1969–)		x
	3. Moro National Liberation Front (1972–)	x	
Singapore	none		
Thailand	1. Barisan Revolusi Nasional (1960–)	x	
	2. Communist Party of Thailand (1965–)		x
	3. CPT-related minority group (1965–)	x	
	4. Pattani United Liberation Organization (1967–)	x	
	5. Barisan Nasional Pembebasan Pattani (1971–)	x	
Vietnam (South)	1. National Liberation Front (1958–75)	x	x
	2. Le Front Unifié de Liberation des Races Opprimées or FULRO (1964–75)	x	
	3. Le Mouvement pour l'Autonomie des Hauts-Plateaux (1961–75)	x(?)	x

Notes:

1. Armed rebellions with overt intentions of 'revising' the existing relationships with central governments or the prevailing state boundaries by setting up more

autonomous regional administration, seceding to form an independent state, or seceding to join another state, are considered to be challenging the state as an institution.

2. Armed rebellions with overt intentions of changing in a more or less comprehensive way the political, economic and/or social order prevailing in a given state are considered to be challenging the existing regime as an institution.

3. According to one authority, since 1948, there have been at least 24 ethnically-related rebel groups. See David I. Steinberg, 'Constitutional and Political Bases of Minority Insurrections: Burma', presented at the Workshop on 'Armed Separatist Movements in Southeast Asia' organized by the Institute of Southeast Asian Studies, on 7–9 December 1983 in Singapore.

The first reason is the artificial creation of modern 'nation-states' in Southeast Asia. Today's state boundaries, together with their underlying philosophy, concepts, norms and aspirations concerning nationhood, have been superimposed for administrative convenience by the colonial powers on a region of immense heterogeneity, where at least 32 ethnolinguistic groups and all the world's major belief systems are to be found, and these boundaries in most cases do not correspond to the actual ethnolinguistic and religious dividing lines (see Tables 3.3 and 3.4). Thus, there exist within each Southeast Asian state enclaves of minorities who are not always willing to accept or identify with such an 'alien' construct as a matter of conviction or habit, especially since acceptance or identification often entails subjugation by another ethnolinguistic or religious group. Although the existence of a minority ipso facto does not mean that there will necessarily be an armed rebellion or that if there is an armed rebellion it will inevitably succeed, there have been sufficient cases of ethnic or religious dissidence to suggest that there is an absence of basic consensus concerning what constitutes nationhood and that such an absence, when joined with certain political and socio-economic factors, can lead to a violent rejection of the existing nation-state as an institution.[3]

The second reason is the artificial insemination of western ideas. Partly due to colonialism and partly due to the growth of communications in the post-war world, influences of such beliefs as liberalism and socialism have penetrated the region. This induces a breakdown in basic consensus concerning the values of distributive justice, for not only do such western ideas conflict with each other fundamentally but they also challenge, and often provoke reactions from, the traditional belief systems, particularly religious. At the same time, by clearly holding forth attractive images of ideal political and social orders they are apt to create radical discontentment

Table 3.3: Ethnolinguistic Composition of Southeast Asian States, 1976

State	Ethnolinguistic Groups	Percentage of Population
Burma	Burman	75
	Karen	10
	Shan	6
	Indian-Pakistani	3
	Chinese	1
	Kachin	1
	Chin	1
Cambodia	Khmer	90
	Chinese	6
	Cham	1
	Mon-Khmer tribes	1
Indonesia	Javanese	45
	Sundanese	14
	Madurese	8
	Chinese	2
Laos	Lao	67
	Mon-Khmer tribes	19
	Tai (other than Lao)	5
	Meo	4
	Chinese	3
North Vietnam	Vietnamese	85
	Tho	3
	Muoung	2
	Tai	2
	Nung	2
	Chinese	1
	Meo	1
	Yao	1
South Vietnam	Vietnamese	87
	Chinese	5
	Khmer	3
	Mountain chain tribes	3
	Mon-Khmer tribes	1
Malaysia	Malay	44
	Chinese	35
	Indian	11
Philippines	Cebuano	24
	Tagalog	21
	Ilocano	12
	Hiligaynon	10
	Bicol	8
	Sumar-Leyte	6
	Pampangan	3
	Pangasinan	3

Table 3.3: Ethnolinguistic Composition of Southeast Asian States, 1976 — *continued*

State	Ethnolinguistic Groups	Percentage of Population
Singapore	Chinese	75
	Malay	14
	Indian-Pakistani	8
Thailand	Thai	60
	Lao	25
	Chinese	10
	Malay	3
	Meo, Khmer and others	2

Table 3.4: Distribution of Ethnic Groups in Southeast Asia

Name of Ethnic Groups	Country of Residence	Approx. Number
Meo		
Other names: Miao, Hmung,	China	2,500,000
Hmong, Hmu Meo, Mlao,	North Vietnam	219,514
Mnong, Miao-Tseu, H'moong,	Laos	300,000
Meau, Mong, Lao Som	Thailand	58,000
Yao		
Other names: Kim-Mien, Kim	China	660,000 to 745,985
Mun, Yu-Mien, Mien, Mun,	North Vietnam	186,071
Man, Zao	Laos	5,000
	Thailand	19,000
Kachin		
Other names: Chingpaw,	China	100,000
Jingpaw, Singhpo, Kakhieng,	Burma	350,000
Theinbaw		
Lahu		
Other names: Mussur, Musso,	China	139,000
Laku	Burma	66,000
	Thailand	18,000
	Laos	2,000
Karen		
Other names: Karean,	Burma	2 to 3 millions
Kariang, Kayin, Yang	Thailand	200,000
Under following groups		
(a) Kayah		
Other name: Karenni	Burma	75,000
(b) Pao		
Other name: Thaungthu	Burma	200,000

Table 3.4: Distribution of Ethnic Groups in Southeast Asia — *continued*

Name of Ethnic Groups	Country of Residence	Approx. Number
Chin Other names: Lushai, Kuki Koochie, Mizo	India Burma	821,000 200,000
Naga	India Burma	550,000 75,000
Mon Other names: Mun, Peguan, Taleng, Talaing	Burma Thailand	350,000 60,000
Thai Names of different groups: Thai Yia or Shan Thai (black, white, red)	China Burma Thailand South Vietnam Laos	About 9,500,000 Thais distributed among all 1,000,000 50,000 385,191 235,000
Tay	North Vietnam	503,995
Nung	North Vietnam	313,998
Ahom	India	345,000
(a) Rhade	South Vietnam	100,000
(c) Jarai	South Vietnam	150,000
Groups of primitive autochthonous hill tribes speaking one language of origin, i.e. Mon-Khmer		
(1) Kha or Lao-Teng	Laos Thailand	750,000 16,000
(2) Phnong or Khmer Loeu	Cambodia	54,000
(3) Moi	South Vietnam	500,000
(4) Wa or Kawa	China Burma	286,000 334,000
(5) Paulang Aborigines	Burma Malaysia	60,000 50,000

Source: Martial Dasse, *Montagnards Revoltes et Guerre Révolutionaries en Asie du Sud-Est Continentale* (D.K. Book House, Bangkok, 1976), pp. 236–8, translation from French by authors.

with the existing, transitional ones. Armed Communist rebellions, which have occurred in every Southeast Asian state with the exception of Singapore, and armed 'religious' rebellions, such as Dar'ul Islam and the Moro National Liberation Front, are the most dramatic, but by no means sole, manifestations of the absence of basic value consensus in the domestic politics of the region.

Apart from these structural factors, the lack of unconditional legitimacy can also be explained in terms of 'process'. Three other meanings encompassed by the Weberian concept of legitimacy are: a *claim* by an individual or a group of individuals to the right to rule over a given political and social order; a *justification* for the existing form and pattern of political rule or domination which entails unequal shares of scarce values, rights, privileges and opportunities for self-advancement in society; and *promises*, overt or implied, that that form and pattern of political rule or domination will contribute justly and effectively to the material and spiritual well-being of the ruled.[4]

Partly because of the structural problems discussed above, partly because of their own failings and impatience, and partly because of additional problems generated in the process of change, regimes and governments in Southeast Asia have seldom been able fully to justify their claim to the right to rule and make good their promises to confer benefits to the ruled.

In the immediate aftermath of independence, 'national self-determination', 'civil liberties' and 'individual rights' were justifications and promises made by the regimes and governments to make good their right to rule. However, these 'political goods' have not been fully delivered. Structural problems brought forth pains of birth and adolescence, as it were, and because they could not be easily coped with, concerns for 'unity', 'stability', 'order' and 'security', which were all too often identified with regime preservation, became of paramount importance. Accordingly, national self-determination came to mean little more than an imposition of the most powerful ethnic group's will upon the rest for the sake of 'national unity'; democracy and political participation became at best 'guided' in accordance with the values of distributive justice of the rulers for the sake of stability and order; and civil liberties and individual rights became circumscribed by more or less coercive and repressive measures for the sake of 'national security'. In this way, what might be termed an impulse towards authoritarianism has acted as an antithesis to the process of legitimation as originally

Table 3.5: Average Growth of Gross Domestic Product

Country	Average Growth Rates (per cent)*	
	1960–70	1970–81
Burma	2.6	4.8
Indonesia	3.9	7.8
Malaysia	6.5	7.8
Philippines	5.1	6.2
Singapore	8.8	8.5
Thailand	8.4	7.2

* Average growth rates are weighted by country GDP in 1970 dollars.

Source: The International Bank for Reconstruction and Development, *World Development Report 1983* (Oxford University Press for IBRD, New York, 1983), pp. 150–1.

conceived by Southeast Asia's regimes and governments.

In more recent years, the focus of the legitimation process especially in non-Communist Southeast Asian countries has shifted, though not entirely, to the economic sphere. Justifications and claims to the right to rule are now predominantly based on promises of economic performance which would bring 'development', 'progress', 'justice', 'resilience' and 'security' to the ruled. To a certain extent a good deal of success has been achieved, particularly in terms of economic growth (see Table 3.5). However, a number of problems have arisen in the process of economic change which serve to undermine the quest for legitimacy through promises to deliver 'economic goods'.

One such problem is the issue of distribution or equity. Development strategies generally chosen and implemented by non-Communist Southeast Asian governments are aimed at bringing about rapid economic growth with focus on urban-based industrial promotion and utilization of advanced technology in an environment of free enterprise. The underlying assumption is that sooner or later there will be 'trickle-down' effects and any maladjustments in terms of distribution will automatically be corrected. In that eventuality equity in terms of equal shares will not be achieved, but everyone's demands and requirements will be 'satisfied' and there will be further incentive to work for another round of growth and trickle-down effects.

However, this 'percolation theory', as it were, has not fully

Table 3.6: Income Distribution

Country/Year	60% Lowest Income Households' Share of Total Household Income (per cent)	10% Highest Income Households' Share of Total Household Income (per cent)
Burma	n.a.	n.a.
Indonesia 1976	27	34
Malaysia 1973	23.6	39.8
Philippines 1970–1	27.0	38.5
Singapore	n.a.	n.a.
Thailand 1975–6	29.1	34.1

worked in practice. The 'self-adjusting' mechanisms have not operated quickly or effectively enough, and consequently large and growing disparities in income and wealth exist between those who have and those who have not, in particular between the urban-industrial sector and the rural-agricultural sector (see Tables 3.6 and 3.7). Despite many a declaration of good faith by the governments that they would attempt to minimize the trade-off between growth and equity, for example by redistributional measures such as land reform, promotion of agricultural productivity and rural development, and progressive taxation, little has been achieved because the regimes concerned have not been willing to take the political risks inherent in such measures, and indeed themselves have vested interests in the continuation and preservation of the status quo. Since the justification for their rule has been based on promises to bring progress to all, failure to bring about a more just distribution of benefits cannot but serve to undermine the process of legitimation. The crucial importance of failure is underlined by the fact that with a few exceptions, minority groups which, as discussed above, already have grievances against central governments, are seldom beneficiaries of overall economic growth.[5]

The second problem concerns dynamic socio-economic forces unleashed in the process of economic growth and change especially in non-Communist countries. During this process the economies become complex with growing division of labour between various sectors, criss-crossing patterns of production and exchange, and formation of interest groups; significant movements of population from rural to urban areas taking place (see Tables 3.7 and 3.8);

Table 3.7: Sector Distribution of Production and Population in 1960 and 1981

Country	Agricultural Production as % of Total GDP		Rural Population as % of Total Population		Industrial Production as % of Total GDP		Urban Population as % of Total Population	
	1960	1981	1960	1981	1960	1981	1960	1981
Burma	33	47	81	72	20	23	19	28
Indonesia	50	24	85	79	25	53	15	21
Malaysia	36	23	75	70	27	54	25	30
Philippines	26	23	70	63	48	62	30	37
Singapore	4	1	—	—	30	71	100	100
Thailand	40	24	87	85	32	48	13	15

Source: *World Development Report 1983*, pp. 152–3, 190–1.

Table 3.8: Demographic Indicators

Country	Population in mid-1981 (million)	Projected Population (million)		Average Annual Growth Rate of Labour Force (per cent)			Average Growth Rate of Urban Population (per cent)	
		1990	2000	1960–70	1970–81	1980–2000	1960–70	1970–81
Burma	34.1	42	52	1.1	1.4	2.2	3.9	3.9
Indonesia	149.5	179	216	1.7	2.5	2.0	3.6	4.0
Laos	3.5	4	6	1.0	0.7	2.7	3.7	5.2
Malaysia	14.2	17	21	2.8	2.9	3.1	3.5	3.3
Philippines	49.6	62	76	2.1	2.5	2.9	3.8	3.7
Singapore	2.4	3	3	2.8	2.7	1.3	2.4	1.5
Thailand	48.0	58	69	2.1	2.8	2.3	3.5	3.4

Source: *World Development Report 1983*, pp. 148–9, 184–5, 188–9, 190–1.

Table 3.9: Education

Country	% of Population Enrolled for Higher Education		Adult Literacy Rate	
	1960	1979	1960	1980
Burma	1	4	60	66
Indonesia	1	n.a.	39	62
Laos	n.a.	n.a.	28	44
Malaysia	1	3	53	60
Philippines	13	25	72	75
Singapore	6	8	n.a.	83
Thailand	2	13	68	86
Vietnam	n.a.	3	n.a.	87

Source: *World Development Report 1983*, pp. 196–7.

and, partly as a result of higher standards of living and partly as a result of this country-to-town migration, a rapid expansion of literacy and higher education ensues (Tables 3.8 and 3.9).

These trends have three major consequences. One is that a pluralism of conflicting and irreconcilable demands, requirements and interests, often with elite groups, is created. The second is that social mobilization takes place at a fast pace, creating rising expectations, which are political as well as economic, and also rising frustrations where those expectations are not fulfilled. The third is that an ever increasing number of people are uprooted from their traditional, land-based values and, while still imperfectly acculturated to the 'new world', remain an unpredictable factor, a potential source of dissent and discontent.

In this context the parameters of the legitimation process become transformed. Regimes and governments may be able to continue to deliver more economic goods, but for some 'more' may not be 'enough', either because a greater share is going to another interest group or because much more is expected not only in terms of economic well-being but also in terms of political participation or freedom, while for others more may be 'too much', given many Southeast Asians' innate conservatism, as evident from the growth of Islamic fundamentalism in the region. The transformation of the parameters of the legitimation process puts regimes and governments squarely in a dilemma. On the one hand, continued economic growth and development are still seen to be necessary for their legitimation, but, on the other hand, socio-economic changes

Table 3.10: Growth of Exports and Imports of Non-Communist Southeast Asian Countries

Countries	Exports (million US$)	Imports (million US$)
Indonesia		
1965–7	731	620
1971–3	2,063	1,654
1977–9	12,692	6,700
Malaysia		
1965–7	1,232	1,131
1971–3	2,146	1,854
1977–9	8,179	6,009
Philippines		
1965–7	843	923
1971–3	1,348	1,446
1977–9	3,699	5,297
Singapore		
1965–7	1,007	1,253
1971–3	2,515	3,760
1977–9	10,610	13,802
Thailand		
1965–7	645	1,015
1971–3	1,159	1,615
1977–9	4,276	5,728

Source: Rechain Chintayarangsan, 'ASEAN's Primary Commodity Exports', in United Nations Economic and Social Commission for Asia and the Pacific *ASEAN and Pacific Economic Co-operation* (UNESCAP, Bangkok, 1983), p. 22.

generated by economic growth and development greatly complicate and indeed undercut the quest for legitimacy. This dilemma in all probability can only be resolved by implementation of thorough-going institutional and political reforms which, given Southeast Asian leaders' impulse towards authoritarianism, may not be easily or painlessly forthcoming.

The third problem, which has emerged in the process of economic change to undermine the quest for legitimacy through promises to deliver 'economic goods', is the growth of inter-dependence. Economic strategies based on high growth and free enterprise serve to open up the economies of non-Communist countries and increasingly link them to the world trade, investment, credit and energy systems (see Tables 3.10, 3.11, 3.12 and 3.13), as

Table 3.11: Private Direct Investment Inflows for Non-Communist Southeast Asian Countries 1967–1980 (million US$)

Year	Indonesia	Malaysia	Philippines	Singapore	Thailand
1967	− 10	43	− 9	34	43
1968	− 2	30	− 3	26	60
1969	32	80	6	38	51
1970	83	94	− 29	93	42
1971	139	100	− 6	116	39
1972	207	114	− 21	191	68
1973	15	172	54	389	77
1974	− 49	571	4	596	189
1975	476	350	97	611	86
1976	344	381	126	331	105
1977	235	406	209	335	106
1978	279	467	163	739	53
1979	219	647	73	911	50
1980	184	928	40	1,454	186
Cumulative Total 1967–80	2,152	4,383	704	5,864	1,155

Source: Development Planning Division, UNESCAP, 'ASEAN Investments from Pacific Sources' in *ASEAN and Pacific Economic Co-operation*, p. 188.

Table 3.12: Foreign Capital Borrowing of Non-Communist Southeast Asian Countries (outstanding, end of year)

Country	Foreign Capital Borrowing
Indonesia (1979)	17,002.0
Malaysia (1980)	4,696.3
Philippines (1980)	9,637.2
Singapore (1977)	1,188.5
Thailand (1980)	5,921.9

Source: Yen Kyun Wang, 'Monetary Interdependence among ASEAN and Pacific Countries' in *ASEAN and Pacific Economic Co-operation*, p. 258.

well as, inevitably transnational influences of tastes, ideas and belief-systems. The trend has two major consequences. One is that regional economies become increasingly sensitive or vulnerable to fluctuations in the world market, monetary system and energy supply, as well as a long-term decline in the terms of trade (see Table 3.14). The other is that domestic socio-economic systems become mirror images, albeit somewhat distorted and on a reduced scale, of the global systems with their pluralism of demands,

Table 3.13: Energy Consumption and Import of Non-Communist Southeast Asian Countries

Country	Average Growth Rate of Consumption (%)		Per Capita Consumption (KG coal equivalent)		Energy Import as % of Merchandise Exports	
	1960–74	1974–80	1960	1980	1960	1980
Burma	4.3	5.8	60	87	4	n.a.
Indonesia	4.3	9.0	129	266	3	8
Malaysia	4.1	7.7	616	818	2	13
Philippines	9.7	4.4	159	380	9	41
Singapore	10.1	6.6	2,111	8,544	17	36
Thailand	16.3	6.5	63	370	12	44

Source: *World Development Report 1983*, pp. 162–3.

Table 3.14: Terms of Trade of Non-Communist Southeast Asian Countries

Country	Terms of Trade (1975 = 100)	
	1978	1981
Indonesia	95	154
Malaysia	109	101
Philippines	98	68
Singapore	102	n.a.
Thailand	87	62

Source: *World Development Report 1983*, pp. 164–5.

requirements, interests and issue-specific or functional group formations; or to put it another way, the openness of the regional economies accelerates the trend towards domestic pluralism.

In this context, the parameters of the legitimation process are further transformed. Delivery of promises is not only made dependent on uncontrollable, unpredictable, exogenous factors but also rendered more complicated and difficult to attain by transnationally induced pluralism. Once more regimes and governments are put squarely in a dilemma. On the one hand, openness is necessary for the process of legitimation, but, on the other hand, if uncontrolled it may undercut the very quest for legitimacy.

Thus, the shift in focus to the economic sphere in the process of legitimation has not been without difficulties despite the relatively high economic growth within the region, and there is no reason to surmise that these difficulties will diminish in the years ahead. On the contrary, with the average growth rates of the labour forces predicted to be mostly above 2 per cent for the rest of this century (see Table 3.8) and the approaching exhaustion of agricultural land frontiers, especially in Indonesia and Thailand, and indeed of a number of raw materials, the demands and constraints on the economies and economic planners are likely to multiply and not subside. In this connection, it should be pointed out that although the discussion concerning claims and justifications being based on promises to deliver economic goods is mainly concerned with the non-Communist countries of Southeast Asia, most notably the five original members of ASEAN (Indonesia, Malaysia, Philippines, Singapore and Thailand), it may in a not so distant future also to a degree apply to the Communist countries: as illustrated by the existence of a large black market economy in Vietnam, to a certain extent the demand for the delivery of economic goods especially consumer items is already there and may increase once the economy is demobilized from its war-footing.

The foregoing suggests that for reasons of structure and process there is in Southeast Asia a relative lack of unconditional legitimacy which is usually enjoyed by western states. It does not follow that regional states are weak in terms of disposable power and likely to disintegrate or that their regimes are always unstable and shortlived. But it does follow that Southeast Asian states are more or less fragile in nature, and this fragility is reflected in the absence of effective political institutionalization, last-resort dependence on instruments of coercion however subtly disguised and manipulated,[6] and propensity towards delegitimation, or 'the process of making explicit, self-conscious rejections and attacks on the ultimate grounds on which a system of legitimacy is predicated',[7] with the potentiality for domestic violence that such a process entails.

The internal problem of legitimacy becomes externalized with consequences on regional security as previously defined in a number of interrelated ways.

The first is through intervention and subversion from the outside. As Mohammed Ayoob succinctly puts it, 'fragile polities, by definition, are easily permeable'.[8] Southeast Asian states because of their fragility and permeability are easily susceptible to external interference. Voluminous tomes have already been written about great power intervention and subversion in this region, especially the United States' activities in Indochina and the People's Republic of China's (PRC) support for Communist movements in Burma, Thailand, Malaysia and Indonesia. However, it needs to be pointed out that great powers have not been alone in conducting such activities but that Southeast Asian states' permeability makes them equally, or perhaps more, vulnerable to frequent interventions and subversion from their neighbouring countries. A number of cases can be cited: Thailand's armed support of the rightists in Laos in the early 1960s and the policy of encouraging, directly or through strategic 'absentmindedness', minority resistance to the Rangoon government; Vietnam's continuing interference in neighbouring Indochinese states culminating in the accession of a strongly pro-Vietnamese Pathet Lao government in 1975 and the 1978–9 intervention in Cambodia; Indonesia's subversion, punctuated by token invasions, of Malaysia during the *Konfrontasi*; and some Malaysian groups' support for Moslem separatist movements in Thailand and the Philippines. The problem of external interventions and subversion is likely to be an unending one, for Southeast Asian states' fragility and permeability, arising from their lack of unconditional legitimacy, not only provide the requisite conditions for such interference but are to a great degree also exacerbated by them. One eminent authority even claims that:

> The one ingredient most vital to revolutionary success or to indefinitely sustaining a rebellion is substantial foreign support. While foreign support exists, the game can go on — perhaps even without significant domestic resources . . . — and when foreign support is cut off or withdrawn, insurgencies die. The historical record in Southeast Asia seems clear on the vital nature of external support . . . Without it, success is probably impossible; with it, failure can almost always be prevented.[9]

The second way through which the internal problem of legitimacy becomes externalized with consequences for regional security is the growth of militarization. Southeast Asian states' lack of unconditional legitimacy and the fragility emanating therefrom force them more or less to depend on instruments of coercion of which armed forces and paramilitary formations form an indispensable part. Two implications follow from this. The first is that although, with the exception of Vietnam whose small economic base supports some 1,200,000 men under arms, regional states' defence expenditures as percentages of their incomes are not usually high (see Table 3.15) and their armaments are not always of the latest vintage or of the most formidable power,[10] there is a constant propensity to increase such expenditures over time (for one estimate, see Table 3.16) with procurement of increasingly modern weapons, some with undeniable offensive capabilities.[11] The second is that although much has been said about the need to find political solutions to problems of internal dissent, armed or otherwise, there seems to be a constant predisposition to use military or para-military force to control and suppress such dissent, an example being Thailand whose governments have often proclaimed the desirability and the efficacy of political offensives and yet have never ceased to launch military ones against the Communist Party of Thailand and the Communist Party of Malaya.

These 'tendencies' can adversely affect regional security in a

Table 3.15: Defence Budgets as Percentages of Gross Domestic Products[1] of Selected Countries in the Asia-Pacific Region

Country	1980–81	1981–82	1982–83
Australia	2.80	2.94	3.17
Bangladesh	1.31	1.13	1.27
India	4.63	4.59	4.26
Indonesia	2.89	3.18	3.14
Japan	0.86	0.92	0.98
Korea, North	8.55	9.67	11.11
Korea, South	6.13	6.38	7.86
Malaysia	6.50	5.90	8.29
New Zealand	0.18	2.17	2.19
Pakistan	6.70	7.82	7.00
Philippines	n.a.	2.33	2.40
Singapore	5.32	5.44	6.00
Sri Lanka	1.66	0.68	0.89
Taiwan	8.00	7.84	7.14
Thailand[2]	3.27	3.53	3.68

Notes:
1. GNP where GDP not available.
2. Sources: Budget Bureau, Government Budget in Outline for FY 1982–83 (Bangkok, 1983) and the National Economic and Social Development Board.

Source: International Institute for Strategic Studies, *The Military Balance* (IISS, London, various years) and Far Eastern Economic Review, *Asian Year Book* (FEER, Hong Kong, various years).

number of ways. First of all, military build-up requires arms procurement and arms generally can only be procured from great powers; thus militarization provides channels through which the latter can become more permanently involved and accordingly the logics of their fears, ambitions and interests become more firmly embedded in regional security issues with all the uncertainty and potentiality for violence that such a course of events entails. Secondly, military build-up, though predominantly for internal purposes, enhances threat perceptions of enemies and rivals and consequently the level of tension existing at any given moment in the region. Thirdly, while increased armed strength can deter, it can also ensure that violence once precipitated can escalate beyond bounds of logic or rationality, as the Iraq-Iran War has clearly demonstrated. And lastly, police actions or counter-insurgency operations can spill over into contiguous territories and thus cause or exacerbate bilateral conflicts such as in the cases of Thai-Malaysian and Thai-Burmese relations.

Table 3.16: Growth of Armed Forces and Defence Expenditures in Southeast Asia 1969—78

Country		Armed Forces (thousands)	Military Expenditure (MILEX)	MILEX Per Capita	MILEX/Central Government Expenditure %
		(million US$ constant 1977)			
Burma	1969	173	156	6	31
	1978	212	156	5	25
% change		23%	0%		
Indonesia	1969	358	784	6	42.7
	1978	250	1,480	10	13.4
% change		−30%	89%	67%	
Malaysia	1969	46	207	19	13.5
	1978	82	615	46	14.3
% change		78%	197%	142%	
Philippines	1969	55	140	3	8.8
	1978	156	610	13	18.3
% change		183%	336%	333%	
Singapore	1969	12	191	95	38.9
	1978	64	409	178	18.9
% change		433%	114%	87%	
Thailand	1969	175	309	8	15.7
	1978	250	670	14	17.9
% change		43%	117%	75%	

Source: Richard Tanter, 'Militarization in Asia', a paper presented at the Asian Peace Research Association and International Peace Research Association Workshop on Militarization and Society, Tokyo, 3—8 April (1982).

The third way through which the internal problem of legitimacy becomes externalized is the promotion of external conflict behaviour as a means of unifying a divided or fragile state.

It has long been postulated by students of politics that there may be a direct linkage between domestic politics and external conflict behaviour of a state. The existence of an enemy or a common problem, real or imagined, can act as an integrative force for a social group: it helps to define the group's boundaries, override centrifugal tendencies with a stong uniform impulse and channel all the energies of group members towards one common end, that of confronting or fighting the enemy.[12] Thus, in the face of mounting internal problems which threaten the position of a regime and/or the unity and survival of a body politic, leaders may use an external conflict as a means of promoting internal cohesion as well as preserving the existing structure of power within that body politic. As Ernest Haas and Allen Whiting wrote:

> Groups seeking self-preservation and no more may be driven to a foreign policy of conflict — if not open war — in order to defend themselves against the onslaught of domestic rather than foreign enemies. In times of extreme tensions among elites, a policy of uniting a badly divided nation against some real or alleged outside threat frequently seems useful to a ruling group.[13]

Although the debate whether this linkage is statistically verifiable remains and is likely to remain unresolved,[14] the theory is intuitively attractive in the context of Southeast Asia where states suffer from an absence of unconditional legitimacy. At the risk of overindulging in a feast of theorizing, one might draw up a possible list of the type of external conflict behaviour Southeast Asian states have engaged in out of considerations of domestic unity, along with some cases as illustrations:

External Conflict Behaviour	*Cases*
1. Public demonstrations against an 'enemy'.	Thailand *vis-à-vis* Indochinese states on several occasions since 1976, including during the 1983 constitutional debate.
2. Doctrinal offensive/War of words.	Indonesia under Sukarno against OLDEFOS, Communist states as a practice.
3. Establishment of a 'bogey' to explain failure or disunity and to promote unity.	Indonesia under Sukarno against OLDEFOS; 'New Order' Indonesia *vis-à-vis* PRC.
4. Negative sanctions.	Thailand vis-à-vis Laos since 1975.

External Conflict Behaviour	*Cases*
5. Maintaining a strong military posture 'in face of surrounding threats'/Image-building of leaders as great 'warriors'.	Thailand since 1981, with the rise of General Arthit Kamlang-ek.
6. Territorial claims.	Philippines' claim on Sabah.
7. Territorial aggrandizement.	Indonesia and the West Irian issue; Indonesia and the *Konfrontasi*.

Such internally motivated external conflict behaviour inevitably has an impact on regional security. At best it is apt to raise the level of tension within the region and at worst may lead directly to violence by accident or design.

So long as Southeast Asian states have problems of legitimacy, these externalizations are likely to remain and in conjunction with other factors may serve to undermine regional security for the foreseeable future. We can now turn our attention, somewhat more briefly, to other internal dimensions.

Threat Perceptions

The second internal dimension is the problem of threat perceptions which in Southeast Asia are diverse, complex, multilevel and not easily susceptible to change — or reason.

As Harold and Margaret Sprout have pointed out,[15] policymakers move simultaneously in psychological and operational environments. Policies are formulated not on the basis of objective reality as such but on the basis of interpretations of that reality. These interpretations may or may not correspond to the reality because the process of receiving and transforming real data into analyses and decisions has a tendency to be influenced by preexisting psychological predispositions including images of enemies and perceptions of threats emanating therefrom.[16] Thus, any study of regional security issues should embrace a consideration of regional states' threat perceptions which may not be direct causes of regional conflicts but can exacerbate tensions and put into motion an escalatorial process leading to violence.

Moreover, given Southeast Asia's history of turmoil and the

fragility of its states, an analysis of threat perceptions in the region is even more crucial. As Klaus Knorr wrote:

> Threat perception is experientially easy for societies, especially weak ones, that have been subject to repeated attack and military pressure. They are naturally sensitive to the signs of danger or to its sudden eruption . . . For materially weaker societies, the margin of survivable error is small, and historical experience produces alertness . . . The absence of immediate threat is not necessarily reassuring.[17]

To reduce the complexity of the issues involved, factors influencing threat perceptions in Southeast Asia can be divided into six categories or dimensions which are by no means mutually exclusive.[18]

The first is the geopolitical dimension. Threat perceptions may arise from a number of factors: (a) geographical proximity or contiguity, (b) discrepancy in size, (c) geographical disadvantages (location, form, topographic features), (d) discrepancy in geostrategic capabilities. At the risk of oversimplification, one might summarize Southeast Asian states' geopolitically-induced threat perceptions as follows:

Geopolitical Dimension

Country	Source of Perceived Threat	Underlying Factors
1. Burma	China	(a), (b), (d)
	Thailand (?)	(a), (d)
2. Cambodia	Vietnam	(a), (b), (c), (d)
	Thailand	(a), (b), (c), (d)
3. Indonesia	—	—
4. Laos	Vietnam (before 1975)	(a), (b), (c), (d)
	Thailand	(a), (b), (c), (d)
	China	(a), (b), (c), (d)
5. Malaysia	Vietnam (?)	(a)
	Philippines (?)	(a), (b)
	Indonesia	(a), (b)
6. Philippines	Japan	(a), (d)

Country	Source of Perceived Threat	Underlying Factors
7. Singapore	Malaysia (?)	(a), (b), (c)
	Hostile power with naval presence (USSR?)	(a), (d)
	Indonesia (?)	(a), (b)
8. Thailand	Vietnam	(a), (c)
	China	(a), (b), (d)
	Burma (?)	(a)
9. Vietnam	Thailand	(a), (c)
	China	(a), (b), (c), (d)
	Philippines (US bases)	(a), (d)

The second is the historical dimension. Most persons and institutions have memories of 'bad' experiences from which come images of those thought to be responsible for such experiences. An image of an enemy once formed is not easily changed, for more often than not it is preserved in school textbooks and in oral history, thus becoming part of the socialization process or concretized in government policies, contingency plans and such like. These experiences can come from: (a) past wars (b) past domination or occupation by foreign power(s), or (c) particular 'traumas'. Again at the risk of oversimplification, one might summarize Southeast Asian states' historically-induced threat perceptions as follows:

Historical Dimensions

Country	Source of Perceived Threat	Underlying Factors
1. Burma	China	(a), (b)
	Thailand (?)	(a)
2. Cambodia	Vietnam	(a), (b)
	Thailand	(a), (b)
3. Indonesia	China	(c)
4. Laos	Vietnam (before 1975)	(a), (b)
	Thailand	(a), (b)
	China	(a), (b)
5. Malaysia	China	(c)
	Indonesia	(a), (c)
6. Philippines	Japan	(b), (c)

Country	Source of Perceived Threat	Underlying Factors
7. Singapore	Malaysia	(b), (c)
8. Thailand	Burma (?)	(a), (c)
	Vietnam	(a)
	China	(c)
9. Vietnam	Thailand	(a)
	China	(a), (b)
	USA	(a), (b)

The third is what might be termed the doctrinal dimension. Each state has its own value and belief system; this is inculcated into individuals more or less as part of the socialization process and forms prisms or lenses through which they view the world. Where two parties' value and belief systems conflict, there is a tendency towards polarization and mutual threat perception. Such is the situation in Southeast Asia where since the end of colonialism there have been conflict and polarization between those countries which are Communist and those which are not. Although various degrees of détente and 'neighbourliness' have been brought about most notably by Malaysia and Indonesia, it is highly unlikely that, given the fragility of Southeast Asian states, vastly differing conceptions of order and justice can be sufficiently reconciled to lessen with any permanence the prevailing threat perceptions.

The fourth is the socio-cultural dimension. As discussed above, Southeast Asia is a heterogeneous region where a number of different ethnic, cultural and religious groups live in close proximity to one another and where post-independence political boundaries are by no means coterminous with ethnic, cultural or religious dividing lines. Thus, for Southeast Asian regimes the task of building unity out of diversity, of forging modern nationhood out of centrifugal elements, is a most immediate, demanding and sensitive one. In this context, perceptions of threat can arise from a number of factors: (a) enmity or antagonism with another socio-cultural group which may be rooted in the past, (b) fear that another country may give help and succour to a (potentially) dissident or rebellious group within one's country, (c) another government's suppression or persecution of a socio-cultural group similar or identical to one's own and (d) fear that one's socio-cultural balance may be upset by another government's actions, behaviour or influence. These threat perceptions may be tabulated as follows:

Socio-Cultural Dimension

Country	Source of Perceived Threat	Underlying Factors
1. Burma	Thailand	(b)
	China (?)	(b)
2. Cambodia	Vietnam	(b), (c)
3. Indonesia	China	(a), (b)
4. Laos	China	(b)
	Thailand	(b)
	Vietnam (before 1975)	(b)
5. Malaysia	China	(b), (d)
	Thailand	(c)
6. Philippines	Malaysia	(b)
7. Singapore	China	(d)
8. Thailand	Vietnam	(a), (b)
	China	(a), (b)
	Malaysia	(b)
	Laos	(b)
9. Vietnam	China	(a), (b)

The fifth is the economic dimension. Threat perceptions can arise from either: (a) fear of economic domination by a minority group within one's country which may have ties with a foreign country or (b) fear of economic domination or exploitation by another country or group of countries.

Economic Dimensions

Country	Source of Perceived Threat	Underlying Factors
1. Burma	Foreign countries in general	(b)
2. Cambodia	Vietnam	(a), (b)
	Thailand	(b)
3. Indonesia	China	(a)
	Japan	(b)
4. Laos	Vietnam (before 1975)	(b)
	Thailand	(b)

Country	Source of Perceived Threat	Underlying Factors
5. Malaysia	China	(a)
6. Philippines	Japan	(b)
7. Singapore	—	—
8. Thailand	China	(a)
	Japan	(b)
	Singapore	(b)
9. Vietnam	China	(a)

The sixth is the structural dimension. Political or bureaucratic machineries and institutions tend to be rigid in their viewpoints in that they are predisposed to gather, select and analyze data to conform with the logic of their vested interests and past advocacy of certain standpoints or policies. These viewpoints may be influenced in the first place by a number of exogenous factors but once formulated acquire a life, momentum and importance of their own, and dissent within the machineries or institutions concerned is minimized through institutional self-doctrination, structure of rewards and promotion and force of habit. Thus, if a bureaucracy or a political machinery is a highly influential one within the body politic, 'national' interests and 'national' threat perceptions may be no more than the interests and threat perceptions of that bureaucracy or political machinery which may or may not conform to the prevailing reality. In Southeast Asia, the following threat perceptions may be highly influenced by structural factors: non-Communist states' *vis-à-vis* Communist states in general, and vice versa; 'New Order' Indonesia's *vis-à-vis* China; Malaysia's *vis-à-vis* China; Thailand's *vis-à-vis* Vietnam and China.

Thus, threat perceptions in Southeast Asia are complex, diverse and multilevel. Although there is no method whereby the degrees of their intensity may be measured, one can identify certain consequences which emanate from them.

The first is that these threat perceptions create and preserve a relatively high level of tension in the region where the possibility of outbreak of violence is constantly present. In particular, there are a number of potentially explosive dyadic relationships, namely between Vietnam and China, Vietnam and Thailand, Thailand and Burma, Thailand and Malaysia, and Malaysia and the Philippines.

The second is that there is a predisposition on the part of regional states to seek patrons or protectors. Threat perceptions create insecurity and uncertainty which may only be allayed by close relationship with a friendly great power and the latter's presence in the region. The differences between Thailand and the Philippines, on the one hand, and Indonesia, Malaysia and Singapore, on the other, concerning the necessity for the United States to play a role in Southeast Asia are differences in degree not in kind. The fact and prospect of continuing involvement by great powers, as discussed previously, constitute additional, unpredictable variables in the calculus of regional security questions.

The third, again as discussed above, is that there is a tendency towards militarization, both in terms of growing defence expenditures and in terms of the use of force to suppress dissident groups, which serve to preserve or heighten the existing level of tension and potentiality for inter-state violence.

At this point, one can turn briefly to the third internal dimension, namely national role conception.

National Role Conception

Related to threat perceptions are nations' conceptions of what their roles should be in the external environment or, to put it another way, their definition of the general types of decisions, commitments, rules and actions appropriate for themselves and of the functions they should perform in various geographical or issue milieus. These national role conceptions may be more strongly held by one group of leaders or at one point in history than another, and indeed like all things in life are subject to change, transformation and obsolescence. However, once formulated, they tend to have a permanence, force and momentum of their own which transcend specific changes of governments and even regimes, and act as influences on discrete acts performed by those espousing them.[19] At the risk of oversimplification, some of Southeast Asian states' salient role conceptions, the more or less specific policy outputs or acts these conceptions lead to and the consequences, actual or potential, on regional security, have been tabulated in Table 3.1 (pp. 58–9).

If this tabulation is accepted, a number of further observations can be made. The first, and the most self-evident, is that within Southeast Asia there is a fair variety of national role conceptions, which reflects the fundamental heterogeneity of the region. The second is that perhaps with the exception of Indonesia's conception of its own role as a leader of anti-colonialist forces, their continuity and quality of permanence can easily be seen. The third is that although a number of role conceptions seem to be exerting positive influences on regional security, most notably Indonesia's and Malaysia's 'active-independent', 'regional sub-system collaborator' and 'conciliator' roles, most of the role conceptions seem to be contributing in one way or another to conflict, tension and violence in the region, especially in the case of Thailand and Vietnam, the rivalry between whom is currently manifested in the Kampuchean problem. And the fourth is that if it is correct to detect a quality of permanence in these national role conceptions and at the same time to attribute to them a number of negative influences on regional security, then the prospect for Southeast Asia is hardly an attractive one. Although major wars between regional actors may not eventuate because of the existence of certain mitigating factors, conflict, tension and varying degrees of violence seem likely to be part and parcel of regional politics for the foreseeable future.

Some Afterthoughts

The foregoing is an attempt to examine the linkages, and the consequences emanating from such linkages, between the main internal dimensions of Southeast Asian states, that is the problem of legitimacy, threat perceptions and national role conceptions and regional security. Although the degree of insecurity, instability and violence prevailing in Southeast Asia should not be exaggerated, it seems evident that these internal dimensions tend to have adverse impacts on regional security especially in the context where certain external dimensions, for example conflict and rivalry between great powers, also exist as crucial determinants of questions relating to war and peace within the region.

Indeed, one can say that in the present conflict over Kampuchea one has one of the clearest cases of regional security problems arising from a convergence of various dimensions, a number of which can be enumerated as follows:

(a) The utter failure of four successive regimes in Kampuchea to establish and maintain even a modicum of legitimacy;

(b) Mutual threat perceptions between Vietnam and Thailand which arise mainly from geopolitical, historical and ideological factors;

(c) Mutual threat perceptions between Vietnam and China which are based on geopolitical and socio-cultural factors;

(d) Vietnam's conception of its own role as the leader of all Indochina, champion of anti-imperialist forces and revolution which stands in juxtaposition to Thailand's conception of its own role as the frontline state, a faithful ally and 'Big Brother' to Laos and Kampuchea, and indeed also to the PRC's conception of its own role as a great power, the champion of the Communist Revolution and the protector of the past glories of the Middle Kingdom; and

(e) Conflict and rivalry between the PRC, the Soviet Union and the United States.

Furthermore, the stalemate over Kampuchea also demonstrates that, because of the existence of a number of converging dimensions, regional security problems are not easily resolved. In particular, there is no self-evident way of influencing or transforming the *internal* dimensions of regional security. For example, confidence-building measures, functional or sub-regional co-operation, and the use of international organizations may — and this is also doubtful — serve to reduce the level of mutual threat perceptions but are likely to leave unaffected the problem of legitimacy and national role conceptions which are firmly rooted in a number of historical processes and protected by the principles of sovereignty and national self-determination. For many these are cardinal guarantees of freedom but ultimately mean nothing more than a freedom to persist in errors, misconceptions and illusions of grandeur which a more judicious reading of one's past should be able to correct without too much difficulty. A failure to do so means that the prospects for security in Southeast Asia and indeed in the international system as a whole are unlikely to improve in any substantive way, and that one's oft-proclaimed duty to mankind's noble precepts of peace, order and justice will for the most part continue to be conceived and discharged within the narrow confines of self-interest and statism.

Notes

1. Mohammed Ayoob (ed.), *Regional Security in the Third World*, Chapter 1.
2. Joseph Bensman, 'Max Weber's Concept of Legitimacy: An Evaluation' in Arthur J. Vidich and Ronald M. Glassman (eds), *Conflict and Control: Challenge to Legitimacy of Modern Governments* (Sage Publications, Beverly Hills, Ca., 1979), pp. 17–48.
3. For further elaboration, see Sukhumbhand Paribatra and Chai-Anan Samudavanija, 'Factors behind Armed Separatism: A Framework for Analysis' in Lim Joo Jock with S. Vani (eds), *Armed Separatism in Southeast Asia* (Institute of Southeast Asian Studies, Singapore, 1984).
4. See Bensman.
5. See Paribatra and Samudavanija.
6. This is one of the points which emerged from the project on 'Development, Stability and Security in the Pacific-Asian Region', organized by the Institute of East Asian Studies, University of California at Berkeley, and the Centre for Strategic and International Studies, Jakarta, for which a final conference was held from 17–21 March 1984.

Political institutionalization has been well defined by one eminent authority as 'a process whereby a political structure is made operational in accordance with stipulated rules and procedures, enabling regularized, hence predictable performance with respect to such key functions as the selection of leadership, the making and implementation of policies and execution of justice. Ideally, political institutionalization enables a movement away from the erratic practices and arbitrary decisions stemming from a high dependence upon personalized rule. In its success, it also precludes abrupt, drastic changes in basic structure, including revolution, since change is made possible in a legal, evolutionary manner via established procedures.' See Robert A. Scalapino, 'Political Institutionalization in Asian Socialist Societies', a paper prepared for the project cited above, p. 1.

7. Bensman, p. 40.
8. Ayoob, p. 14.
9. Jackson, pp. 34–5.
10. For the latest summary of armaments, see The International Institute of Strategic Studies, *The Military Balance 1983–1984* (IISS, London, 1984).
11. For good summaries of weapons procurement agreements, see Far Eastern Economic Review, *Asia Yearbook 1982; 1983; 1984* (FEER, Hongkong, 1982, 1983, 1984 respectively).
12. See Lewis A. Coser, 'Conflict with Out-Groups and Group Structure', and James N. Rosenau, 'Theorizing Across Systems: Linkage Politics Revisited' in Jonathan Wilkenfield (ed.), *Conflict Behaviour and Linkage Politics* (David McKay & Co., New York, 1973), pp. 15–24 and 25–8 respectively.
13. Ernest B. Haas and Allen S. Whiting, *Dynamics of International Relations* (McGraw-Hill, New York, 1956), p. 62.
14. For negative conclusions, see R. S. Rummel, 'Dimensions of Foreign and Domestic Conflict Behaviour' in D. G. Pruitt and R. C. Snyder (eds), *Theory and Research on the Causes of War* (Prentice-Hall, Englewood CLiffs, New Jersey, 1969), pp. 223–6; R. S. Rummel, 'Dimensions of Conflict Behaviour Within and Between Nations' in Wilkenfeld (ed.), *Conflict Behaviour and Linkage Politics*, pp. 59–106; Raymond Tanter, 'Dimensions of Conflict Behaviour Within and Between Nations 1958–1960', *Journal of Conflict Resolution*, vol. 10 (1966), pp. 41–64.

For more positive conclusions, see Jonathan Wilkenfeld, 'Domestic and Foreign Conflict' and John N. Collins, 'Foreign Conflict Behaviour and Domestic Disorder in Africa' in Wilkenfeld (ed.), pp. 107–23 and 251–93 respectively.

15. Harold and Margaret Sprout, 'Environmental Factors in the Study of International Politics', *Journal of Conflict Resolution*, vol. 1 (1957), pp. 309–28.

16. For an excellent discussion of the psychological dimensions of conflict, see C. R. Mitchell, *The Structure of International Conflict* (Macmillan, London, 1981), pp. 71–119.

17. Klaus Knorr, 'Threat Perceptions' in Klaus Knorr (ed.), *Historical Dimensions of National Security Problems* (University of Kansas Press, Lawrence, Kansas, 1976), p. 98.

18. The following is an adaptation and extension of the paradigm used by Robert O. Tilman in *The Enemy Beyond: External Threat Perceptions in the ASEAN Region*, Research Notes and Discussion Paper no. 42 (Institute of Southeast Asian Studies, Singapore, 1984).

19. See K. J. Holsti, 'National Role Conceptions in the Study of Foreign Policy', *International Studies Quarterly*, vol. 14 (1970), pp. 233–309. The differentiation between various types of roles used in the passage immediately following is derived from this work.

COMMENTS

Felipe B. Miranda

The authors provide a feast of ideas, combined with various tables of comparative information. Three basic dimensions have been looked into: *regime legitimacy, threat perceptions* and *national role conceptions.* Their internal dynamics and configurations are explored historically and sociologically before their 'externalization' (to borrow the authors' felicitous terminology), or their impact on regional security, is explored. Paribatra and Samudavanija conclude that 'these internal dimensions tend to have adverse impacts on regional security especially in the context where certain external dimensions, for example conflict and rivalry between great powers, also exist as crucial determinants of questions relating to war and peace within the region'. Using in particular what they feel to be the lessons of Kampuchea, they note, perhaps with a trace of sadness, that 'there is no self-evident way of influencing or transforming the *internal* dimensions of regional security', and that unless the historical evidence in Southeast Asian countries is more critically read, we can anticipate regional (and indeed even the broader international) security conditions to be primarily a function of parochial national interests and statism.

There are some specific data and data interpretations which I would question, but there is nothing in the authors' explicit thesis which I fundamentally disagree with. I believe, however, that some further elucidation might be attempted as regards a common thread which runs through the discussion of regime legitimacy, threat perceptions and national role conceptions. Ultimately, security conceptions, defined in terms of dynamically active levels of actual or potential social violence, must go beyond analyses of elite politics or authoritarian governments. Even in Southeast Asia, the popular underpinnings of national and, therefore, regional security cannot be ignored much longer.

The various processes of social change (whether in the economy or the polity) in most Third World countries have one remarkable feature which distinguish them from those which occurred in earlier, 'pre-modern' times. This character is the demand for popular, mass involvement and the presumption of the legitimacy of mass involvement. Even in the most authoritarian states in Southeast Asia, the formal social philosophy is one of outright commitment to, or eventual adoption of, democratic ideals (however culturally modified). The crisis of national security (and by implication of regional security) is precisely that a significant number of increasingly better organized citizens demand that the democratic rhetoric become operational reality. Particularly because material (say economic) growth has been a demonstrable historical experience for most Southeast Asian nations, the popular expectation and demand that equity concerns be attended to has increasingly become more acute. To the extent that regimes facilitate rather than obstruct these expectations and demands, to that extent may popular support for these regimes be anticipated. Adopting the language of the authors, the 'fragility' and 'permeability' of states within the region might then be minimized.

I should also like to develop a related thought. Usually we are prone to understand stress conditions and destabilization processes or phenomena as indicative of threatened national security. Perhaps, at least in some cases rigorously understood, some of this stress and destabilization might be positive indicators of an improving condition of national security. Specially in societies where due to colonial or imperialistic processes, artificial structural features are induced which contribute to long-term social tension, the very processes which seek to neutralize imposed structural characteristics might be understood as investments in long-term social stabilization and thus of improved national security.

There is a reverse phenomenon of apparent tranquillity as an indicator of a volatile security condition. Imposed social peace may be successfully achieved through militarization, a phenomenon which our authors correctly indicate as increasing national and regional permeabilities, particularly to great power as well as intraregional state intervention. The absence of overt dissidence or insurgency might be better appreciated as we follow our authors' advice to undertake a 'judicious reading' of historical evidence in our part of the world.

Analyses of security conditions have been largely predicated upon assessment of elite capabilities and historical reflections on past popular actions. Perhaps the time is ripe for analysts to undertake truly systematic analysis, examining the full context of security concerns by paying at least equal attention to the dynamic roles of increasingly demanding and better organized national constituencies. Popular perceptions and organized actions may have to be monitored more effectively. Perhaps there should be more attempts at social weather reports and forecasts (however suspect the 'scientific' reliability of the latter), and at monitors of national political pulses if only to anticipate potentially explosive stress build-up in the political system. In current times, there is a necessity in any serious study of national and regional security to conjoin judicious historical reading with prudent, systematic, even loosely speaking scientific, efforts to scenario alternative futures. This conjunction of methodologies permits ruling elites, restive subjects and concerned academics like us productively to consider a wide range of social options, instead of being reduced to passive historical reflections and/or conservative trend extrapolation.

4 INTERNAL CLEAVAGES AND REGIONAL CONFLICT: THE CASE OF LEBANON

Sami Mansour Ahmed

This paper is based on three basic hypotheses:

First: A revolution is underway in Lebanon. It has all the components, the characteristics and the causes of one, but at the same time it is an impossible, ineffective revolution because it cannot attain its objectives in the light of the current regional situation.

Second: Lebanon has the components of a modern state, but lacks the infrastructure and the characteristics of a real nation. It is a transient entity which some people wished to endow with permanence, but which, unfortunately, is not possible.

Third: Lebanon has specific characteristics proper to it, and a unique trait, namely that changing variables govern and direct events and not permanent factors as is the case in most communities. Lebanon is not the sole case of this sort on the international scene, but these are exceptional cases.

These three hypotheses shape the current Lebanese situation. It is, therefore, essential to study the interaction of these hypotheses and prove the validity of each one of them and the extent to which they remained valid at the outbreak of the civil war in the middle of the 1970s.

The Impossible Revolution

Income distribution in Lebanon reflects the true economic and social situation, 2 per cent of the population monopolize one-third of the national income, and 4 per cent enjoy half the national income, whereas industrial, agricultural and handicraft workers — who constitute 50 per cent of the Lebanese population — get 20 per cent of the national income.[1]

Not only is wealth concentrated in the hands of a minority, but the capital, Beirut, monopolizes most of the economic and social activities. It accommodates 75 per cent of the workers of the industrial sector and 75 per cent of those employed by the public services sector. In other words, Beirut attracts approximately 60 per cent

95

of the working population in Lebanon. Such an unusual concentration of economic activity resulted in the absence of any substitute for Beirut and, hence, those looking for job opportunities outside the agricultural sector had to go to Beirut.[2] The Lebanese economic system was then called 'ferocious capitalism'. It is an economy based on the service sector which yielded 70 per cent of the national income.

This percentage was around 50 per cent in the 1950s. Financial activities constitute the essence of that sector. The major characteristics of the monetary market in Lebanon is that two-thirds of its activities are in the hands of foreign banks and the other third is hardly diversified. Banks consolidate the service sector, thus limiting the development of the productive sectors. The contribution of the agricultural sector to the national income dropped in the 1970s to 10 per cent against 15 per cent in the 1960s. The production rates of food crops deteriorated in favour of commercial crops for export. This also occurred in the industrial sector, which promoted manufacturing and assembling industries.

This phenomenon left its effect on manpower structure. Agricultural workers, who formed 45 per cent of manpower in the 1960s, dropped to 18 per cent in the 1970s, while workers in the service sector increased from 34 per cent to 57 per cent. The net result was the shrinking of manpower in productive sectors which indicated a lower contribution of the productive sector to the national income and, consequently, the control of commercial capital.

With the advent of the 1970s, Lebanon lost its role as an intermediate agent between Arab funds on the one hand, and western investments on the other. The growing rates of accumulated monetary surpluses together with rising oil prices motivated the West to quickly exhaust such surplus and, consequently, limited to a certain extent the intermediate role.

Suffice it to say that Arab deposits in the Lebanese banking system in 1974 did not exceed US$3 billion, whereas the revenue of the oil producing countries exceeded US$50 billion, most of which were channelled to the international monetary market. It became quite evident that Lebanon was losing its role as a transit centre for Arab funds.

This was linked to the economic crisis in the capitalist world to which the economy of Lebanon was organically related, and which fell prey to an unbridled inflation. Prices soared to incredible levels.

All conditions, economic and other, that could trigger a revolution were at hand. We can draw a vivid picture of the events from developments in one day. On 4 February 1974, in Lebanon, one year before the outbreak of the civil war, the title on page 3 of *Al Nahar* newspaper — in no way a left-wing paper — read: 'Mass dissatisfaction at inflation in all areas.' The following line read: 'Authorities are accused of collusion with monopolizers, and some trade union leaders are accused of collusion with the authorities.'

The paper then published pictures of demonstrations in all Lebanese cities and fierce speeches against the regime delivered on such occasions. These public demonstrations were not a sudden development, but had at their origin the debate that had taken place in 1974, in the form of seminars on 'Committed Thought'. All Lebanese political parties took part in these seminars but failed to arrive at a solution to their problems. Changes were then felt in the student's movements, and in the trade unions.

Not a single day passed without demonstrations in one or more cities in Lebanon, while the different factions started arming themselves and forming militias in preparation for 'Judgement Day', to the extent that *Al Nahar* newspaper in 1975 devoted a supplement to 'Armament and Militia'.

The situation exploded and, although violence escalated, the system did not reach a breaking point and the objectives sought by these explosive events was never achieved. It appeared as if the explosion was an end in itself. The explosion of 1975 was not the first in the history of Lebanon; it had been preceded by others, principally in 1958, which was brought to an end by American military intervention. However, although revolutions or attempts at revolutions were recurrent, it still remains an impossible revolution due to the special characteristics of Lebanon and the Arab region. The specific conditions of the Lebanese situation created a congruence of interests between sectarian leaders and the rich elite — meaning a congruence between the economic situation and the stands adopted by the sectarian leaders. The conflict became governed by sectarian disputes.

People have come to think of Maronites as capitalists, though a large majority of them are poor. Socialism is linked to the Druze though a majority belongs to the conservative wing. The Shiites are associated with Communism though there is an ideological conflict between Communism and Shia Islam. In general terms, we find that the composition of the religious sects is the following: the rich are Maronites whereas the poor are Muslims.

All this is not absolutely true, but on the whole it is true. Hence we are faced with a revolution which took the shape of a sectarian war, and not a revolution of the poor against the rich, or of the productive people against the exploiters. That is why the revolution never succeeded.

The Marxist explanation looks at it as class conflict deeming that transit capitalism is inherent in the nature of Lebanon, and that the middle class, from the scientific point of view, is a social layer and not a class structure because classes relate to relations of production. In the absence of relations of production, a class as such, party to a social conflict, does not exist. Lebanese society is a multi-category society rather than a class society. There is no one class with some common consciousness at production level. The rule is that class does not exist unless there is class consciousness.

Class consciousness is the basic component in the class concept. Thus Lebanon is composed of different and interlocked classes whether horizontally or vertically, as regards the type of work, interest and outlook of the community. It would be more correct to say that there are distinctive class categories,[3] thus preventing the outbreak of a comprehensive revolution.

In addition to a lack of sense of belonging to the nation as a result of the sects' structure where there is a feeling of affiliation to the sect, rather than to the country, and similarities between economic and sects' conditions, the privileged and affluent classes were impelled to seek outside help in order to secure protection against the revolution of the needy.

They also impelled those who had a stake in the revolution to look outside Lebanon's borders and so both sides looked for non-Lebanese help to attain their objectives. The Phalangists looked for assistance from the Syrians to prevent the National Lebanese movement from attaining a decisive victory, and then resorted to Israel's help to get rid of the Syrians, and finally asked the United States to help expel both Israelis and Syrians. This was the case on both sides. Once more the Lebanese Revolution despite its long duration cannot succeed because of foreign interference whether from Arabs or non-Arabs.

The fact remains that a revolution rages in Lebanon although it cannot achieve its objectives because of the characteristics of its social and economic structure. What is of interest at this point is the awareness of all sides, that due to sectarian connotations, they all had to seek outside help. There is general political and social acceptance of outside help that is neither penalized nor condemned.[4]

A State without Real Institutions

The second hypothesis is that Lebanon has the shape of a state with a president, a parliament, parties and an army, but in fact it is a question of form and not of substance.

Sectarianism in Lebanon is linked to social, political and economic activities, to the extent that to be affiliated to a sect is the only guarantee for political and economic ability to act. Affiliation to a sect has turned into loyalty to the sect surpassing all commitments including loyalty to the nation. The sect has become the nation in actual practice. The situation is further aggravated by the fact that the sects are centred in certain regions of Lebanon. The Maronites are stationed in the mountains, the Sunnis in the north, the Shiites in the south and the Druze in the Shouf. The former Lebanese President Charles Helu summing up the situation said: 'Being Lebanese is not a nationality, but a profession'. The Phalangists' party newspaper was even more explicit in saying: 'The National Charter was turned into a trade contract, even into an investment company for jobs and sects'.[5]

The political system distributes power among the 17 recognized sects, according to the national charter and constitution, but in fact, the texts add the word 'provisionally' and the other provisions are in complete opposition to sectarianism.

Time alone cannot turn the formula of a provisional homeland into a permanent one. A sectarian entity is not a phase leading to the establishment of a homeland, but delays the establishment of one, specially since Lebanon lacks a constitutional court to which could be referred laws encouraging sectarianism for consideration and codification. Jobs were distributed according to loyalty to the sect and not on the basis of scientific or professional criteria.

Even the party system consolidated the concept of loyalty to the sects. The Lebanese parties on the whole are sectarian parties ruled by tribal and family methods in terms of jobs and hereditary leadership. That is why parties do not work out policies, they are just instruments. Despite the fact that some ideological-political parties were formed in recent years, they could not spread effectively at the level of all sects, and remained contained within intellectual circles.

Parliamentary membership is governed by sectarian considerations, ministries are distributed according to loyalty to the sect, and key positions, indeed, even the most junior posts, are distributed according to sectarian criteria. Furthermore, the army itself reflects that dangerous disease, although admittance to the armed forces calls for special specifications, the most important being discipline and loyalty to the authority representing the nation and a common objective.

The absence of a state as such, and a lack of consensus on the identity of Lebanon, whether Arab or a bridgehead for the west, as the Maronites claim[6] — a pending question until the Lausanne Conference in 1984 which stated that Lebanon is an Arab country — prevented the establishment of an army. Moreover, the Phalangists in particular, and the Maronites in general, justified this situation by saying: 'Lebanon derives its power from its weakness', meaning that Lebanon's weakness will prevent others, out of compassion, from attacking it.

The truth is that the greatest obstacle to the establishment of a strong army is its sectarian structure. Military ranks were distributed proportionally among sects, but even these proportions favoured one sect at the expense of the others. In 1972, 85 per cent of unit commanders were Christians against 15 per cent Muslims.[7]

Through sectarianism, the army entered the field of politics during the crisis of 1958 and afterwards; the army became a sectarian army and not a national one. Suffice it to say that the air force attacked Beirut, the capital, to strike at the centres of the National Movement and the Palestinian forces, but disappeared when Israel attacked Lebanon. Moreover, the army was removed from the jurisdiction of the executive authority and placed under the authority of the president.

Armament was a new element which helped destroy the real Lebanese army. The nature of economic activities in Lebanon turned the concept of armament from a national duty into a commercial enterprise, and, according to the Lebanese system, bribery was called commission and cheating described as lack of experience and ignorance. The armament records of Lebanon abound with cases of bribery and cheating. At the beginning of the 1970s, the Lebanese army was equipped with weapons dating from the Second

World War which most armies had relegated to warehouses and maybe to museums. It was no surprise then, that when the Israelis invaded Lebanon, the Lebanese army was not among the forces which stood up to Israel although it was the legitimate body to do so being the national army of the country invaded.

It is quite evident that Lebanon did not develop its institutions, and hence they do not reflect the real Lebanese community. Furthermore, these institutional bodies being a matter of shape and not of substance, opened the door wide to an unlimited crisis. As Sheikh Maurice Gemayel, the uncle of the current president, said: 'If the state does not wage a legitimate revolution, we will witness a revolution on legitimacy'.[8] The former President, Fuad Shehab, further clarified the situation by refusing to stand for re-election saying: 'The political institutions in Lebanon, and the conventional enforced methods of work no longer constitute an effective instrument for the development of Lebanon. The institutions lagged behind new systems, and election laws are dictated by transient and momentary events. The economic system encourages monopolies which do not allow for serious work'.[9]

Other variables in the Lebanese community further distorted this situation and widened the scope of the Lebanese crisis. Among the most salient factors was the emergence of the Shiites as a power to be reckoned with in the political arena having at their disposal political institutions and armed militia not commensurate with their political participation in the system.

The National Lebanese Movement also appeared on the political scene seeking to build up the nation, and liquidate sectarianism in all its forms. The economic and social conditions helped magnify the role of the movement. Another variable was the armed Palestinian presence, especially after being expelled from Jordan in 1970. The absence of state institutions in Lebanon also magnified the Palestinian role and its influence.

I believe that the most influential factor in increasing distortions and deepening the crisis was the fragmentation of forces contrary to what is commonly believed outside. The widespread notion nowadays is that of a conflict between the Maronites and the Druzes or the Shiites, and differences between Shiites and Sunnis, as if there was a single Maronite, or Shiite or Druze stand; but that is not the case in Lebanon. The Maronites themselves are divided into many factions, the three largest each with a military wing, being the Marada (Suleiman Franjieh), the Leopards (Camille Chamoun) and the Phalangists (Al Gemayel). These factions have even regional frontiers between them such as Al Madfoun between the Marada and the Phalangists. The Phalangists themselves are divided into three factions, one siding with Sharon, the second with France and the last with the party leadership. Each faction wants to impose its rule through military force as Beshir Gemayel did on the other Maronite military wings, or on the Phalangists not loyal to him. It is also thought that the Shiite Amal movement is one movement but in fact it is composed of seven wings, with Iranian, Saudi, American and even Israeli allegiances.

Equally there is a common belief that the Druze are a cohesive force, but they are in fact divided into three factions: the first a conservative right wing, the second siding with Israel and the third and most well known with Walid Jumblat.

The above substantiates the second hypothesis, namely that Lebanon has the form of a state but lacks effective state institutions, because of the absence of the infrastructure that goes into the making of a nation.

What I wish to emphasize in this paper is a corollary of this hypothesis, namely that the absence of an effective state is, in itself, an element which attracts outside powers, Arab or foreign, to interfere in the internal affairs of Lebanon and exploit them to attain their aims. Moreover, the absence of a real state together with sectarian conflict that escalates into civil war between factions greatly encourage foreign powers to interfere and exploit the civil war to achieve objectives in no way related to the war itself. In fact, the objectives of the civil war could be the victim of such an interference. Interference can be through direct military invasion or through supply of armaments or training of troops. It can also take indirect means through secret channels.

Variables and Constants

The third hypothesis is that variables rather than constants govern events and situations in Lebanon which lends a special characteristic to Lebanon which does not exist in most countries of the world.

The general rule is that each community has permanent political lines and beliefs that represent the community's strategy. This strategy is relatively stable but flexible in the face of events. However, as a result of the specific characteristics of Lebanon, the variables are at the origin of any development and cancel out the constants as if they had never existed.

To clarify the notion on which rests the third hypothesis, we will review the recent events — at the time of writing this paper — to give a tangible expression of Lebanese realities.

According to the statements made by the factions' and militias' leaders there is a general agreement on the uselessness of pursuing the war. It has been going on for nine years without attaining the objectives of any faction except those of the Lebanese arms' dealers. Ending the war is an imperative need. To achieve this end, the different parties should arrive at a compromise in order to modify the Lebanese structure which collapsed and caused all this damage.

Almost all parties concerned convened in Lausanne, in Switzerland, and not in Lebanon. These leaders, who wish to restructure Lebanon, could not guarantee the safety of the conference if held in their country. Nevertheless, agreeing to the date of the conference generated some optimism and gave hope for an agreement on ending the war. But the transient variables undermined this opportunity.

Unexpectedly, the date of the conference coincided with news of a crisis in Syria and rumours that Rifaat Al Assad, the brother of the Syrian President, was preparing a coup during the illness of President Hafez Al Assad, and had established contacts with American circles.[10] These rumours as well as other factors motivated the parties concerned to secure the failure of the Lausanne Conference as long as the outcome of the power conflict in Syria had not become clear.

The different parties attended the conference in organized fronts and left it in newly organized fronts. The front which was established with Syrian support and was composed of Walid Jumblat (Druze), Rashid Karami (Sunni) and Suleiman Franjieh (Maronites of the north), split up and fought each other during the conference.

The National Movement, which shared a common goal and destiny, broke up by the end of the conference, one group — the Druze — waged armed battle against another group, the Murabitoun or the Nasserite organization. The Druze won and took over the positions and the broadcasting station of the Murabitoun, who were considered the only military organization — though limited in size — of the Sunnis in Beirut.

Strangely enough, the Druze — the socialist party — liquidated one of its allies in the National Movement, while its leader, Walid Jumblat, held secret talks with an enemy from the Maronite front. He met in London Dany Shamoun, the son of former President Camille Shamoun, a leader of the Maronite front, a few days after the Lausanne Conference.[11]

The delegations left Lausanne having ascertained the stability of the Hafez Al Assad regime and the resumption of his control over the situation. Contacts started again, and a summit meeting between the Presidents of Syria and Lebanon took place where they agreed to ask Rashid Karami to form a Cabinet.

Syrian influence was quite evident. It was logical to expect that the forces supported by Syria would be the first to accept to join the Cabinet and the opposition would be the last to accept, if they did at all. But what actually happened was exactly the opposite.

What is of import is that this hypothesis means that one of its dimensions provides optimal internal conditions for external interference whether regional or international; it also allows international conflicts to take place on the Lebanese scene turning Lebanon into a mere playground.

This ties the three hypotheses triangle encompassing all the issues, powers and interests within its framework, or as commonly stated, they become immersed in the sands or water of Lebanon.

The Lebanese Specific Characteristics

The three hypotheses interacted and created a number of traits governed by the degree of interaction of its components, such as:

1. Every single one of the major groups has a foreign alliance whether Arab or foreign. The effectiveness of each group is subject to the extent of influence of the external ally and his ability to use this alliance to attain part of his objectives.

2. Alliances between internal and external powers are limited in scope as well as in duration. The Lebanese describe these alliances as 'alliances with a ceiling' in the sense that they are restricted and not unlimited.

3. Internal alliances with external forces are sometimes incompatible if not conflicting beyond any logic. For example:
   — One group of the Phalangists has an alliance with Syria,

another with Israel and the United States, meaning external forces which are originally in conflict.
— The Druze have alliances with Israel and at the same time are allied with Syria which supplies them with arms, while they are trained by Israeli officers.
— The Shiite have alliances with Iraq and Syria who are foes, with Iran, despite its war with Iraq, even with the United States which is deemed an enemy by the majority of Shiites. Some of them have even established communication channels with Israel because it occupies the south.
— The Maronite factions have traditional alliances with France, but also participated in the American plan to expel France from Lebanon. They helped Washington to become the only one in control, and following the US failure in Lebanon, they are trying to restore to France an effective role.

Lines of communication are thus confused to the extent that they often neutralize each other and this increases the complexity of the situation in Lebanon. Moreover, Lebanon has become a world centre for espionage and exchange of information. It has become impossible to imagine that there could be any secret in Lebanon to which one could not have access.

4. The failure of alliances and external intervention in achieving radical internal benefits in favour of any party. There could be transient gains but they soon fritter away under strong counter-pressures. The rule of no winners/no losers has been adopted by those who believe that maintaining the present structure of Lebanon is the only way by means of which their intervention can be pursued.
5. The conflicting parties end up with the opposite of what they wished to achieve and sometimes their original objective is lost because of the interaction of numerous parties.
— The Phalangists, for example, started the civil war in 1975 to prevent a revolution and protect their wealth. After ten years of war, whose end none can predict, Lebanon has been totally destroyed economically and socially, and the revolution has grown in strength and influence.
— The Maronites raised the banner of the sovereignty of Lebanon over its territories and the need for expelling the

Palestinians. They ended up by having Lebanon occupied by more than one country, and the sovereignty of Lebanon only exists on paper.

— Syria entered Lebanon to contain the Palestine Liberation Organization, and acquire further bargaining power through its influence in Lebanon. This gave rise to an armed conflict with the PLO and with other forces in Lebanon, especially those which could make use of their troops. The Syrian army is now a hostage in Lebanon and is a likely cause for the possible outbreak of an Arab-Israeli War.

— Israel invaded Lebanon to strike at the PLO and to work out another Camp David accord with Lebanon. It ended up with a Shiite militia who are more violent and more persistent in hitting at Israeli objectives, in addition to economic and social consequences in Israel itself. I believe that in the long run it will be seen that it has saved the PLO from being destroyed and caused the Palestinians to take up their cause and intensify their activities in the occupied territories rather than living in Lebanon.

— The United States entered Lebanon to prevent Syria from scoring a political victory and achieve what Israel had left unfinished by an agreement between Israel and Lebanon. What happened was a disgraceful exit, an entrenchment of the Syrian role and the abrogation of the Lebanese-Israeli agreement before it came into effect. What is more important is that the United States intervened to demonstrate its exclusive power in the region and put an end to the Soviet role. But it departed, leaving the Soviet Union with a greater role than it had had before the American intervention.

The specific characteristics of Lebanon with their three hypotheses managed to sink all parties in a bottomless pit and made Lebanon's problem part of the region's problem.

Linkage with Regional Conflicts

The Lebanese problem merged with the regional conflicts despite the efforts of the Maronites to separate it from the Middle East problem. It is most evident that the Maronite parties failed to understand how the civil war related to foreign intervention and, in particular, that inviting external intervention means turning an internal conflict into a regional and maybe an international issue.

Several studies have dealt with the phenomenon that foreign intervention in internal conflicts always escalates the conflict instead of solving it.[12] In fact, the interaction of the three phenomena which are at the origin of the Lebanese problem determined the linkage of that problem with the conflicts of their region.

The Arab-Israeli Conflict

Because of the geographic location of Lebanon, it is one of the Arab countries which border on Palestine. These countries which are called frontline countries are Jordan, Syria, Lebanon and Egypt. Lebanon, being a member of the Arab League, is bound by Arab policies, specially those related to the Arab-Israeli conflict. Due to the Palestinian presence in Lebanon since 1948, and the organic link between the PLO and the National Movement in Lebanon,[13] it became the most effective frontline country in the conflict, especially after the other frontline countries curbed the activities of the PLO and forbade it to attack Israel from their territories.

While the PLO had close relations with the Lebanese National Movement, some Maronite factions, and especially the Phalangists, were co-operating with Israel. The relations between the Phalangists and Israel date back to 1951, when Pierre Gemayel asked for financial help from Israel to fight the Lebanese elections in the spring of that year. Furthermore, one of the party leaders had made contact with Israel during the 1948 War, specifically with the World Zionist Organization in the United States.[14] Concurrently, in its early days, Israel had drawn up its security theory on the basis of an attack against Arab unity, by establishing statelets based on religion such as a Maronite state, a Druze state and a Kurdish state to create passages and partitions through Arab territories forming a safety belt around Israel. It would also be establishing states which like itself would be based on religion and, by so doing, would alleviate the moral pressures brought to bear on it.[15] In fact, according to a study undertaken by the Israeli paper *Jerusalem Post*, this idea had originated with the American Zionist movement which had published booklets calling for the establishment of a Maronite state.

All three elements taken together were determining factors in turning Lebanon into an arena for the Arab-Israeli conflict. The unfolding of events as well as the changes in Arab stands especially after the 1973 War, left Lebanon as the only place where the Palestinians, whether positively or negatively, could pursue their activities and where the Phalangists, the opponents of the Palestinian Revolution, could counter them.

Several efforts were made to regulate relations between Lebanon and the Palestinian Revolution, but these positive and negative factors rapidly undermined all agreements and opened the door to military confrontation.[16] Despite the desire of some Lebanese leaders to dissociate the Lebanese problem from the Arab-Israeli conflict, objective factors established an organic link between the two problems.

The Islamic-American and Israeli Conflict

The contradiction between American strategy in the Arab world and national Arab aspirations is a genuine one. The history of this conflict dates back to the 1950s. The American side wants to impose its supremacy by alliances and strategic consensus, whereas the Arab side strives to attain a free political and economic will.

A radical change occurred in the stand of some Arab regimes toward the United States, but this change did not coincide with a similar change on the part of general Arab opinion. Indeed, it was impossible to occur, given the unchanged American policy. The Arab regimes repeatedly called for such changes on the part of the United States, or at least some moderation, what some people call neutralizing the United States in the Arab-Israeli conflict.

As a result of several factors Lebanon became the field where this conflict was reflected. Then the Iranian Revolution broke out which added a new dimension and intensified activities in the Lebanese arena by the introduction of a new party to the conflict, a party that had close links with the Shiites of Lebanon. This development was concurrent with the growing role of the Shiites in Lebanon.

On the other hand, the Israeli policy in southern Lebanon was activated through the Phalangists to arrive at the Camp David concept, and was a concomitant of the increasing involvement of the Americans in the Israeli expansionist projects in the region. This was no surprise, but came as a result of the evolution of their security theory which culminated in a strategic co-operation agreement. American involvement was based on the American viewpoint, namely that the Arab regimes could not possibly react against the United States and not from the premise that it did not run counter to American interests in the Arab world. This is a correct viewpoint to a large extent and the events of the past three years confirm it.

There is also the strange role played by American diplomacy during the Lebanese civil war. It told each party what it wanted to hear, and offered encouragement that contradicted the encouragement given to the other parties. It appeared as if out of ignorance of the Lebanese problem it wished to perpetuate the civil war, or was deliberately seeking to partition Lebanon into religious statelets. Furthermore, the US approved a decision to open a NATO liaison office in Beirut to arm the Maronites. This decision was taken at the time when Alexander Haig was the commander of the NATO forces.[17]

Events unfolded until international forces were stationed in Lebanon composed of forces from some of the NATO countries, primarily the United States, which provided a real opportunity to entrench the American military presence in Lebanon. This, however, turned it into an easy target, and Lebanon became the only place in the region where attacks could be aimed at the American presence in the area. Yet, before this the largest effective Arab arena against the American presence did not go beyond the mass media field.

American-Soviet Conflict

The main objective of the American policies during the 1970s was to remove the Soviet Union from the Arab World. The United States succeeded to a large extent in achieving this, helped by various factors. But it is important to point out that throughout this stage Lebanon was, because of its circumstances, the field of the media war between the two superpowers. Two events greatly influenced the nature of the conflict between the two superpowers in Lebanon:

1. The Israeli invasion of Lebanon on 5 June 1982. American involvement in Israeli expansionist policies reached its peak when the US participated in the invasion either by mere approval, such as indicated by Haig in his memoirs,[18] or by effective participation with the AWACS planes which helped deliver a crushing blow to

the Syrian air force. News reports indicate that the Soviets knew about this attack but lacked the technological capability to intervene.[19] Soviet standing dropped to its lowest level since the 1973 War. American involvement in the invasion was deemed the final blow to Soviet prestige and presence in the region.

2. The death of Brezhnev on 11 November 1982, five months after the Israeli invasion, and the appointment of Andropov as his successor. In fact, it was not a mere change of persons but a change of policies. The Soviet Union started to counter American policies in Lebanon; it provided Syria with more modern arms, especially for those troops station in the Beka'a. It was even said that Soviet missiles in the Beka'a were threatening the American sixth fleet and were kept under direct Soviet control. An agreement was also signed with Syria to counter the strategic agreement between the United States and Israel. Despite the fact that the agreement does not apply to the Syrian presence in Lebanon, any conflict between Syria and Israel should be carefully studied in the light of the Soviet-American conflict, and the possibilities of a confrontation between the two superpowers in the Middle East.

Inter-Arab Conflict

Lebanon in the Arab world is similar to Oscar Wilde's *The Picture of Dorian Grey*. Whatever occurs in the area and whatever actions are committed against regional interests and objectives are reflected in Lebanon. Lebanon made it possible for the Arab regimes to express their viewpoints without officially signing them or having to remain committed to them. This was a source of wealth in Lebanon as well as a means whereby to express the covert differences between regimes.

Differences turned into conflicts and the region witnessed a deterioration in values as well as in dealings between the Arab regimes, and Lebanon reflected each passing phase in the relationships within the Arab world.

Thus, the lines of internal conflicts in Lebanon interlinked with regional conflicts creating a mutual interaction of the two sides. Regional conflicts escalated and sustained the internal conflicts while, in turn, the latter sharpened the acuteness of the regional conflicts.

Consequently, the search for a solution to the Lebanese problem merged with the quest for solutions to regional conflicts, in particular the Arab-Israeli conflict which posed the major obstacle to the solution of the Lebanese situation.

Available Alternatives

While the Lebanese problem seems to defy solutions, four alternatives could be defined:

1. The partition brought about by the civil war could become a recognized partition. Although the most likely alternative, it is nevertheless not as easy as it seems. The conflicting parties cannot bear the responsibility of official partition, given the fact that they are fully aware of the possibility of incorporation into neighbouring entities, a situation doomed to failure. No one wishes to bear this burden and awaits the initiative from others. All parties concerned seem eager to maintain the Lebanese entity either in the form of a confederal state or of a union of cantons. There is no general consensus among the major powers, which means that this alternative stands no chance of permanency.

2. Agreement of all internal parties — this agreement could be achieved if all parties realize how impossible it is to attain their respective objectives through a war that has been going on for ten years. A decisive victory fulfilling all the objectives of one party is impossible in the light of the current situation, but all parties concerned must realize this fact. They should also realize that they cannot rely on an external party without being involved in the objectives of this external party. Under such circumstances, the internal party might lose what it strove to attain through an external party.

The statements and attitudes of the Lebanese leaders seem to indicate a degree of awareness of this reality, but it is also evident that although the new Cabinet is composed of most leaders, the fighting has not abated. Moreover, the degree of awareness has not reached the extent of coming to an agreement on a solution. A similar solution occurred in 1943, with the difference that at that time there were great leaders and today they are just midgets.

Furthermore, so much blood had not been shed impeding agreement by all parties. There would still be a chance for agreement if the present formula was modified, meaning if the privileged could be convinced to waive some of their privileges instead of losing them in their totality. Consequently, the ten years of war would become just a means to modify the formula and not to change it. In other words, the sectarian concept would remain, but with a widening of the circle of participating sects and a change in the quota of each sect, without abolishing sectarianism. A general consensus by the internal parties on the abolition of sectarianism is a most difficult exercise although it is advocated by them all.

3. Agreement of all external parties — it implies that all major external parties agree to a formula and impose it on the Lebanese. Such an agreement has precedents in history — the most important being that of 1958, after the American military intervention. The United States and Nasser's Egypt reached agreement on a common candidate for the presidency, namely Fuad Shehab. The president was chosen by agreement among the external parties allied with the internal parties.

The difficulty in that alternative is that Israel has become one of the external influencing parties and Syria has replaced Egypt, hence an agreement now is more difficult if not impossible. The United States could negotiate on behalf of Israel and Saudi Arabia on behalf of Syria. All depends on whether Israel and Syria wish to use third parties. It does not seem possible at present, especially since Syria has succeeded in getting the Lebanese-Israeli agreement abrogated.

4. Popular revolution — it is a possibility if the people of Lebanon realize that sectarian leaders are the only beneficiaries of the war. They are amassing millions of liras either through trade in arms or external assistance leaving the Lebanese to reap death and destruction.

Lebanon is partially aware of this fact but not to the extent of reacting in a revolt against the leaders. The demonstrations of women of all sects and the children's demonstrations are but expressions of opposition to the trading by the leaders in Lebanese blood. The arms circulating without any control could turn opposition into a revolution and the building up of a modern state. This is still a remote possibility because the elements that go into the making of a popular revolution, primarily the emergence of great leaders rising above sects, enjoying revolutionary consciousness and genuine feelings of belonging to the nation, are still in the age of infancy.

Thus these alternatives remain but mere queries seeking an answer; no one can foresee what this answer will be. Time, and time alone, can determine the alternatives and consequently the solution.

Notes

1. Anver Khoury, *The Crisis in the Lebanese System* (American Institute for Public Policy Research, Washington DC, 1976).

2. Riad Tapata, 'The Supremacy of Beirut and Development Policy', *Al Nahar*, 11 June 1977, in Arabic.

3. Nasef Nassar, *Toward a Better Society* (Al Talia, Beirut, 1975), in Arabic.

4. Sami Mansour, *The Great Lebanese Massacre: The New War of Attrition* (Arab Centre, Cairo, 1978), in Arabic.

5. *From the Harvest of Days: The Lebanese Question 1974/1976* (Dar Al Nahar Special Studies, Beirut, 1975), in Arabic.

6. George Hanna, *From Occupation to Independence* (Al Talia, Beirut, 1944), in Arabic.

7. Fuad Lahoud, *The Tragedy of the Lebanese Army* (Al Nahar Publishers, Beirut, 1975), in Arabic.

8. *Al Nahar*, 27 October 1968.

9. *Al Nahar*, 5 August 1970.

10. *Washington Post*, 25 April 1984.

11. *Sunday Times*, 25 March 1984.

12. K. Rasler, 'Syrian Intervention in the Lebanese Civil War', *Journal of Conflict Resolution*, no. 27, September (1983), and Piorson, 'Foreign Military Intervention and Domestic Disputes', *International Studies*, no. 18 (1974).

13. Ferhan Saleh, *Palestinian Revolution and the Evolution of the National Question in Lebanon* (URRJ, Beirut, 1975), in Arabic.

14. B. Morris, 'The Phalange Connection', *Jerusalem Post*, 1 July 1983.

15. Al Ahram Centre for Political and Strategic Studies, *The Zionist Military* (Al Ahram, Cairo, 1974), in Arabic.

16. W. Khalidi, *Conflict and Violence in Lebanon: Confrontation in the Middle East* (Harvard University Press, Cambridge, Mass., 1974).

17. Sami Mansour, 'American Involvement with Israel in Lebanon', *Al Watan*, November (1982), in Arabic.

18. Alexander Haig, *Caveat: Realism, Reagan and Foreign Policy* (MacMillan, New York, 1984).

19. *The Observer*, 6 May 1984, and *Jeune Afrique*, 16 May 1984.

COMMENTS

Richard Pennell

Mansour's paper makes a very useful and important point: that the war in Lebanon, despite the involvement of foreign states, is fundamentally a *civil* war. It has local causes which are not responses to foreign intervention, but which are part of the political structure of Lebanon. Indeed they invite foreign intervention. This is quite true. It would seem to be obvious that foreigners can only mediate in a conflict if the basis for a conflict already exists. It does, however, bear restating.

Where Mansour's paper falls down, however, is in its lack of a historical framework. Lebanon has broken down into civil war before, and foreign forces have intervened — notably in 1860 and 1958. These issues are not discussed, but they are important.

It is crucial to realize that every previous attempt at solving the crisis between the communities in Lebanon, or at preventing it from breaking out into open warfare, has been based on the principle of legitimizing sectarianism, of organizing government deliberately along confessional lines, giving a certain amount of power to Maronites, a certain amount to Druzes, to Sunnis and so on, precisely *because* they are Maronites and Sunnis and Druzes. That was true of the Qaimaqamate of the 1840s, the Mutasarrifate of the 1860s, the political system which emerged under the French in the inter-war period and the National Pact of 1943.

All the constitutional arrangements from 1860 onwards were directly or indirectly responses to foreign intervention. Thus the powers had a direct role in the appointment of the Mutassarif; the French held a direct mandate after the First World War; the National Pact came about in order to balance Lebanon both internally, defining relations between sects, and externally, defining relations with the West and the other Arab countries. When they broke down (1860, 1958) external forces (the French, the Americans) intervened to return apparent order.

However, power was not handed directly to the members of the sect as a group, but to individual members of the elite of each sect. Mansour correctly identifies the present conflict as one between the members of elites. But that is only part of the story: leaders need followers, and simply looking at the present does not explain why they were followed. A historical view shows some interesting, and rather disturbing, patterns. It seems fairly clear that the old communal leaders are no longer in complete control. This is to a considerable extent the result of the changes of the 1960s. The pre-eminence of the Phalange, which really took off in the 1950s and 1960s in the Maronite community, can be seen as a challenge to the traditional leadership. In the case of the Shi'is the traditional leadership was almost entirely replaced — hence the rise of Nabih Berri. However, both he and the Gemayels have to some extent become prisoners of their own movements and are no longer in control of them. That helps to explain the inability of the leaders to come to an agreement at Lausanne. They simply no longer had the power to do so. Indeed, the leadership of the most prominent Sunni militia, the Murabitun, was not represented at Lausanne. Thus Mansour is correct in describing the struggle with the communities as he does, rejecting the simplifications of the Christian versus Muslim, or Maronite versus Sunni and Shi'i and Palestinian — which is only slightly more sophisticated.

It is however difficult to accept that a revolution is underway in Lebanon. Mansour rightly describes a potentially revolutionary situation — inequalities of wealth distribution, employment and so on. He writes that 'All conditions, economic and others, that could trigger a revolution were at hand', but the arming of militias was not a revolutionary development: on the contrary it was a return to communalism.

Once the fighting had begun, and given the multiplicity of armed groups within each community, weapons had to come from somewhere. Hence the further involvement of outside powers. Of course, there is nothing new in this: it has been the pattern of Lebanese history in the last one hundred years or more. What is new, however, is that the outside powers could only contribute to the fighting, they could not end it. Previously one of the external powers has been strong enough to intervene decisively. That option no longer exists. The local groups are too divided, and too well armed, and the external powers — Syria, Israel, the United States — are too rigidly opposed to each other.

Another alternative might be a revitalised Lebanese state. Mansour is quite right in suggesting that in the past the state has lacked reality, being more formal than actual. The symbol of this powerlessness was of course the army. Despite the Maronite influence in the army, it was probably true that it was non-sectarian. It had to be, or it would have broken up. In 1958 General Shehab was praised for his wisdom in not risking the army's unity by intervening — but what is the use of an army that cannot act? The point is that if it had acted it would have had to be in defence of the existing order: that is the protection of 'Lebanon' defined in terms of Maronite domination. Lebanon within its present boundaries was set up to be the largest area the Maronites could safely dominate. However, since the 1920s, the demography has changed, and any attempt to preserve Lebanon in those terms must be doomed to failure.

Because Lebanon itself is defined in sectarian terms, both at the level of the state and at every level throughout society, because the sects are themselves the arenas for the power struggle and because no outside power can impose a solution, the problems are likely to continue indefinitely.

PART 3: INTER-STATE DIMENSIONS OF REGIONAL SECURITY

5 THE KAMPUCHEAN CONFLICT AND REGIONAL SECURITY: A SUGGESTED SOLUTION

Arthur Lim Joo-Jock

More than six years after Vietnam invaded Democratic Kampuchea (DK) in order, in her terms, to secure her borders which were alleged to have been threatened by the forces of the Pol Pot government, the Kampuchean problem remains as intractable as ever, and seems no nearer solution than it did in January 1979. Vietnam, in a masterly application of a form of modern warfare characterized by swift moving, air-supported, armoured and motorized columns, rapidly took over a major portion of the country, toppling the Pol Pot government in the process, and setting up another more sympathetic to Hanoi's security interests and to its predominant position in what was the old Indochina, ruled by the French. Hanoi has frequently couched its position in terms of Communist solidarity in Indochina with Vietnam the *de facto* leader of the group. The regime installed through Vietnamese force of arms, referred to as the Heng Samrin government or the People's Republic of Kampuchea (PRK), appears to accept Hanoi's hegemony.

However, the solution which was sought through force of arms has eluded Hanoi's leaders. The urban centres have been largely secured, through what could be permanent garrisoning, but much of the countryside, especially in the west, is unsettled, allowing for anti-Vietnamese guerrilla infiltration. The setting up of the Heng Samrin administration, and attempts at elections, have failed to rally the people of Kampuchea in support of Vietnamese policies in Kampuchea. Vietnam now appears as an occupying power and has to maintain a strong military presence in Kampuchea, without which the PRK government is likely to be ousted by the anti-Vietnamese coalition government consisting of the Khmer Rouge, the Son Sann group and loyalists backing Prince Sihanouk. These are estimated to number 40,000 to 60,000 Khmer Rouge, 10,000 to 15,000 of Son Sann's men and about 5,000 or so Moulinaka, the armed wing of the Sihanoukists. They oppose the Vietnamese force in Kampuchea estimated to number between 150,000 to 180,000 men, and their attendant PRK forces, functioning in an ancillary role. If the estimates of Kampuchean resistance forces and of the

119

Vietnamese forces in Kampuchea are correct, then the ratio of Vietnamese forces to those of the resistance does not appear favourable to a rapid military solution of the problem by Hanoi. Hanoi's policy-makers now find themselves involved in what would appear to be a long drawn out guerrilla war.

In this protracted struggle, the Vietnamese army of occupation sees the gains of its annual dry season offensives whittled away, or even wiped off, by expanded guerrilla action in the wet seasons when mist, fog, rain and low clouds inhibit the counter-insurgency tactics of the Vietnamese which are beginning to look more and more like the American efforts in Vietnam with an increasing reliance on heavy equipment, heavy artillery, tanks, helicopters and aircraft to subdue small, foot-mobile guerrilla units. In other words, the armed opposition to the Vietnamese occupation of Kampuchea is an important factor to be considered in any analysis of the possibilities for a solution of the Kampuchean crisis. This, however, does not suggest that the Vietnamese have begun to lose. They still retain the initiative during the dry seasons. They are still able to choose most of their points of attack and, moreover, they have declared their firm intention to weather the present protracted guerrilla war. Nevertheless the current position is one of strategic stalemate which in the kind of analyses of liberation wars as propounded by Mao is the second stage of a protracted war of resistance, preceded by a stage of strategic rearguard actions taken by the resistance, with a stronger foe on the offensive. In this analysis the strategic stalemate is likely to be followed by expanded guerrilla action leading gradually to a stage when the occupying forces are put on the strategic defensive.

The strategic impasse is of such a nature that any attempted solution of the Kampuchean problem, even if it is of necessity a political one as all protagonists claim it should be, cannot entirely ignore the military situation on the ground. In guerrilla strategy, any stalemate in which resistance forces are preserved, regrouped and consolidated is a victory for the cause of the resistance. The momentum of the Vietnamese military drive has slackened and would appear to have been lost during the last two years. The coalition forces on the other hand have gained strength in numbers and arms and in cohesion of political purpose. The efforts at political consolidation of the PRK government by Vietnam, and the attempted policies to gain the support of the Khmer people of Vietnamese-controlled areas seem to have met with only limited success. There have been reports of disillusionment and of growing resentment of the Vietnamese control of all sectors of activity. The influx of Vietnamese settlers in both urban and rural areas has added to Khmer apprehensions.

The 'Irreversible' Vietnamese Policy

When Vietnam occupied most of the lowlands of Kampuchea and when it was confronted by UN and ASEAN demands that it withdraw from Kampuchean soil, it constantly reiterated that the situation, that is the Vietnamese presence in Kampuchea, was 'irreversible'. In early 1984, this was repeated by Vietnam's principal supporter, the USSR, when Soviet Foreign Minister Gromyko reportedly told his Indonesian counterpart, Mochtar Kusumaatmadja, then visiting Moscow, that 'the clock (on Kampuchean events) cannot be put back'. This attitude, however, needs to be seen, as indicated earlier, in the light of the military situation in Kampuchea itself.

With this background of a Vietnamese posture of claimed irreversibility in the midst of strategic stalemate, it would be useful to examine the factors which would influence the germination, and eventual direction of, a Kampuchean solution. It is widely held that the solution of this problem would be the first step towards attaining any degree of regional stability. In this view, the basic cause of regional insecurity is the war in Kampuchea. Thus, irreversibility, bringing with it continued pressure, military from the Khmer coalition and political through the concerned efforts of ASEAN to effect a situation of 'reversibility', lies at the root of the problem of regional instability. In this interpretation, the basic cause of conflict is Vietnam's intention to remain in Kampuchea.

Opponents of Vietnam would advocate a combination of military and diplomatic approaches. While pressure is being applied by an externally-aided resistance coalition, efforts should be made in the political arena to persuade Vietnam to withdraw. Thus far, however, Vietnam has, with aid from the USSR, successfully withstood this pressure. There is no reason to believe that she will change her mind under the present circumstances. This lends credence to the view that Vietnam will only withdraw if forced to do so. Nevertheless, it could be useful to examine the factors as a prelude to any suggestion of a possible mode of solution of the problem.

Underlying Factors in the Kampuchean Crisis

What then are the factors which might make the Vietnamese more amenable to a solution involving their withdrawal from Kampuchea? These factors reflecting, as they do, Vietnamese interests, would need to be seen in the light of the interests of all parties to the dispute.

Factors which underlie any solution to the Kampuchean crisis would include the following:

1. Vietnam's perception of the threats to her security. The perceived security, by Hanoi, of Vietnam is fundamental to the problem.
2. The security of Thailand. Thailand's concern for her security brings in the concern, on the part of ASEAN, the US and the PRC, for the preservation of a Thailand free from Vietnamese pressure.
3. The role of the groups working for Kampuchean independence. Any attempted solution which does not address the interests of the Kampucheans, particularly the armed groups — the Khmer Rouge, the Son Sann group and the Sihanoukists — is much less likely, or unlikely, to succeed.
4. The PRC's concern for security on its southern borderlands and for the instability caused by what Beijing sees as aggressive, expansionist Vietnamese policies aimed at preserving Hanoi's dominant position in an Indochina federation consisting of Vietnam, Kampuchea and Laos. Beijing has often said that to the PRC the security of its southern border, that is, peace with Vietnam, is inextricably linked with Vietnam's unconditional withdrawal from Kampuchea and with its relinquishing any claim it has of hegemony over Kampuchea. The PRC has demonstrated that she is willing and capable of using force on a large scale to counterbalance any Vietnamese military gains in Vietnam's southern borderlands. The PRC has also stated that any Vietnamese attack on Thailand would bring China directly into the conflict.
5. The policies and the competing and often conflicting strategic interests of both the USSR and of the US in Southeast Asia in the context of their global policies.
6. The position taken by ASEAN which so far has not moved from the original call for Vietnamese withdrawal.

Global Powers and Kampuchea

A glance at these factors would suggest that any purely 'regional' solution to the question of regional security is out of the question. Any attempt at a solution which rests on the assumption that external powers are ultimately and directly responsible for the conflict in Kampuchea and that to keep out external powers would lead to a condition more amenable to an 'internal' regional solution, would be unrealistic. It is unrealistic simply because the external powers just cannot be kept out, even if all local protagonists agree that they should be kept out.

The US and the USSR, for their own security reasons, actively implement global policies which are aimed at countering or minimizing any strategic gain one has over the other. Besides, the pressures engendered by the ongoing hostilities in Kampuchea, and the ensuing economic and political strain, ensure that some of the protagonists, like Vietnam, would have to rely heavily on external financial and military aid. In Vietnam's case, it is partly in exchange for Soviet access to naval and air bases in Vietnam. The use of warm water ports, a strategic asset for the USSR's policy of naval participation in global affairs, would make the USSR extremely reluctant to accept any Kampuchean solution which would not compensate her for an envisaged withdrawal from the bases at the hypothetical close of the conflict in Kampuchea. It would be worth noting that the Soviet Union, through its media, constantly reiterates the theme that Southeast Asia is of vital interest to the Western, namely, capitalist, world because of its rich resources and its maritime strategic location. In this Soviet view the West is deeply involved in the region. It would be reasonable to assume that if this reflects Soviet strategic thinking then in the global competition with the West, and especially the US, the Soviet Union would not want to be left out of the region.

When external powers are so closely involved for the foreseeable future, what then are the really significant factors internal to the region which have a direct bearing on regional security, and which may possibly outweigh external considerations?

Any attempted answer to this question would depend crucially on the definition of the geographical limits of the Southeast Asian region. If the region were to be defined in the normal fashion, that is the zone lying between India and China and comprising Burma, Thailand, Malaysia, Singapore, Laos, Kampuchea, Vietnam,

Indonesia, Brunei and the Philippines then two further questions can be raised as a consequence.

First, what is the role of China? Is she beyond the region and thus external or is she of the region without being totally in it?

Second, since Southeast Asia is divided into two camps, are we discussing total regional security or are we discussing the security of ASEAN? ASEAN can be described as a security region just as Western Europe is in fact the NATO security region. It is not the intention in this paper to discuss the security of the ASEAN region alone. It would be more fruitful to examine the security of the entire Southeast Asian region. It would be naive, moreover, to assume that the PRC can be quarantined out of Southeast Asia, merely by declaring that she is external and that she is a long-term threat to the region.

Essentially then, there are five sets of interests that have to be accommodated in any search for a solution. These are Vietnam's (and of the governments friendly to it in Laos and Kampuchea), ASEAN's which devolve largely on Thailand's security, China's which centre on a desire to see a regional order to her south more accommodating to her larger security interests and finally those of the US and the Soviet Union.

Kampuchea and Perceptions of Security

Here we shall discuss the security of Southeast Asia as a whole starting from the cockpit of Kampuchea. The political confrontation, and the 'war atmosphere' in northern Southeast Asia springs, quite simply, from the Vietnamese armed presence in Kampuchea, and her control of the present government in Phnom Penh. It is assumed also that a solution to the Kampuchean problem would bring greater security to the region, though there are indications that the elimination of the Kampuchean issue could well lead to the mushrooming of other, latent, disputes within the region — disputes which have been shelved for the time being because of the existence of the Kampuchean problem.

What are some likely solutions which would stand some chance of acceptance by all parties concerned? The choices are restricted. Vietnam links the removal of what she regards as the Chinese threat in her north to any Vietnamese withdrawal from Kampuchea. China, on the other hand, insists that Vietnamese withdrawal should precede any normalization of relations between Beijing and Hanoi. This is a perfect example of a deadlocked situation and portrays the essential aspects of the Kampuchean problem, that is a vicious circle which has so far defied all attempts to break it.

Thailand sees Vietnamese troops close to her borders as a threat to her security, and the ASEAN group rallies behind Thailand on this point. Thailand insists that Khmer guerrilla encampments and bases are not on Thai soil, while Vietman is equally insistent that she could crush Khmer resistance if the latter did not have sanctuary in Thai territory. The increasingly frequent confrontation and fighting, usually between small units of Thai and Vietnamese armies, reported incursions of Vietnamese troops into Thailand and the spilling over of fighting between the Vietnamese and the Khmer coalition heighten the tension between Thailand and Vietnam.

Thailand, bereft of this historical buffer, sees herself as a frontline state facing a hostile, well-armed Vietnam which has pursued aggressive policies since its victory over the US and South Vietnamese forces in 1975. The policies of Hanoi appear, moreover, to receive Soviet support, materially and politically, adding to Thai, and ASEAN, apprehensions. Basic to any solution is the question of a physical separation of Vietnamese and Thai troops and the extinguishing of any physical basis for confrontation.

A Solution Based on the UN Resolution Calling for Vietnamese Withdrawal

In a solution close to that first advocated by ASEAN, it could be argued that a first step would be the disengagement or separation of forward Vietnamese and Thai army units. The Vietnamese themselves have suggested a buffer zone on both sides of Kampuchea's border with Thailand. However, there is no guarantee that such a buffer zone can be effectively policed, especially since the transborder country is remote, inaccessible and in places poorly mapped. Any buffer zone involving Thai territory, when Thailand is not regarded as an aggressor, would be seen in Bangkok as an unacceptable concession on Thailand's part. There is also the possibility that Vietnam might use this opportunity to eliminate resistance bases near Thailand. Besides, it could be argued that a trans-border buffer zone should only be an interim measure, to be followed up rapidly by a second phase which should go some way in implementing a policy of reduction and eventual withdrawal of Vietnamese troops in Kampuchea.

Some Other Considerations

The kind of solution mooted above is of course hypothetical. To the Vietnamese it would appear to be close to an ideal solution which is favourable to ASEAN interests.

At this point some questions can be raised. Does Vietnam really want to withdraw from Kampuchea or has she long-term designs on the thinly populated lands and resources of Kampuchea? The prize could be well worth the price of Chinese hostility which could be offset by Soviet power. Again, would the Soviet Union allow Vietnam to take this course, during which she could well be less dependent on the Soviet Union and on its aid and hence lessen the bargaining power the USSR presumably had when she obtained the use of air and naval bases in Vietnam? This question is of considerable importance, if only because the Soviet Union has for the first time obtained the use of air and naval bases in Southeast Asia, thereby strengthening her capacity to 'contain' China, to interdict shipping using the sea narrows of the region, to project her new naval power more effectively into what is essentially a maritime region, to more effectively confront the US fleet in the region and to protect her own interests in the sea lanes which connect the Pacific and the Indian Oceans. If we were to assume that a controlling influence in the Gulf and the Middle East would be a decisive factor in the competition between the Soviet Union and the US (and her allies), then the Soviet Union would not easily relinquish its use of the bases in Danang and Camranh Bay. Conversely, the Soviet Union would support Vietnam in its Kampuchean policy as long as it obtains, in return, benefits such as the use of the bases in Vietnam. For Vietnam, the compensation among others is that the Soviet presence gives a strong assurance that she will not be overly pressured by the PRC.

It should be noted that the PRC has repeatedly stated that Vietnamese withdrawal would be the precondition of stability to China's south. But would the PRC apply pressure again on Vietnam for reasons other than the Vietnamese policy towards Kampuchea?

Finally, could it be that all parties concerned (apart from the Kampucheans) prefer the status quo in Kampuchea? For the Thais the sensivity of the border and the proximity of the Vietnamese army to the Bangkok area is a cause of primary concern. Yet for those opposing the Vietnamese policy in Kampuchea, a scenario could be drawn in which Vietnam is bogged down in the Kampuchean conflict and consequently her will or capacity to launch a new adventure is neutralised. On the other hand, for Hanoi, as indicated earlier, the longer the status quo lasts, the greater the opportunity to consolidate its hold on Kampuchea and to draw her into the Indochina political and economic sphere dominated by Hanoi. The continued presence of the Soviet navy and air units gives added comfort to the Vietnamese faced as they are by the PRC in the north.

It is possible that opponents of Vietnam would like to continue seeing Vietnam being 'bled white' in Kampuchea, though this discounts the fact of heavy Soviet aid to Vietnam, and the benefits Vietnam derives from its membership of COMECON. Equally, it can be said that the Vietnamese would willingly pay the price of a guerrilla war provided they feel they are assured of substantial long-term gains. Retardation of domestic economic development could be seen as a temporary setback and as being well worth it, if Vietnam could be finally in control of the lands to her west and southwest, and if Hanoi could be assured of safe borders for the Vietnamese ethnic homeland and also of access to the wide spaces for the transmigration of Vietnamese from the more densely populated parts of Vietnam. This migration has already begun not only into the remoter northeast of Kampuchea, but also along the rich riverine tracts in eastern Kampuchea, by the shores of the Tonle Sap, the fish-rich central lake which provides Kampuchea with much of her protein needs and in the main cities as well. This would fit into the historical pattern of expansion of the Vietnamese ethnic lands at the expense of weaker, less developed neighbours.

Thus, is Vietnam really being bled, or is she in fact, with Soviet aid, expanding the sphere of her power and that of the USSR as well? It is well worth repeating that losses in terms of retardation of economic development might, in this context, be seen by a war-bred leadership, inured to hardship, as a price worth paying for the long term gains inherent in a dominant position in the old French Indochina — gains which include direct access to a larger resource base by a densely populated country short of natural resources. The north of Vietnam shows heavy population pressure on land and is a chronically food-deficient zone.

The dangling of a resumption of economic aid to Vietnam *per se* would not carry much weight either, since whatever can be donated by the western countries, and Japan, could not match the flow of current Soviet aid to Hanoi. At most it would only supplement Russian aid, relieving the pressure on the Soviet economy. A seeming Vietnamese eagerness, expressed through diplomatic channels and in international meetings, to maintain and forge contacts with the West and to ask for western aid, needs to be seen in this light by potential donors. Any offer of resumption of aid would need to be made in the context of a web of concessions and counter-concessions contained in the basket of a peaceful solution.

It must be borne in mind that Vietnam has repeatedly rejected out of hand any kind of solution which calls for withdrawal from Kampuchea. Naturally, she sees this as an unacceptable concession without prospect of a compensatory settlement. Also, both sides, ASEAN and China on one hand, and Vietnam and her supporters on the other, appear to believe that time is on their side, and that a prolongation of the current stalemate would weaken both the physical condition as well as the negotiating position of the other.

A Proffered Solution: The 'Expanding Central Corridor' Concept

With such an entanglement of the factors involved, perhaps the best way to initiate a discussion — which is the purpose of this chapter — is to give a perspective incorporated in a suggested method of *implementation* of a peace scheme which tries to take in as many of these factors as possible.

With this in mind, any proffered solution must necessarily be hypothetical, even highly speculative. The suggested solution offered here contains significant concessions to Vietnamese feelings about their national security and recognizes that Vietnam's economy needs rehabilitation.

The chief concerns are assumed here to be as follows:

1. Assuring Kampuchea's independence.
2. Assuring the security of Thailand's border with Kampuchea.
3. Assuring Vietnam's security in the areas bordering Kampuchea.
4. Assuring Vietnam of security on her northern borders and

decreasing her fear of China.

5. Satisfying the PRC that Vietnam would not dominate Kampuchea or mainland Southeast Asia.

6. Meeting the Soviet need for bases and a role in Southeast Asia.

7. Assuring the US that there is no diminution of her role in Southeast Asia and that none of her strategic interests in the region are compromised, or made worse than the existing position.

The solution offered is based essentially on the physical separation of Vietnam from Thailand, and on trying to meet most, if not all, of the needs mentioned above. It assumes some degree of willingness on the part of Vietnam to negotiate a peace settlement in Kampuchea. It also assumes that Vietnam's poor economic situation would be a factor in helping Hanoi decide to use western aid. It also assumes that Hanoi has no designs for hegemony in the old French Indochina.

The following steps could be taken:

The first step in this proffered mode of solution would be the creation of a central zone under UN supervision around Phnom Penh with access to the sea via Kompong Som and with Vietnamese forces to the east and Kampuchean forces to the west.

The complete withdrawal of all opposing forces from this zone to be supervised by a UN peace-keeping force.

All propaganda barrages from all protagonists to cease, particularly those emanating from Beijing, Hanoi and the various capitals of ASEAN.

The setting up of an interim or caretaker Kampuchean government, to be headed by Prince Sihanouk leading the coalition, to the exclusion of Pol Pot and his immediate circle, but not the Khmer Rouge as a political party. The presence of the Khmer Rouge in the government will, however, present problems, as its much publicized record of harshness makes it anathema to opinion in the West, and is a political liability — although a military asset in any opposition to Hanoi — to ASEAN policies. Sihanouk has in early 1984 expressed the view that he is willing to include Heng Samrin and his followers in any caretaker government in the context of a Vietnamese withdrawal.

Phased withdrawal from the western zone by the Kampuchean forces, with an accompanying gradual but steady expansion of the area controlled by the UN for the interim government.

Simultaneous phased withdrawal to the east by the Vietnamese.

A progressive expansion of the area controlled by the UN.

A belt along the Thai border retained for the encampment of Khmer forces. This is to be a temporary measure and is also to be UN supervised.

Similar arrangements to the Vietnamese-controlled border zone to the east, with Vietnam allowed to station troops in a UN-supervised belt in the border region. However, the rugged northeast of Kampuchea, where these Vietnamese military concentrations have been reported since the Vietnam War, would be difficult to supervise.

The holding of UN supervised free elections when all, or nearly all, populated areas of the country, come under UN control.

The independent Kampuchea to receive aid channelled through the UN.

China to be persuaded not to attack Vietnam during this process.

All parties to agree that the question of Soviet bases in Vietnam to be a matter strictly between Hanoi and Moscow. In return, Vietnam and the USSR are to undertake not to oppose the presence of US bases in Southeast Asia.

UN forces to remain for as long as requested by the Kampuchean government. Some UN regional bodies to be based in Phnom Penh, capital of an independent Kampuchea.

A guarantee, underwritten by ASEAN, Vietnam and China that the new Kampuchean government will be neutral and neutralist, as on the Burmese model, and equidistant from all contending parties.

In the closing stages of this exercise China would sign a non-aggression pact with Vietnam in return for the Vietnamese withdrawal from Kampuchea and the relinquishing of the Vietnamese concept of an Indochina federation.

The difficulties for this kind of solution would be:

(a) From the perspective of Hanoi the concessions will be almost entirely on Vietnam's part, unless military pressure in the field compels her to agree to a solution which, in fact, does go a long way in preserving her security interests. Vietnam will have to vacate a valuable piece of real estate.

(b) Infiltration of Vietnamese and Khmer forces into the central corridor cannot be stopped entirely.

(c) Any of the large powers, especially the PRC and the Soviet Union, could block the delicately balanced arrangement.

Factors favourable to this approach would include the assurance to Vietnam of her border security in the south (Kampuchea) as well as to her north (China). Moreover, she is free to maintain her links with the Soviet Union as an added assurance against possible PRC pressure. Incidentally, this kind of strengthening of Vietnam would also suit Indonesian interests, embodying, as they do, a perception of the Chinese threat. Vietnam would no longer need to be on a constant war footing, though this may well give rise to internal tensions presently obscured, because of the distraction of war in Kampuchea and the constantly repeated Chinese threat.

In theory this approach could be a basis for discussion. But in the final analysis, any attempt to persuade the Vietnamese to agree would partly depend on their perception of the benefits they could or could not obtain. This being so, an Aid Vietnam Club could be formed, with convincing proof that a worthwhile aid programme awaits Vietnam should she agree to the plan. India and Indonesia, as two past and current beneficiaries of western aid, could be asked to explain to Vietnam the scope and the range of benefits accruing to recipients who are willing to follow the rules in this kind of western-derived aid programmes.

Finally, because the initial step involves the relinquishing of western Kampuchea by the Vietnamese, this mode of solution would be acceptable to the Vietnamese only if conditions in western Kampuchea were to be made highly unfavourable to the continued maintenance of Vietnamese garrisons.

Concluding Remarks

Before this progress towards peace can be initiated, it needs to be said that Vietnam is more likely to agree if the military situation in Kampuchea is made untenable for her through the process of a classic Maoist protracted struggle of Khmer national liberation. The danger for all concerned is that this very continuation of the war could lead to a larger conflagration, with its potential for spillover into Thailand and an avowed 'second lesson' to be meted out by Beijing to the Vietnamese. Ironically, the best guarantee so far against the war being carried into Thailand is probably the demonstrated PRC willingness and capacity to invade Vietnam should this happen, despite Soviet support for Hanoi. Knowledge of this aspect of China's role in the internal affairs of the region reinforces Vietnam's fears of her northern neighbour and strengthens her desire to enjoy a close relationship with the Soviet Union thus ensuring the continuation of superpower rivalry in the region.

The vicious circle, beginning and ending in Kampuchea, is again evident. For the time being, the 'central expanding corridor' solution, based on the assumption that Vietnam is in Kampuchea for reasons of national security alone, remains an academic exercise even though it would seem to satisfy most of the various conflicting interests in the region. The one major imponderable remains Vietnam's real intentions. Indonesian officials, after an attempt in early 1984 at sounding out Vietnam about the possibility of a peaceful negotiated settlement, have expressed some disappointment at Hanoi's equivocal tendencies. Vietnamese Foreign Minister Nguyen Co Thach, for example, when discussing Kampuchea tends to say different things to ASEAN and to other interested parties, such as the Australian leadership and media. During the Vietnam War the US had experienced this Vietnamese tactic in her negotiations with North Vietnam. Beijing, on its part, has consistently questioned Vietnamese intentions in Kampuchea.

COMMENTS

Leszek Buszynski

It can be very easy to debunk suggested solutions to intractable problems in international affairs and for this reason I have some sympathy for Lim's efforts. Those who tend to put forward solutions such as the Kampuchean dispute often become targets of criticism and their well-intentioned efforts can stimulate or even excite the censorious proclivities of many an observer. Lim's task is a very difficult one. My own job in commenting on his paper is by contrast considerably easier. I hope I will not fall into the trap, outlined above, of misusing the advantage conferred by the right to comment merely to indulge in a critical exercise in the negative sense.

Any suggested solution to the Kampuchean dispute has to satisfy the conflicting interests of five parties. Three participants can be called immediate contestants in the sense that their security interests are directly threatened and their margin of compromise is sufficiently narrow to exclude the possibility of their coming to an agreement at the present moment. These participants are China and ASEAN on one side and Vietnam on the other; all are involved in a multilevel conflict in which political interests appear to be contradictory. China is adamant that without a Vietnamese withdrawal from Kampuchea there can be no agreement. The Vietnamese seek negotiations before any withdrawal in an attempt to legitimize their occupation of Kampuchea; ASEAN has consistently pressed for a Vietnamese withdrawal while realizing that a solution of this nature without safeguards would benefit China regarded by Indonesia and Malaysia to be the region's long-term threat. ASEAN is faced with the exasperating difficulty of attempting to support China over the Kampuchean issue, to the extent that both seek a Vietnamese withdrawal, while disengaging itself from Chinese aims which in this dispute include utilizing the Khmer Rouge as a means of pressure against Vietnam.

Outside the region are the two indirect participants, the United States and the Soviet Union, though it is obvious that the Soviets have more at stake in this issue than the Americans. Within the region it was once considered possible to persuade the Soviet Union

133

to press Vietnam into negotiating on the Kampuchean issue. The Soviet Union, it was thought, would become a major factor in the search for an acceptable solution. The Soviet Union, however, has little to gain in pressing for a Vietnamese capitulation over the Kampuchean issue. The Soviet interest is to prolong the dispute to ensure Vietnam's dependence upon Moscow to secure the use of naval facilities for the Soviet Pacific fleet in southern Vietnam. If the Soviet Union has any interest in solutions it would be in terms of legitimizing the Vietnamese position in Kampuchea which could involve an agreement with ASEAN which would separate ASEAN from China. The United States is the least involved of all the great powers yet one whose global interests have been affected none the less. A discrepancy exists between the low level of involvement of the United States in the Kampuchean dispute and the fact that strategic gains for the Soviet Union, in the form of the acquisition of base facilities in Vietnam, have been at the expense of the United States. That discrepancy is accounted for by American reliance upon China over the issue which makes the difficulty of disentangling the ASEAN position from that held by the Chinese that much more complex.

Where does Lim's suggested solution fit in? The near-impossible task of decoupling the political interests outlined above calls for the following features in Lim's solution: a Vietnamese withdrawal from Kampuchea; the establishment of a neutral Kampuchea guaranteed by ASEAN, Vietnam and China; and assurance to Vietnam that she can retain links with the Soviet Union as insurance against China. The major problem with the suggested solution is one of political incentive. There is an absence of incentive for most of the parties to agree to the proposal while success is still thought possible in the guerrilla battlefields of western Kampuchea. First, as Lim recognizes, there is the problem of the Khmer Rouge who will always represent Chinese political interests in Kampuchea as far as the Vietnamese are concerned. To that extent there is little incentive for the Vietnamese to consider withdrawal if the immediate beneficiaries will be the Khmer Rouge, as the most powerful anti-Vietnamese Kampuchean faction, and their Chinese patrons. The problem of the Khmer Rouge would present overwhelming difficulties for any UN peace-keeping force or administration which could always be accused of unwarranted intervention into the affairs of a sovereign state.

Secondly, there is little political incentive for the other

participants to agree to the proposal that Soviet bases in Vietnam should remain a Vietnamese concern. One of the factors in Chinese involvement in the Kampuchean issue has been Vietnam's steady incline towards the Soviet Union since 1975 which culminated in the Soviet-Vietnamese alliance of November 1978. China's rigid posture over the Kampuchean issue is not only a consequence of Vietnam's invasion of Kampuchea, it is also linked to Vietnam's strategy of underpinning its interests in Indochina by embroiling the Soviet Union close to China's borders. Vietnam's regional move extended Sino-Soviet rivalry into Southeast Asia. To that extent, the Chinese seek not just a Vietnamese withdrawal from Kampuchea but a downgrading of the Soviet presence in Vietnam as part and parcel of the process of normalizing Sino-Vietnamese relations. The problem arises when limited aims are attributed to the Chinese whose real interests extend beyond the immediate issue of the Vietnamese occupation of Kampuchea and are related to the Soviet presence in the region.

Further, there is no political incentive for the Soviet Union to accept a solution which could entail a loss of advantage in Indochina. The suggested solution calls for a means to detach Kampuchea from the Sino-Soviet dispute which could then continue unabated without, however, affecting ASEAN once a neutralized Kampuchea is accepted. A neutralized Kampuchea, however, would represent a loss for the Soviet Union in that, first, Kampuchea symbolizes an attempt to build socialism thereby vindicating its relevance to Third World conditions, and, secondly, a socialist Kampuchea would be one factor in bringing political pressure to bear upon ASEAN which is seen to be moving in a provocatively pro-American direction. Limitation of the area of Soviet influence to Vietnam would be an unacceptable reversal for Soviet leaders.

The suggested solution proffered by Lim is, therefore, incapable of practical fulfilment at the present time as long as the major contestants believe that their interests can be better served by prolonging the conflict. Nevertheless, suggested solutions may be required one day when one or other side or both have exhausted themselves or when, as a consequence of the increasing strength of the KPNLF and Sihanouk's group, the Khmer Rouge present less of a problem to a negotiated solution. Many other factors may change and transform the conflict in the future; a new Vietnamese or Soviet leadership may view the dispute differently, a split may emerge between China and ASEAN and so on. Then, suggested solutions like the one outlined by Lim will be much sought after.

6 THE ARAB-ISRAELI CONFLICT: A VIEW FROM CAIRO

Abdul-Monem Al-Mashat

Introduction

There is no doubt that the Arab-Israeli conflict provides an excellent example of a protracted social conflict.[1] It is a conflict of multidimensional aspects where social, political, ethnic and strategic issues intermingle. In studying the Arab-Israeli conflict there is a tendency either to overemphasize one aspect, for example, demographic or ethnic, or overemphasize the rights of one side while undermining those of the other. Moreover, the role of the states and their security claims have not been thoroughly examined. For instance, the Arabs believe that the security claims of Israel are not real but a mask for its expansionist policies to achieve a grand imperialistic design and dominate the region. As for the Israelis, they don't recognize the Arab need for security. They see themselves as threatened not as a threat to others' security. They believe that the Arabs aim at the annihilation of Israel. Consequently, they are not willing to recognize the right of self-determination for the Palestinians.

Such incompatible perceptions have led to the perpetuation of hostilities in the region. Each actor tried to manipulate the conflict to its advantage and deprive other actors from achieving any benefit. Both sides tried to externalize their domestic problems in the form of conflicts and wars. Each side attempted to penalize the other too severely to be able to retaliate. Each party tried to secure international support for its claims. The super and great powers found a chance to make their strategic deals elsewhere at the expense of the indigenous peoples of the Middle East. Hence, the conflict has been internationalized.

In the middle of such a vicious circle comes the peaceful settlement between Egypt and Israel as an indicator that there may be a way out of such an impasse.

Hypothesis

The main hypothesis of this chapter is that the resolution of the Arab-Israeli conflict cannot take place unless the security issues both on the state and the regional levels are settled.

In order to examine the forementioned hypothesis there are some assumptions which guide our analysis. First: the analysis of security issues presumes that Arab 'regional' security is indispensable no matter what can be achieved on the 'state' level. That is to say, Arab regional security has its own dynamism which can disturb or destabilize bilateral settlements which are based on territorial compromise that overlook the interests of the rest of the regional actors. In this context, our analysis is built on the fact that Arab states compose a region, that is the Arab regional sub-system.

Second: Israel is analyzed as an intruder into the Arab regional system. It intends to intensify the destructive effect of the centrifugal forces in the region while pushing for regional recognition and acceptance. In this regard, Israel has the advantage of maintaining a clear strategy and a high level of national consensus regarding its national goals. Hence, Arab initiatives do not alter the Israeli strategy. Instead, they give Israel a kind of manoeuvreability to shift its options between military and political means. Analyzing Israel as intruder means that while it may be physically located *in* the Third World, it is not *of* the Third World. Therefore, Israeli security is linked directly to issues of systemic security.[2]

Third: hostilities and violence between the Arabs and the Israelis are triggered off by regional and inter-state conflicts. The super and great powers play a secondary, but indispensable, role. Hence, the resolution of the conflict will most probably be confined to the regional and domestic environmental setting. Exogenous initiatives would not work without their acceptance by the parties to the conflict. This may explain why Sadat's initiative in 1977 was able to change the conflict pattern to a greater degree than any external initiative.

Environmental Setting: Perpetual Conflict and Parties' Insecurity

The contending goals of the Arabs and the Israelis led to the impasse in the Middle East. While the Israelis do have a well-defined set of national goals towards their future the Arabs do not.

Israel: Intruder in Search of a Role

The Israeli strategy is built on the necessity to penetrate the Arab sub-system. The objective is to create inter-state contradictions and increase the role of the centrifugal forces in the sub-system. It also tries to reach the central regional power in order to ally itself with it or replace it. In this regard, Israel has the advantage of maintaining a developed set of goals which confronts the amorphous, ambiguous Arab goals.

Before elaborating on some of the Israeli goals, it may be useful to notice that the Israelis try to make use of every available chance to make their security viable. Their perception regarding the vulnerability of their state is real and hence a part of their collective psyche. On the other hand, while Israelis were the most vocal advocates of peace in the 1960s, their concept of peace is a peculiar one. It aims at establishing societal interactions in the social, economic, political and strategic domains before conducting any accord. In the Geneva Conference (1974), for instance, Abba Eban declared that peace doesn't mean a ceasefire; the real guarantee for peace is the existence of joint regional interests which are characterized by intensity and diversity.[3] In addition to this, Ben Gurion stated that the Israeli concept of peace doesn't mean the signing of an accord on a piece of paper, it is 'friendship and mutual co-operation'. Also, the Israeli concept of peace is built on power and deterrence. The former Israeli Prime Minister, Yitzhak Shamir, mentioned that as long as there is power, there is peace; power gives opportunity for peace.[4] Conceptually, the Israeli definition of peace is equivalent to the Arab concept of co-operation. Such conceptual differences were reflected in the negotiation process between the Arabs and the Israelis.

On the other hand, the Arabs don't recognize the core of the conflict — that it is a conflict over political role and strategic interests of both sides. This led them to confuse the Israeli goals and mix them with those of the US.[5] No matter what such goals are, the Israelis are more capable of manoeuvring than the Arabs because their goals are clear and their options are open and numerous. Among the Israeli goals we will discuss the following three: maintaining military superiority, achieving regional acceptance and defending special and advantageous relations with the US. There are instruments, of course, to achieve these goals such as expansion into the Arab territories by occupation or settlement, the Jewishness of the state, or the rejection of the establishment of any Palestinian entity.

The Maintenance of Military Superiority. Israeli military superiority has been perceived by the Israelis and the world Jewry, particularly the American Jews, as the essential element for the survival of the state.[6] Such a superiority may be a goal in itself in the case of states which are built on isolated, intrusive settlement, for example Israel and South Africa. It is also a means to enforce their regional acceptance without the need to change their priorities or *raison d'être*. Israel has survived *only* because it is militarily and technologically stronger than the Arabs.

For the Israelis, military superiority is essential in order to achieve their security which is based on the existence of an independent deterrent force. Israeli security is built on maintaining strong defence forces and effective standing offensive forces.[7] Also, the Israeli strategic doctrine is founded on the idea that it must fight its wars outside its own territory. Qualitative superiority, that is military technology, is important also to sabotage any attempt by their adversaries to build up their military power. One-third of the Israeli budget allocated to science and development is dedicated to research in military fields.[8]

Added to all this, is the fact that Israel possesses nuclear bombs.[9] This serious and devastating strategic dimension intensifies the military imbalance between the Arabs and Israel. One justification for Egypt's peaceful settlement with Israel is related to such an imbalance. Mustafa Khalil, the former Egyptian Prime Minister, told Yigal Yadin and Ezer Weizmann: 'We know that we would not have a chance of winning a war and we also know that you have the atom bomb. Egypt doesn't have a military alternative and we have to seek a different solution.'[10] Table 6.1 discloses the extent to which the military imbalance exists between the neighbouring states and Israel. In areas like combat aircraft, jet fighters, armoured vehicles and armed manpower, Israel enjoys superiority over any of its Arab neighbours. It is interesting to notice that in spite of the peaceful settlement between Egypt and Israel, Israeli military expenditure has increased drastically — from $3.3 billion in 1977 to $7.2 billion in 1980.

The foregoing description reveals the quality of Israeli military power. It became clear since the 1967 War that Israel wants to utilize its military forces in order to achieve its optimal goals, that is to play an important, if not a decisive, political role in the region.

Table 6.1: Military Balance between Israel and its Arab Neighbours*

	Combat Aircraft Strength	First Line High Performance Jet Fighters	Army Manpower (in thousands)	Medium Tank Strength	Other Armoured Vehicle Strength
Egypt	429	251	320	2100	3300
Jordan	94	74	65	616	992
Syria	534	450	170	3990	3862
Israel	769	614	450	3600	8000

*Source: International Institute for Strategic Studies, London (1982).

On the other hand, for much of the period between 1967 and 1973 Egypt appeared to have relinquished its role as leader of the Arab world. Even during the war of attrition Egypt's impotence seemed at least as much in evidence as its power.[11] In addition, after the 1967 defeat Arab leaders had come to grips with reality and recognized the need for a *modus vivendi*, but a *modus vivendi* that met some of their needs too. They had reached the stage long sought by Israel — that is one of readiness to accept a negotiated settlement including recognition of Israel's existence.[12]

In the last few years alone Israel has tried to emphasize its ability to play the decisive political role in the area. Its raid on the Iraqi nuclear reactor, its invasion of Lebanon, its military aid to Iran and its growing military co-operation with some African countries are just examples of what is meant by a political role. We may, moreover, argue that the Camp David Accords (1978) and the peace treaty (1979) between Egypt and Israel are a culmination of that role.[13]

Israeli strategists divide the Arab world into three strategic regional circles: the Nile valley, the Arab peninsula and the Fertile Crescent. Its strategy is directed toward an alliance with the first strategic circle or at least to prevent an alliance between the first and second circles.[14] Added to the above is the US strategy to sustain Israel's superiority, especially air superiority, against all Arab front-line states combined.[15]

Regional Recognition and Acceptance. Looking at Israel as an intruder or a pariah state brings out all the psychological complexes accumulated between Jews and Gentiles. Historically, the Jews lived in ghettos. Israel, as an intruder, provides another contemporary large-scale ghetto inside the Arab sub-system. Since its existence in 1948 Israel has tried to achieve both recognition and acceptance. While recognition is a legal procedure which may have very limited impact on the role of the state except at the symbolic level, acceptance is of a more substantial nature. It is related to societal and non-official types of interactions as well. It goes beyond peaceful co-existence, that is strategic peace so to say, deep into social, cultural and economic co-operation. This process is of great importance for the Israelis because it means that they do not have to change into Middle Easterners to be accepted. It means also that they can keep their 'western cultural superiority' from being contaminated by the Arab, Middle Eastern culture and yet be accepted on their own terms in the Middle East. The concept of acceptance corresponds to Nahum Goldmann's idea that the real Israeli superiority is in its quality, its nature, its talents and technological progress.[16]

Associated with this are the new attempts by the Israelis and the American Jews to establish and organize what can be called a technological diaspora in order to make use of the revolution in production especially in communication, space and data management. Israel's acceptance has to be reflected in the volume of economic exchange with its neighbours, that is the Arab market. The Israelis want to duplicate in the Arab countries their success in the economic and know-how exchange with the Africans. In spite of the troubles which face Israel in the diplomatic domain in Africa, its exports to that continent increased from US$41.5 million to US$190 million between 1970 and 1980 while its imports increased from US$30.1 million to US$135.7 million in the same period.[17] Moreover, Israel was able to provide both socialist states, for example Ethiopia, and capitalist states, such as Zaire, with military aid. The largest African state, Nigeria, is debating the issue of establishing diplomatic relations with Israel in order to reflect the increase in their economic interaction.

The Israeli goal of acceptance dominated the negotiation process between Egypt and Israel. The negotiators used the term normalization to indicate acceptance.[18] Normalization, in the context of this paper, means an increasing role of the Israeli economic and cultural sub-systems in the region compared with those of the Arab states.

Preservation of Special Relations with the US. Undoubtedly, Israel maintains special relations with the US. The *raison d'être* of such relations is not the emotional link between the two, but their mutual national interests and their joint security considerations.[19] These relations go back to the 1940s when the US worked hard for the adoption by the UN of the partition resolution in November 1947.[20] In May 1948 the US was the first to recognize the newly established state of Israel. The understanding concerning strategic issues between the two countries goes back to the 1950s. In 1952 both states signed the Assistance Agreement concerning mutual defence according to which military services, tools and weapons provided by the US to Israel would only be used for legitimate self-defence or participation in the defence of the area within collective security arrangements.

The US considered the maintenance of Israeli power and security as the cornerstone of its Middle East policy.[21] Israel is seen in the US as an indispensable strategic asset in the area. American intelligence circles in particular believe that Israel is the most reliable ally in the area against the Soviet Union.[22] Israel receives the lion's share of American military aid. Between 1950 and 1982 American military sales amounted to US$17 billion. On the other hand, the Israelis themselves know very well that they cannot survive without American aid.[23] For the first time in recent years both countries have started to put their commitments down in writing. In 1979 the US issued a Memorandum Agreement which was followed in April 1981 by another commitment by Secretary of State Alexander Haig to provide Israel with what is needed in order to develop its military industry. Both commitments became part of Haig's vision of strategic consensus in the Middle East. He wanted to create regional consensus against the Soviet Union with Israel as its dependable base. Hence, both sides concluded a Memorandum of Understanding on Strategic Co-operation in November 1981. This memorandum was activated in 1983 after the Israeli invasion of Lebanon. Such a special relationship means an invitation to one of the superpowers to have a foothold in the area. It means also that the Arab states may either try to establish their own special relations with the US (e.g., Egypt) or to enter into similar agreements with the Soviet Union (e.g., Syria). All this means that the Arab-Israeli conflict is mainly a regional conflict with an international dimension, almost at the disposal of the regional parties to the conflict.

The coincidence of the aforementioned goals would help Israel to influence, if not decide, the patterns of regional interactions, and the patterns of regional alliances. What will add to the self-steering mechanisms of these goals is the national consensus in Israel regarding such goals. Both the Likud coalition and the Labour Alignment are committed to these goals. They have a narrow tactical difference regarding the instruments to achieve them or the sequence regarding the implementation of the shared goals.

Arab Undefined Goals

The Arab goals regarding the Arab-Israeli conflict are neither defined nor clear. Moreover, there is a lack of Arab national consensus over what the Arabs want. It is true that the Arab sub-system is perceived as an integrative system.[24] None the less, certain changes took place in the region through which the role of the regional central power, Egypt, has been challenged. In the 1950s and 1960s Egypt had been recognized and accepted as the leader of the Arab sub-system. However, other regional actors — Saudi Arabia and Iraq — started to challenge it in the 1970s.[25]

By and large, we can depict three different Arab strategies towards Israel and towards the resolution of the conflict. These strategies are: rejection/confrontation strategy, taming/manipulation strategy and recognition/acceptance strategy.

Rejection/Confrontation Strategy. This is the oldest, and most well-established strategy of all. It started in the 1920s and 1930s when the Palestinians, the Syrians and other Arabs fought against the Jewish settlements in Palestine. It reached its zenith when the armies of seven Arab states entered Palestine to fight the Jewish army and related terrorist groups. The same strategy was implemented in the 1956, 1967 and 1973 Wars. The rejection was based on the fact that Israel is founded by intruders on Arab territory and that it created a real threat to Arab security. Israel was also perceived as a spearhead for the imperialist powers, especially the US. In other words, Israel was perceived as a dependent state and as a watchdog or a policeman in the area. The Arabs tried to institutionalize the confrontation strategy. The charter of the League of Arab States indicated that one of its objectives is the liberation of Palestine and the achievement of its independence. In 1950 the Council of the League adopted a resolution that laid down the basis for the rejectionist strategy. It stated that 'No member of the League is allowed to negotiate unilateral peace accord or any political, economic or military accord with Israel or actually reach such peace or accord. Any member state which does such a thing will be dismissed immediately from the League according to article 18 of the Charter.'[26]

Another attempt in this regard was the 1950 Mutual Defence and Economic Co-operation Agreement between the members of the League of Arab States which prohibited any member from reaching any political agreement which may not be in accordance with the objectives of that agreement. Added to this were the resolutions in the Khartoum Arab Summit after the 1967 defeat which stated that no peace with, no negotiation with and no recognition of, Israel can take place.

It was hard for such a strategy to succeed for more than one reason. First and foremost, it has been designed on the basis of a limited, deformed and erroneous concept of security. It is a concept which deliberately separates the internal and societal prerequisites for security from external threats. It has also been founded on the misconception that better military preparedness could be sufficient to confront Israel. This led to two fatal developments. The Arabs neglected the social process which is required in order to reach a consensus. Instead, they thought that the external threat, namely, Israel, would be enough in itself to create such consensus. They did not distinguish between spontaneous or deliberate mobilization and national consensus. Consequently, they simultaneously failed to create a generation of high calibre or a modern and efficient army. On the other hand, the pronounced Arab strategy led Israel to emphasize its military superiority against the whole Arab world. Hence Israel decided to have its own military industry and its own weapon systems.[27]

Associated with this strategy was the creation of the Palestine Liberation Organization (PLO) by the Arabs in 1964. The *raison d'être* of the PLO is rejection of the state of Israel. Articles 19–22 of the Palestine National Charter emphasize the rejectionist strategy. The PLO suffered from the same Arab problem — a declared strategy without the means to achieve it. There is no doubt that the failure of the PLO in Lebanon in 1982–3 was due to the inconsistency between its goals and the means at its disposal.

The strategy of rejection led to the greater presence of world powers in the region through the supply of arms, military experts, training and the transfer of know-how. For instance, the share of the Middle East of world arms imports increased from 18.3 per cent to 33.1 per cent between 1971 and 1980. It reflected an increasing role of major weapons exporting countries in the Middle East, especially the US and the Soviet Union.[28] Accordingly, Middle East security arrangements will most probably be tied to the strategies of the big powers.

Taming/Manipulation Strategy. This strategy is aimed at neutralizing the Israeli danger without the need for overt interaction with its implacable foe. It is a position which is adopted on the assumption that the Arabs can neither defeat Israel nor accept it since it is not ready to accept the rights of the Palestinians and withdraw from the occupied Arab territories. This position is also built on the idea that the Arabs need time to achieve their development goals, including the development of their armies. As long as it is impossible to deal simultaneously with the national cause, liberation of the land, and the social cause, the development issue, it becomes inevitable that they try to tame Israel.

The Arabs tried this strategy after their defeat in 1948. All the armistice agreements between the Arab confrontation states and Israel in 1949 can be explained in this context.

Another attempt was made by Egypt in the mid 1950s (1953−4) when Nasser opened channels of communications with Moshe Sharett, the Israeli Foreign Minister and Prime Minister.[29] Nasser's objectives were limited to taming Israel during the negotiations with the British concerning evacuation from the Suez Canal zone and to preparing an army for any confrontation with Israel. However, this attempt came to an end when Ben Gurion became the Prime Minister and the Israelis launched their raid against Gaza. All Arab attempts in the UN and its specialized agencies to condemn Israel and isolate it were also part of the taming process. This strategy failed because of the lack of confidence and high level of misperception between the two sides. Added to this is the fact that most of the attempts — between Egypt and Israel and between Jordan and Israel — were mainly bilateral and not based on a regional consensus.

Recognition/Acceptance Strategy. This strategy is not confined to the bilateral settlement between Egypt and Israel, but it goes back to the pre-1967 War era when in 1965 Habib Bourguiba, the President of Tunisia, initiated a three-point proposal for the resolution of the conflict.[30] It was followed by another proposal in July 1973 with almost the same principles. The Egyptian responses to Jarring, the UN representative, in 1968–9 provide a well-defined framework for a resolution of the conflict which includes the recognition of Israel. The Jordanian initiative in 1972 concerning the establishment of the United Arab Kingdom meant recognizing Israel as well.

There is no doubt that the 1970s witnessed a large number of peace proposals by many international actors. However, the parties to the conflict expressed very little enthusiasm about them.

The Egyptian initiative in November 1977 was a turning point in the recognition/acceptance strategy. It was an attempt to accomplish two objectives. On the one hand, it aimed at the sabotage of the increasing role of the superpowers in the conflict. (The US and the USSR shared the chairmanship of the Geneva Conference in December 1973. They issued a joint communiqué in October 1977 which called for the necessity to resolve the conflict and achieve Palestinian rights.) On the other hand, Sadat wanted to retrieve the Egyptian role *vis-à-vis* the emerging role of the Saudis.

The Egyptian initiative resulted in a series of Arab proposals which shaped the strategy of recognition. In August 1981, Saudi Crown Prince Fahd — now the King — launched his initiative which included among other points the implicit recognition of Israel. On the other hand, Egypt announced a new proposal in April 1982 based on mutual and simultaneous recognition between the Palestinians and the Israelis. Moreover, the Arab summit conference held in Fez, Morocco, in September 1982 issued a new proposal based on the recognition strategy. Subsequently, when the Lebanese government concluded a peace accord with Israel in May 1983, the Arab states did not sever their diplomatic relations with Lebanon in accordance with article 19 of the Charter of the League of Arab States (the same article which was invoked against Egypt after the Camp David Accords).

What binds the three strategies is the perception of Arab actors that Israel represents the main threat to Arab security. In spite of the different strategies to deal with such a threat, time has proved that the last one is probably becoming the most viable especially after the Israeli invasion of Lebanon and the Fez proposals.

Camp David Accords and Regional Strategic Imbalance

What were the motivations of both Israel and Egypt to reach a settlement agreement and what are its consequences?

Motivations

After the 1967 War the phenomenon of status-inconsistency emerged. On the one hand, Israel's unchallenged victory led to its acquiring a high achieved status while its ascribed status was low. On the other hand, Egypt's unexpected defeat led to deterioration of its achieved status while it insisted on maintaining a high level of ascribed status as the leader of the Arab sub-system (hence, Egypt initiated the October 1973 War in order to rescue its role and status). However, as a result of the October War, Saudi Arabia emerged as a new actor which enjoyed a high level of achieved status through its financial capabilities while suffering from a low level of ascribed status. Each one of these actors tried to redress the gap between their ascribed and achieved status.

After the first and second disengagement agreement between Israel and Egypt, it became clear that a settlement between the two countries was possible. What Israel wanted was an Egyptian recognition of Israeli power and role. Israel had completed its nation-building process and had started to look for an active regional foreign policy. At the same time, Egypt wanted to regain Sinai, open the Suez Canal to international navigation and to change the course of its political and economic conduct. Egypt wanted its land back, but also a new friendship with the US.[31] Egypt under Sadat had changed its perception of its main enemy in the Middle East and Africa and had transferred this role to the Soviet Union. At the same time, Egypt wanted to dissociate itself from the Arab states which started to pursue more active policies in the region. The deal — recognition versus withdrawal — was a viable one within that context.

Consequences

First, what the Camp David Accords and the peace treaty did was to get Egypt out of the leadership of the Arab sub-system and allowed Israel to promote its own role in the Middle East. Saudi Arabia and Iraq tried, through the peripheralization of Egypt, to obtain the central power status. Syria and Libya wanted to sabotage the Egyptian-Israeli moves. Hence, Egyptian-Arab interactions fell off suddenly in 1977, while Egyptian-Israeli interactions started to grow.

Instead of utilizing the accords as a means to increase the chances of Israel's acceptance in the region, both Egypt and Israel formed, in a sense, a peripheral, pariah sub-system, while other vulnerable Arab sub-systems emerged, for example, the Gulf Co-operation Council, the Egyptian-Sudanese sub-system and the rejectionist Arab sub-system.

The Iranian Revolution of 1979, and the Iraqi-Syrian hostilities which led Syria to support Iran against Iraq, added to the vulnerability of the Arab sub-system. All this was reflected in the political and military status of the PLO. Without an Arab regional centre of power, the Palestinians became vulnerable and ineffective.

Secondly, Egypt's relative military power became weaker than in 1973. Now Sinai is demilitarized and the army is very dependent on the US which is committed to protect Israel. Egypt, so to say, has been tamed in regional or international conflicts in which the US or Israel are involved. Hence, Egypt's role in the Lebanese War, the Iraq-Iran War and in the Western Sahara problem has been totally minimized. Even Egypt's role in the 'autonomy' talks for the West Bank and Gaza has come to an end.

As a result, Egypt's moves are directed toward Africa. It seems that whenever Egypt's role in the Arab East decreases, its role on the southern front, i.e. Sudan and Africa, increases. However, this front is not, and has never been, the prime Egyptian sphere of interest.

Thirdly, the accords created a security vacuum. Israeli power cannot be utilized for the protection of the other regional actors. The US did its best to create a strategic consensus, a new pact, between Israel, Egypt and other conservative Arab states. However, Israel is perceived by most of these actors as the main threat to their security.

Alternatively, the US created its own forces to be used in case of urgent threat to its interests in the area, namely, the Rapid Deployment Force now known as the Central Command (Centcom). The US also tried to gain military facilities in Egypt, Somalia, Oman and Saudi Arabia. Moreover, the US started to conduct joint military manoeuvres (Bright Star) with the Egyptian army and other Arab armies. Simultaneously, the US and Israel reached a new Understanding on Strategic Co-operation in the Middle East. Consequently, the security of the Middle East has become more linked to world order than ever before.

Alternatives for the Future

There is a consensus in the Arab world that without the solution of the Palestinian question there cannot be durable peace in the Middle East. None the less, another consensus prevails in the Arab world, i.e. that the existing power imbalance between the Arab states and Israel forces the Arabs to settle the conflict by peaceful means. What also makes that trend viable is the division of the Arab world into more than one camp, and the wars in the Gulf, in Lebanon and the recent weakening of the Palestinian movement.

In the light of all this, one can visualize three different scenarios. First, that the status quo will continue with more Israeli expansion and domination and the impasse over the Palestinian issue. It means an active role for the US, more potential for violence and probabilities for more wars in the area. Second, a return to a more dominant role by Egypt and more consolidation of forces in the Arab sub-system. It is a return to a non-acceptance strategy and a minimum role for the US and probably more active role for the Soviets. It means a more effective Arab defence policy and more control over regional security. However, this scenario will lead to pre-emptive offensive attacks by Israel, i.e. more intense violence. Third, Arab and Israeli mutual acceptance and participation in regional security arrangements. The prerequisites for such a scenario include the Israeli recognition of the Palestinian right of self-determination and the withdrawal of its troops from occupied Arab land, and Arab readiness to accept Israel and open their borders and markets to the flow of Israeli goods and personnel. The superpowers will not be interested in the last scenario because it deprives them of their active role in regional security arrangements, although it is the only one that appears to be a viable solution for the perennial Arab-Israeli conflict.

Notes

1. E. Azar, *et al.*, 'Protracted Conflict in the Middle East', *Journal of Palestinian Studies*, Autumn (1978), pp. 41–60.
2. Mohammed Ayoob (ed.), *Regional Security in the Third World*, Chapter 1, p. 13.
3. Abba Eban, *An Autobiography* (Random House, New York, 1977).
4. Yitzhak Shamir, 'Israel's Role in a Changing Middle East', *Foreign Affairs*, Spring (1982), pp. 789–801.
5. H. Nafaa, *Egypt and the Arab-Israeli Conflict* (Centre for Arab Unity, Beirut, 1984), (in Arabic).

6. H. Sharabi, 'The Palestinian Approach to Negotiations', a paper presented at the Centre for Political and Strategic Studies, Al-Ahram, Cairo, March 28–30 (1983).

7. Abba Eban (1977).

8. S. Ghabbour, *Science and Technology in Israel* (Foundation of Palestinian Studies, Beirut, 1982), in Arabic.

9. Abdul-Monem Said, *Nuclear Balance in the Middle East* (forthcoming), in Arabic.

10. D. Hirst and I. Beeson, *Sadat* (Faber and Faber, London, 1981).

11. P. Jureidini and R. D. McLaurin, *Beyond Camp David* (Syracuse University Press, New York, 1981).

12. Ibid.

13. A. Al-Mashat, 'Israel's Strategy Toward the Arab System', published research paper (Cairo University, 1984), in Arabic.

14. Hariubin, *Necessity for Choice* (Tel Aviv, 1980).

15. El-Shazly, *The Crossing of the Suez* (American Mideast Research, San Francisco, 1980).

16. N. Goldman, 'Israeli Foreign Policy: A Time for Re-evalutation', reprinted in *New Outlook*, Israel.

17. *Statistical Yearbook of Israel* (1980).

18. E. Azar and S. Cohen, 'Peace as Crisis and War as a Status Quo: The Arab-Israeli Conflict Environment', *International Interactions*, vol. 6, no. 2 (1979), pp. 159–84. Also see M. K. Ibrahim, *The Lost Peace* (The Saudi Company for Marketing and Distribution, London, 1984), in Arabic.

19. Henry Kissinger, *Years of Upheaval* (Little, Brown & Co., Boston, 1982).

20. Nadav Safran, *Israel: The Embattled Ally* (The Belknap Press, Cambridge, Mass., 1981).

21. Arthur Herzberg, *The Zionist Eden: A Historical Analysis and Reader* (Athaeneum, New York, 1979).

22. H. Sharabi, 'The Palestinian Approach to Negotiations'.

23. Aharon Yariv, 'Reflections on a Solution of the Palestinian Problem' in ATouph Hareven (ed.), *Can the Palestinian Problem Be Solved?* (The Van Leer Jerusalem Foundation, Jerusalem, 1983).

24. A. Hilal and G. Matar, *The Arab Regional System* (Centre for Arab Studies, Beirut, 1980), in Arabic. Also see A. Al-Mashat, 'Contemporary Crisis of Arab National Security' in Al-Mashat *et. al., Regional and International Aspects of the Palestinian Question* (Dar el-Mustaqbal Al-Arabi, Cairo, 1983), in Arabic.

25. Gamal Hamdan, *Egypt's Character*, part I (World of Books, Cairo, 1980), in Arabic.

26. B. Auda, 'The League of Arab States and the Palestinian Question', *Egyptian Journal of Political Science*, July (1970).

27. A. Howaidi, *The Arab-Israeli Conflict: Between the Traditional Deterrent and the Nuclear Deterrent* (Dar el-Mustaqbal Al-Arabi, Cairo, 1983), in Arabic. Also see M. Azmi, 'A Theory of Israeli Security in the Light of the 1973 October War', *Journal of Palestinian Studies*, March (1972).

28. US Arms Control and Disarmament Agency, *World Military Expenditures and Arms Transfers 1971–1980* (USACDA, Washington DC, 1983).

29. H. Nafaa, 'American-Israeli Relations' in Al-Mashat *et. al., Regional and International Aspects of the Palestinian Question*. Also see E. Jackson, *Middle East Mission: The Story of a Major Bid for Peace in the Time of Nasser and Ben Gurion* (Norton & Co., New York, 1983).

30. El-Hur and El-Moussa, *Settlement Proposals for the Palestinian Question 1937–1982* (Al-Galeel Publishing House, Amman, 1983), in Arabic.

31. M. Heikal, *Autumn of Fury* (Andre Deutsch, London, 1983).

COMMENTS

Kamel S. Abu Jaber

Of all the Arabs, only the Egyptians, scholars and sometimes even journalists, can write with such detachment about the Arab-Israeli conflict. Perhaps this is because they are somehow less involved culturally in it and thus, though vocal, less emotionally charged when writing about or discussing it. And although Israel poses as much of a threat to Egypt as it does to the other neighbouring Arab states, the Arab-Israeli conflict as an issue is treated by the Egyptians as if there exists a distance between them and the conflict.

Al Mashat hints at, but does not spell out, the security needs and/or claims of the Arab countries. He states — which is an under-statement in itself — that Israel does not '. . . recognize the Arab need for security'. I found this statement so deliciously detached that I had to reread it several times. The author, coming as he does from Egypt, a country that perhaps lost more than all other Arab countries in terms of men, material and prestige, knows better than that. He knows that Israel's mere creation was, and continues to be, an aggression in itself. Israel's behaviour, politically and militarily, has given so much credence to this statement that it needs no elaboration. Its encroachment on the no-man's lands, its attacks on Arab villages, its collaboration in 1956 with Britain and France in their attack on Egypt, its encroachment on the water resources of the area, its 1967 aggression, occupation of Jordanian, Egyptian and Syrian lands, its illegal annexation of East Jerusalem and the Golan Heights, its illegal settlements programme, its invasion of Lebanon and continued occupation of its south, its continued occupation of the Taba area in spite of a peace treaty with Egypt; indeed its general demeanour of a superior invader-intruder, instrument of violence and terror, both physical and mental, attests to its present and future intents. Surely the question arises as to whether Israel truly searches for peace or expansion. It has been the major cause of the insecurity of the area since 1948.

It should be emphasized that the Israeli-created insecurity has several dimensions besides the military: an insecurity that transcends the bounds of regime, even regional, security reaching global dimensions. Israel seems to the Arabs to be a nation whose very *raison d'être* is the creation and provocation of further insecurity: militarily by the furtherance of its military preponderance with its concomitant reliance on violence in dealing with others, and territorially by its ever-expanding concept of security giving rise to its continued expansion through a settlement programme designed ultimately to legitimize its creeping annexation. Its military outreach extends beyond its immediate frontiers to the area as a whole and sometimes even beyond. Entebbe is a case in point, while its attack on the nuclear reactor in Iraq in 1981, its aid to separatist groups in Iraq or in south Sudan and its aid to Iran against Iraq speak of a role much larger than one would imagine.

Israel's deliberate ambiguity *vis à vis* the peace process is ultimately linked to its concept of the desired Israeli state. Where do the borders of Israel lie? Sometimes they creep while at other times they leap. Surely delineating its borders would enhance the chances of regime, regional and even international security since the neighbouring states would then also know where their own borders lie.

Israel's destabilizing and insecurity-rendering activities take many forms. Its subversive interference in the affairs of neighbouring states is one, while its covert, and sometimes not so covert, support of certain groups is another. Lebanon is one case in point. Viewed from the Arab side Israel's intention is not only to destabilize but to fragment the region into smaller ethnic or religious entities; minorities amongst whom Israel will remain as the dominant power.

I agree with the first two hypotheses of Mashat: the presumption that Arab security is indispensable to the security of the region and, the second, regarding Israel's double strategy; to be accepted in the area while at the same time facing that acceptance and the ensuing normalization process on its own terms. And thus, instead of commencing a meaningful process leading towards peace with its neighbours, it resorts to the dual strategy of elevating the regional conflict to an international one through untiring efforts at bipolarizing and thus freezing it between the two superpowers and through its encouragement of centrifugal forces within the region and thus its further fragmentation. By elevating the Arab-Israeli conflict to the global level Israel succeeds in making it a part of the cold war formula thus providing itself with the breathing space and the time it needs to digest its successive expansions. By encouraging internal centrifugal forces, Israel ensures that no regime or combination of regimes is in a position ever to plan to become a serious threat to its expansionist designs. In the meantime, Israel continues to hold the initiative in timing its own moves, the creation of 'new realities and facts' which it then manoeuvres into becoming permanent because of the existing bipolarization between the superpowers.

This brings me to the third hypothesis of Al Mashat relating to the '. . . role of the superpowers and great powers' which he calls 'secondary but indispensable . . .' He alludes to President Sadat's visit to Israel from which I draw different conclusions. I see that visit and the ensuing Egyptian pro-western, pro-American stance as a dramatic attempt by an Arab leader to take the Arab-Israeli conflict out of the freezer of superpower politics. The role of the superpowers is not at all secondary and this recognition by Sadat caused him to attempt to break the Israeli-Zionist monopoly over the American political process, indeed over the American decision-making process. He saw Israel deliberately offering itself as the only reliable ally and friend of the West while at the same time pushing the Arabs in the other direction. Ironically, and for a variety of reasons, the Arabs helped Israel in isolating or re-isolating Egypt within the Arab camp and thus lessening its credibility as a reliable pro-western power in the region. Later this was one of the major factors encouraging the US, or at least further freeing its hand, to conclude the Strategic Co-operation Agreement with Israel.

The other side of this situation is that while one of the two super-powers is wholly and unequivocally supportive of one side, often to the detriment of its own interests, the other superpower is not to the same degree supportive of the other side. In this regard the author, on the authority of Henry Kissinger, alludes to what Israel deliberately and repeatedly emphasizes as the mutuality of national security and interests between the United States and Israel. It could be argued that such a mutuality not only does not exist but that Israel is ultimately a threat to the medium- and long-term interests of the United States; that if such a mutuality of interests exists, it does so by force of Zionist propaganda and influence alone and strictly on paper and that it is repeated time and time again to further the already existing alienation between the Arabs and the United States. It does not take much wisdom or a tremendous amount of hindsight to realize that Israel was the net beneficiary of the assassination of Sadat and the eventual assassination of his legacy.

7 THE IRAN-IRAQ WAR: REGIME SECURITY AND REGIONAL SECURITY

Kamel S. Abu Jaber

Background

The current war between Iraq and Iran, already into its fourth year, is not an isolated incident between the two neighbours, but yet another battle in a long historical conflict whose onset some scholars and political commentators attribute to the advent of Islam in the seventh century. Even at that early date, Iran already had a distinctive national history, language, literature, art, religion (Zoroastrianism), and a distinctive racial origin (Aryan). Leonard Binder emphasizes that the '. . . Arab invasion, . . . did not break the continuity of Iranian history . . .'[1] That the Iranians took the Shia Ja'fary brand of Islam helped in the maintenance of their distinctiveness and also their separateness from the surrounding Arab Islamic world. 'Shiism in Iran is not only the true religion . . . it is also the distinctive adaptation of Arab Islam to Iranian culture . . .'[2] Ahmed Khasravi (1890–1946), a modern Iranian historian, advocated a return to a form of Zoroastrianism while the Iranvij society, a hold-over group of intellectuals from Reza Shah's time, still argues that the '. . . Arabs never conquered Iran; according to them, Shiism is Zoroastrianism in Muslim clothing . . .'[3]

While one may question some of the conclusions stated above, there remains, of necessity, a certain amount of suspicion in the Arab world about the desire of at least some Iranian leaders and members of the elite to demonstrate that Iranian nationalism is antithetical to Arab nationalism. The problem has become more complicated since the advent of the present Islamic regime and the apparent change from the emphasis on Aryan-Iranian to an Islamic-based nationalism which to Iraq and other neighbouring Arab states poses a clear and present danger. While Iraq claims that Islam only provides a facade behind which Aryanism is at work, the Islamic Revolution of Iran, with its populist appeal in the region, is a more real threat than ever before. From the Iraqi vantage point the Iranian nationalism of the Shah with its territorial and ethnic limitations was less of a danger than the present

155

transnational Islamic ideology of the Imam.

Modern Iran has been a largely independent, unified state with recognized boundaries for more than four hundred years. Its bases of nationals, whether ancient or modern, very strong at the onset, were further strengthened with the establishment of the Pahlavi dynasty by Reza Shah in the early part of this century, and continued by his son, the late Shahinshah Mohamad Reza Pahlavi.

Incidentally, the term Pahlavi adopted by Reza Shah refers to the rulers of ancient Parthia.[4] The late Shah and his father spared no effort in distinguishing Iran from its Middle Eastern milieu by emphasizing the Aryanness of their people and by attempting to revive ancient pre-Islamic Iranian culture. In 1935 the state was officially named Iran to replace the Hellenistic name Persia. Also, at that time, Reza Shah ordered the revision of the language, '. . . with a view to purifying it from Arabic influences', a specific task given to the Iranian Academy of Literature.[5] Iran, according to the late Shah, was the residium of a once great empire and culture. While many of these activities, emphasizing the Aryanness of Iran, including the purification of the language have been discontinued by the Islamic Republic, Iraqi memory of them as well as their reading of the present revolutionary zeal in Iran continue to cause apprehension in Baghdad.

The contrast between what once was, and what now is, produced a sense of unfulfilled nationalism that had to find expression in one way or another. The Shah reached back into antiquity for images and attempted to build up his military to become the greatest power in the region, while the Ayatollah has attempted to build Iranian power and legitimacy on a religious basis: in both cases, Iranian. Hrair Dekmejian ventures the opinion that the 'Leadership potential of Ayat Allah Khumayni is limited to the *Ithna'ashri* (twelve) sect of Shiite Muslims who mostly inhabit Iran and southern Iraq. Therefore, the return to Islamic roots has a "nativistic" and "locatistic" character; at least, in part, as it has developed in response to particular conditions . . .'[6]

The divergence in the history of state formation between Iran and Iraq in the last few centuries, especially since the Safavid assumption of power in 1502 in Iran and the adoption of Shiism as the state religion, was emphasized by the coincidence of Ottoman Sunni rise to power and expansionism. It is thus that historically, as well as now, Islam as current in Iran, perhaps more than in any other Muslim land, flows right along with nationalism. Of course, the point should not be carried too far, but the point is that there exists a latent tendency among the Iranians to distinguish themselves from their Arab and other neighbours. Binder, quoted above, also stated in 1964 that should Iranian power increase (and it did increase militarily in the Shah's time, and certainly morally in Ayatollah Khomeini's time), '. . . it may be expected that Iran will return to more aggressive policies abandoned a century ago . . .'[7]

Iran's claims to supremacy over the Gulf area, and to annexation of certain parts of it, date back to the early sixteenth century. The 1975 Algiers Treaty, attempting to delineate the borders between Iraq and Iran, was the last of a series of treaties dating back to 1535 when the first treaty was concluded between Safavid Iran and Ottoman Turkey. Treaties were concluded in 1555, 1568, 1590, 1618, 1639, 1746, 1823, 1847, 1911, 1913, 1914, 1937 and 1975.[8] Throughout the Ottoman period, the Ottoman sultans frequently mobilized to deter Iran from occupying Iraq which Shah Ismail succeeded in doing in 1508, and which he maintained until 1514 when he was ousted by Sultan Salim I. Its re-occupation in 1529 lasted until 1543. Iraq was again occupied between 1623 and 1639, at which time Sultan Murad IV ousted the occupants and concluded the Zahab Treaty of 1639.

Later attempts to conclude a meaningful and lasting agreement to delineate the border between the two countries met with failure. The fact that Iran lays claim to certain Arab territories in the Gulf area and in Iraq itself continues to be a very important reason for the dispute, further aggravating the situation and deepening suspicions. Iran's claim to Bahrain and her refusal to recognize even Iraq herself at the conclusion of the First World War were disturbing even to the British, not to mention the Arab government of Iraq under the Hashemite dynasty.[9] Her occupation of the three islands of Lesser Tunb, Greater Tunb and Abu Musa at the mouth of the Gulf following their evacuation by the British in 1971 gave further evidence of Iran's intentions. With the advent of the new regime in Iran it was hoped that the dispute would be resolved amicably. From the Iraqi point of view, and despite the initial welcome of the change of regime in Iran, this did not happen. On the contrary, the Iraqis charge that Iran renewed its claim not only to Bahrain but also to Kuwait and, in addition, committed belligerent acts in the Gulf area and in Iraq itself.[10]

Contested borders seem now to be the main reason for the past and present disputes. Going much deeper than the mere contestation of border areas, however important these may be, it is a dispute that is encouraged by mutual fears fed by ancient suspicions of many forms, shapes and colours. It has several levels and roots: national, ideological, religious, psychological, personal; and is, in some of its aspects, even racial. It is also the clash of images between two neighbours who know little about each other; their lack of knowledge causing further fears and suspicions; a clash of two mobilizing ideologies, one the Ba'th of Iraq, with its essentially secular overtones, while the other is essentially religious. The bases of power in the two countries are very different. Iraq, with its multi-religious, multi-ethnic composition cannot very well accept religion as the sole basis of its legitimacy. This, in fact, may lead to further dissension and strife. Secularism, which the regime does not openly emphasize, has to be the cohesive force in Iraq.

The image of Iran from Iraq, indeed from most of the Arab world, is that of a powerful or potentially powerful, dynamic and ambitious neighbour, which has over the centuries been psychologically, sometimes religiously, sometimes nationalistically charged to look across its frontiers to its west. The fact that the Shiite holy places of Najaf, Karbala and al-Kadhimin are situated within Iraqi territory serves as a constant reminder of the tension that exists between the two neighbours; neighbours whose relations have rarely been neighbourly. The Ottoman Empire, and then the British, maintained their protection of Iraqi national integrity. Why is it that the clash, currently in progress, did not take place in the 1960s or even in the early 1970s under the Shah's regime? The question is certainly a difficult one, made more difficult by the fact that, at least initially, the Khomeini regime never made the same claims as those made by the imperial regime of the Shah. On the contrary, the present Iranian regime continues to speak of Islamic brotherhood and solidarity. Perhaps one possible answer may be sought in the fact that both Iraqi-Arab and Iranian nationalisms are thwarted, frustrated and unfulfilled nationalisms; both nationalisms coming to a head at the same time.

Both Iran and Iraq are developing countries undergoing the agonies of transition from one level of life to another. The discovery by both Iraq and Iran of their weakness *vis-à-vis* the western intrusion was shocking. While the discovery of the weakness on the military level was shocking in itself, the more startling was the intrusion of world culture, modernity, or western culture into both societies. The response in both societies was similar in some of its aspects. In both, there was alienation, though more advanced in the Iranian case because of the determined, though, hindsight indicates, short-sighted efforts of the Shah to push the development of his country at very high speed and to such a degree that the average man could not relate to the tremendous changes taking place all at once and encroaching on every aspect of his life, social, physical, personal, psychological and cultural, and leaving him bewildered, uncertain and frustrated.

That both societies toyed with a variety of reforms added further dimensions to the bewilderment. Liberal institutions, once extolled, were later vilified in the name of the revolution and replaced by strict authoritarian regimes. Whether the revolution came from above or from below, the end result, as far as the average man was concerned, was the same; more restrictions, more rationalizations that did not seem rational and more bewilderment, and all in the name of progress.

In Iraq, secular nationalism has, thus far, provided a certain type of certitude. The pressure from Iran, rather than weakening the regime, has caused it to become more cohesive. The prospect of any change at this moment in history is so frightening to the Iraqis that they instinctively rally behind their regime. For the Iraqis have come to appreciate that the most likely direction change may take is to the right, to a fundamentalist-type regime along the lines of the Islamic Republic of Iran. This fear is compounded by Khomeini's demand that President Saddam Hussein be ousted from his position as a condition for peace. As a matter of national pride that call has caused negative reactions. They ask, '. . . how will life be when Iran can dictate who will rule us?' The question is the more pertinent when one contemplates that the Sunni Iraqi elite and leadership rule over a population whose majority is composed of Shi'as. It is significant that the Iraqi Shi'as, despite the repeated calls of Iran for them to revolt against the 'heretical-Baathist regime', have, thus far, not done so. Is it the triumph of secular over religious ideology or is it the result of Arab fear of Iranian hegemony?

It is thus that the conditions for the present conflict were ripe: two frustrated nationalisms that came to fruition at about the same time; disputing a territory led by two highly charismatic, highly volatile personalities; and charged with ancient images and grudges. How dare Saddam Hussein stand up to Imam Khomeini, infallible according to Shia doctrine? It was unfortunate also that

Saddam Hussein, then the Vice President of Iraq, was pressured three years after the conclusion of the 1975 agreement by the Shah to have the Iraqi Chief of Intelligence inform Imam Khomeini that he was to leave Iraq, where he had been residing as a political refugee for 14 years. It is said that it angered the Imam that Iraq yielded to the Shah's pressure. It removed him to far away France which made it more difficult for him to agitate against the Shah's regime. While in Iraq, the government there had provided him with access to the radio station to speak out against the Shah. Ironically enough his removal to France sped up the process of agitation and revolution against the Shah's regime. In France, with his appearance and fiery speeches, he became the focus of the international mass media.

On 17 April 1980, before the outbreak of war, the Imam is reported to have said, 'The Iraqi regime which is attacking Iran (verbally and in propaganda) is, in fact, attacking the Quran and Islam. Iran will take over Iraq and advance until it reaches Baghdad . . .' On 22 April 1980, also before the outbreak of war, he is reported to have addressed the Iraqi armed forces personnel: '. . . leave your barracks, do not suffer any longer from the shameful condition under which you live now and get rid of Saddam Hussein like we got rid of the Shah . . .' Saddam, on the other hand, on 15 April 1980 called Khomeini '. . . that mummy . . .' and on another occasion, on 23 April 1980, stated that the present confrontation is between Arabs and *Furs* (Persians) and that Khomeini is a Shah wearing a turban.[11]

The 1975 Algiers Agreement

The background to the conclusion and later cancellation of the 1975 agreement was that of mutual mistrust, border incidents, provocations and continued disputation. Iran had continued to complain that Iraq was not abiding by the provisions of the Treaty of 1937,[12] especially those pertaining to the revenue from passing ships, while Iraq continued to complain that Iran was still in occupation of certain Iraqi territory. The unfriendly atmosphere, mutual accusations and border incidents continued until Iran, almost one year after the 1968 assumption of power of the Ba'th Party in Iraq, unilaterally abrogated the 1937 treaty.[13] Iran also claimed that Iraq was not abiding by its terms, especially its provisions relating to dual administration over the navigation and maintenance of Shat al-Arab.[14] Iraq, on the other hand, claimed that Iran was taking advantage of its military weakness and the fact that the new regime had barely had time to stabilize the situation in Iraq. The support of the Kurdish rebellion in Iraq by Iran, which collapsed almost overnight upon the conclusion of the 1975 agreement, did not help matters between the two nations. The Shah, too, was very unhappy with the Ba'athist regime in Baghdad while the latter was constantly agitating against the 'reactionary' regime in Tehran. The occupation by Iran in 1971 of the three islands at the mouth of the Gulf added further fuel to the dispute.

It was at the initiative of the late President of Algeria, Houari Boumediene, that the Shah and the then Vice President of Iraq, Saddam Hussein, met in Algiers. In addition to its specific provisions, the 1975 agreement attempted to normalize relations between the two neighbours, calling on both to refrain from interfering in each other's internal affairs. It was thus that the Kurdish rebellion collapsed almost immediately. The treaty called for the delimitation of land borders according to the 1913 and 1914 agreements, and the drawing up of the maritime border according to the thalweg line. Along with its three addenda protocols, it came into effect on 22 June 1976.[15] Iraq was also supposed to receive certain territory previously occupied by Iran which, Iraq claimed, Iran continued to occupy even after the assumption of power by Imam Khomeini in Tehran. Further, the new Iranian regime refused to evacuate the three islands in the Gulf. Some of the new Iranian leaders also began talking of cancelling the 1975 agreement, claiming that Iran was not bound by it.[16]

The cancellation by Iraq of the treaty on 17 September 1980 came as a result of a series of incidents and provocations that Iraq accused Iran of perpetrating. One of them was the bomb explosion at the al-Mustansiriyyah University on 1 April 1980 which resulted in several dead and injured. Another, was the bomb thrown at the funeral procession of the victims of the first bomb on 5 April 1980 which also resulted in several dead and injured. This prompted the oath by President Saddam Hussein that '. . . By God, by God, by God, the innocent blood that spilled at the al-Mustansiriyyah will not have spilled in vain . . .' The mutual accusations, border incidents and border artillery barrages continued throughout the Spring and Summer of 1980. On 4 September 1980 several Iraqi towns along the border were subjected to heavy artillery bombardment. It was this incident that, President Saddam Hussein later stated, prompted the full-scale Iraqi attack on Iran on 22 September 1980.[17]

Very early in the war, Iraq indicated its willingness to cease hostilities and called for direct negotiations through either a third party or the United Nations.[18] Later, Iraq initiated a unilateral ceasefire then withdrew to its international frontiers with offers of negotiations through any intermediary acceptable to both sides.[19] Thus far, and after the passage of nearly five years of a hopelessly senseless and bloody conflict, Iran continues to refuse cessation of hostilities and commencement of negotiations. It continues to insist on its conditions for the conclusion of the conflict: conditions and terms that the Iraqis continue to find not only unacceptable but constituting a national insult as well as interference in their internal affairs. In addition to the demand for reparations which the Iraqis find questionable, Iran, in fact Imam Khomeini, insists that no peace will be concluded with Iraq as long as Saddam Hussein is in power in Baghdad.[20] Further, Iran demands that the new Iraqi regime must resemble the present Iranian regime in its constitution, ideals and organization.[21]

Since the first week of the war Iraq has sued for peace and much Arab, Islamic and international effort has gone into attempts to mediate between the combatants. This, in addition to offers of mediation by the United Nations, the Organization of Islamic Conference, the Arab League, the Non-Aligned Movement, the Gulf Co-operation Council, Pakistan, Egypt, Algeria, the Palestine Liberation Organization and many others.

Perhaps the most novel and imaginative proposal to date came from the Egyptian National Democratic Party which called for an immediate halt to the hostilities and the referral of the dispute to an international Islamic tribunal to be set up at the Azhar in Cairo or at the Ka'bah in Mecca. The proposal also called for those who cherish Islam to participate in peaceful demonstrations in front of the Iranian and Iraqi embassies throughout the capitals of the world bearing the Holy Book, the Quran, and raising the white flag of peace.[22] All these efforts have been of no avail, for Iran still holds to its demands adding yet another dimension of bewilderment to the uniqueness of this conflict.

A Unique War

Miscalculation does not make a situation unique. It is the persistence in miscalculation that makes it so. On the one hand, the Iraqi miscalculation was that the regime in Iran, disorganized as it was in 1980, would quickly disintegrate and the nationalities and separate tendencies within Iran would take the opportunity to rise up against the regime: the Arabs of Arabistan, now Khuzistan, Kurds, the Baluchis, etc.[23]

Iraq misread the situation in Iran thinking that the upper and middle classes created by the Shah in the cities over the past four decades would grasp the chance to topple the reactionary regime. These classes were not only cowed by the onslaught of a powerfully dynamic indigenous ideology that too harkened back to ancient myths and symbols, but many of them either remained silent or crossed over to the Khomeini lines. The fervour of religious ideology found further support from the fact that the Iranian fatherland was being attacked by an Arab secular state. While the Iraqis harkened back to the Battle of Qadisiyyah in AD 636, where occurred the conclusive battle between the Arab Muslim armies led by Sa'd Ibn Abi Waqqas and the Persian armies led by Rustum and in which Persia was defeated embracing Islam, later Shia Islam, Imam Khomeini reversed roles by proclaiming a *Jihad*, a holy war, against the forces of Arab, secular Ba'thist, socialist Iraq, while the Iraqis described the conflict as the 'Second Qadisiyyah' or 'Saddam's Qadisiyyah'.[24] The appeal to the masses of Iranians in the countryside and the cities, already jobless and confused in the political and economic chaos that came in the short span of time between the Islamic Revolution and the war with Iraq, was strong. After all, Imam Khomeini, while in Paris, succeeded in toppling the hated regime of the Shah; who then is Saddam to abrogate treaties with him? The war of right against wrong thus became a war of no compromise regardless of sacrifices.

This is especially true when pronounced by a powerfully motivated religious leader like the Imam, made more venerable by the tragedies of his personal family losses and his advanced age. Declaring those who die in the battle against Iraq to be martyrs and giving them symbolic keys to the gates of heaven, further heightened the zeal and enthusiasm of the people. The symbolism, Qadisiyyah on the one hand and a Jihad on the other, are powerful enough to continue deepening the schism between the two neighbours.

The miscalculation on the part of Iraq while enormous seems plausible in the hindsight of later events. How could a mundane earthly leader foresee the time-bomb with which he was dealing? Could he, could anyone, at that time fathom the real or imagined accumulation of resentment and suspicions that existed? It was like opening an already inflamed wound to be further inflamed through exposure to further contamination. Once one takes hold of the angry tiger's tail, how can one let go? President Saddam not only renounced the 1975 Algiers Treaty but also the 1937 treaty that confirmed Arabistan, now called Khuzistan by the Iranians, as the home of Iran's Arab minority, since it no longer applied.[25] In Richard Cottam's estimate, Iraq's miscalculation was disastrous and played right into the Imam's hands. Imam Khomeini not only had the necessary support from certain classes within Iran, but viewed his role '. . . as a divinely appointed leader of the oppressed peoples of the world . . .'[26] Revolutions should not be responded to with military power. Such a response causes further entrenchment of the revolutionary regime and the galvanization of wavering elements in its support.

Again, hindsight indicates that however disenchanted it was with the new regime in Iran, and, in spite of the high expectations it may have had regarding it, Iraq was impatient in pressing Iran, already in the throes of a revolution, for fulfilment of the 1975 agreement. While Iraq may have wished to take advantage of Iran's internal troubles, the latter was not in the mood for, nor did it regard the timing right for, compromise. It, too, was a nationalist revolution, however much couched in religion it may have been, and, in the wake of ousting the Shah — a nationalistic deed in the people's eyes — it would not have been nationalistic too quickly to begin yielding territory to neighbouring Iraq, regardless of the merits of the situation. It simply was bad timing.

Imam versus President; a nascent pan-Islamic movement versus a pan-Arab movement; one truly transnational, hoping to embrace all nationalities, perhaps all of mankind, in the newly found spirit of a regenerated Islam; the Ba'th, a secular and, at best, a pan-Arab movement, addressed to the Arab peoples alone. The zeal, the fervour and the attraction of the Imam were tremendous. His stern eyes projecting confidence and his call for the re-establishment of an Islamic order were attractive to many beyond the frontiers of Iran. For a moment it appeared that the hurricane building up within Iran would sweep everything before it. Within the Islamic countries he was attractive to the weak, the disinherited, the *mustaz'afin*; internationally, the whole Islamic world appeared weak, disinherited, thus ripe for a new leader with vision, courage and unbounded fearlessness. After all, did not the Imam bring America to its knees throughout the hostage crisis? Who but himself humiliated America, indeed the whole western world, and rendered it helpless; helpless in spite of military might, weapons and missiles? Preaching world revolution, the Imam and many Iranian leaders viewed the international borders with Iraq as a mere 'inconvenience'. The call for the overthrow of the 'evil and atheist' Iraqi leadership did not constitute in their eyes interference in Iraqi internal affairs. The Imam, the then Iranian Foreign Minister, Qotbzadeh, said on 1 May 1980, was '. . . the leader of the Iraqi people, and all Islamic peoples; as he feels responsibility for Iran, he feels responsibility for Iraq . . .' The Iraqis, on the other hand, had other ideas. The Ba'thist regime opposed, and continues to oppose the '. . . use of religion for political purposes' and, taking into consideration the sectarian diversity of Iraq and that the Arab Sunni element constitutes only a minority of about 25 per cent of the total population, the Ba'th must emphasize Arab nationalism, even Iraqi patriotism transcending religious sectarian affiliations. Some Iranian leaders, on the other hand, charged that Arab nationalism contained not Islamic but 'Zionist, Fascist and Nazi doctrines . . .'[27]

That the Imam wanted to export his revolution beyond his frontiers was a frightful prospect to the regime in Baghdad, indeed elsewhere in the Arab and Islamic world as well. Parts of the Third World, both Iran and Iraq, lacked the institutions that could have, or may have, acted as a check against the unlimited powers of their leaders. The 'personalization', the dominance of the regimes in the Third World by their leaders, was very apparent in the case of both Iran and Iraq. The whole nation, national effort, even development, focuses on the person of the leader whose pronouncements become dicta supplying the politico-social, economic and intellectual content of the creed of the country. Ba'thism is a comprehensive, total, wholistic ideology whose precepts attempt to embrace man's life from birth to death and concern every aspect of his existence. It attempts, in its 'Eternal Message', to accomplish a psychological transformation of the values of both the individual and the nation. Khomeinism is no less a total creed with an added touch of divine inspiration. The Islam of the ages, regenerated in the image and the pronouncements of the Imam, himself a venerable sheikh, an old man, was bound to clash with the youth of Ba'thism and Saddam Hussein. The Imam resurrected the spirit of martyrdom and strong pure faith among the masses.

Iraq's abrogation of the treaty was bad enough. Some observers and writers since have indicated that this played right into the hands of the Imam who used the war to consolidate his position within Iran, get rid of any and all internal opposition and entrench his Islamic republic.[28] This may have been the case but its end result is that the war did halt the Imam's thrust and his attraction throughout the Islamic world. In fact, as the weeks of the war turned into months then years, any attraction that may have still lingered for the Imam wore out.

Had Iran magnanimously accepted Iraq's bids for peace early in the conflict, the Imam's momentum would have been resumed with perhaps more vigour and vitality. But, as the war dragged on, the moral fervour of Imam Khomeini was reduced and he, himself, became yet another mortal bent more on revenge than on the pursuance of lofty ideals once pronounced by him. It is thus that both Iraq and Iran have spent, and continue to spend, whatever is left of themselves.

Since only a few Arab countries, Jordan in particular, have come out strongly in support of Iraq, this state of affairs is not displeasing to many parties within the Middle East, those on the periphery, the Europeans, the superpowers and most others. Israel is, of course, delighted with the conflict too; in addition to the sale of arms to Iran, it further weakens the Arab world while at the same time reducing the larger panorama of Islamic fervour and unity. The Soviet Union, bordering on Iran, busy as it is with its own 'affair' in Afghanistan, is happy to be left alone by the Islamic world to do what it is bent on doing. The United States and the West in general are not averse to the continuation of the conflict for a number of reasons.[29] While it trims both aspiring regional powers to size, it provides lessons for other 'ambitious' persons or countries; at the same time, it is transferring wealth from the region principally to the western world, wealth that once posed, or could have posed, a threat to the industrialized world. The refusal of the superpowers to be dragged into the conflict or to make any serious attempt at halting it adds another dimension to this unique conflict. The war further divides the Arab world, with Syria and Libya openly supporting Iran, while the others are maintaining an enigmatic silence or hoping that it will continue still more, till both countries become totally exhausted. 'Plague on both houses' does not seem to be the attitude of only non-Arab, but of many Arab countries as well.

President Saddam Hussein, once viewed as a 'budding Nasser', was just as much a threat to many Arab regimes as was the Imam of Iran. Iraq's strategy to 'contain' the danger emanating from Iran was, in the final analysis, not displeasing to many Arab as well as other states within the region as well as outside it.

The war is unique in a number of other ways: its longevity, considering that it is between two neighbouring Muslim countries; the vast damage to the economy of both nations; the terrible human losses; the intensity, even fanaticism, of the fighting, especially the 'human wave' tactic on the part of Iran, and the advanced weaponry utilized. Its sustenance for so long at such great cost not only to the combatants but to others is in itself an amazing feat. Iraq has had to draw on the resources of neighbouring oil-producing countries. The physical damage, in addition to the approximately two to three million refugees, add additional burdens and attest to the level and the intensity of feeling on both sides.[30]

Security Questions

In his analytical chapter on the question of security of Third World countries, Mohammed Ayoob says that, in many cases, questions of security emanate just as much from within as from the result of outside pressures.[31] Internal tension, caused by 'artificial' boundaries imposed by the colonial powers, tribal, ethnic and religious schisms, the attempt to create a new national identity in addition to the adjustments and dislocations concomitant upon the process of socio-economic development, as well as a host of other factors are, in most cases, the primary reasons behind the insecurity that exists throughout the Third World. Here a most pertinent question comes to mind and it has to do with the function of the armed and security forces in most countries of the Third World. Are they really to protect the country from external aggression, whether regional or international, and can they really accomplish that, or are they there primarily to protect the regime against local dissidence? The question is the more pertinent in view of their inability to sustain a modern war of even medium duration.

Perhaps it is pertinent to begin looking at questions of security, whether on the international, regional or national levels, from a different angle. That is, the angle of the historically continuous presence of insecurity rather than the quest for security, and to begin to deal with the problem as such; to deal with it by searching for ways and means wherby we will have less insecurity rather than continuing the seemingly futile search for security. Would it seem like a naive remark to state that, looking at the problem from the historical as well as the contemporary perspective, it is the ubiquitous condition of international, regional and even national politics to be insecure? The real question then becomes how to live with insecurity and manage crises as they occur, preferably within a long-term strategy of attaining a level of tension tolerable for human existence, rather than undertaking a futile search for security. How do you, or can you, make insecurity more palatable? From the vantage point of the Third World, the western concept of security, at best a static one catering primarily to the status quo of the present power configurations and acceptable to it, should be abandoned or at least ameliorated. The need here is for a manageably dynamic concept of the world and regional orders that will take into account the aspirations and forces of change of the future in orderly fashion rather than a strict and rigid adherence to the existing formulae.

Looking at it from this perspective, it then becomes possible, even less daring, to question whether even the superpowers themselves are secure, whether NATO or the Warsaw Pact countries are secure? Perhaps it makes more sense to suggest that they are a little more secure than others because they have the will and the ability to fight either by proxy on a lesser level through allies, or on their own. The point becomes more lucid when one looks at the experience of the countries and regions adjacent to the superpowers or held vitally important by them, as is the case of Eastern and Western Europe. Here, intra-regional, or national, traditional disputes have been held at bay or resolved partly by the imposition of the security umbrella of the superpowers. France and Germany have become friends, Turkey and Greece may bicker but only a certain level of tension is permitted to them. Frontier adjustments between the countries of East Europe may be made or questions about them raised, but again only at a certain moderate level, rarely escalating to actual fighting.

In the Middle East, a volatile region for many reasons, no such condition exists. The regional or local actors are freer to choose the tools. The Middle East region is an insecure region and the peoples of the area, at least its Arab inhabitants, have come to realize this fact and live with it.

For many reasons, principally those dealing with Israel's imposition in its midst, many of its peoples and their leaders do not wish to see the area calm, not yet anyway. But then, the region is insecure for other reasons too. It is either beset at its core with crises or surrounded by them; crises that interact with and spill over, one way or another, into it. The Polisario-Morocco dispute in Western Sahara, the Chad crisis, the South Sudan crisis with the accompanying tension that involves Egypt, Ethiopia, Libya, Somalia . . . etc., the Arab-Israeli conflict, the Lebanese civil war, the Iraq-Iran War, the Afghanistan affair. These, in addition to a host of other greater or lesser flare-ups like the Cyprus problem and the Kurdish question; all of these, in addition to the tensions within; the tensions, adjustments and dislocations accompanying the process of socio-economic development. And finally, need one mention, the input of the great powers and the superpowers into these tensions and conflicts and the role they play?

The Middle East is indeed an insecure region, made more insecure by the fact that the security of most of its regimes is tied to the security of its leaders. This fact is so important that it seems futile to speak of the question without referring to the leaders. Often lacking institutions altogether, or having institutions whose sole aim is to orchestrate support for the leader, the security of the regime is closely tied to that of the person. That is why regime conflicts in the region quickly degenerate to the personal level more closely resembling feudal wars than modern conflicts with substantial issues behind them. The uniqueness of the present conflict between Iran and Iraq is that it has aspects of both modern and feudal conflict.

The mosaic culture of the Middle East, rich in the diversity of language, culture and religious affiliations, once co-existed within the context of the Ottoman *millet* system. That system that once encompassed the diversity in amicable or semi-amicable working relationships has either been destroyed or drastically changed by the newly emerging nation-state without, as yet, a proper replacement for it. The resort to violence, internally or externally, can thus be viewed as one attempt to marshal the different groups behind the new nation. It is an attempt to divert the attention of dissenters elsewhere, towards a real or created common enemy. This may be a condition that many nations will have to live with until they generate enough national loyalty and a true sense of belonging. Under the *millet* system, the communities simply co-existed with each other, without the feeling of real security. In fact, many of them never knew what it was to have real security always having had to live with a certain amount of insecurity. Each community accepted the presence of the others as a matter of course and fact. There was interaction, sometimes there was friendliness, sometimes tension and sometimes communal strife. If anything, one may conclude that insecurity has been institutionalized in the Middle East, to the point that a search for its anthithesis, at this historical juncture, is premature.

That is alo why the pan-Islamic or pan-Arab aspect of both combatants quickly reverted to the roots, to the original base of support, the original community. At the risk of oversimplification, the leaders of both countries emerged as the leaders of two distinct communities, one Iranian, one Arab. The former Prime Minister of Jordan, Ahmad Obeidat, like many others saw the conflict in this light. In an interview on Jordan television in 1984 he stated that the Shiite Muslim fanatic militance with its roots back in Iran is a threat to our Arab and Islamic identity and that, unchecked, that threat would have effects not only on the immediate countries but also far beyond.[32]

Considerations

Just as the Arab-Israeli conflict has proven, it is easier to start a war in the Middle East, even win battles, than to win the peace. That is why the Iraq-Iran War too may be looked at as a search for identity in an uncertain area, in an insecure world. Once that search began the two sides got locked into their own rhetoric and mutual accusations; a rhetoric, though having substantial factors behind it, that quickly involved the power, position and prestige of the two nations and their leaders.

The war quickly deteriorated into a war of attrition, developing into a stalemate of artillery and verbal barrages from both sides. Iran, too, claims its war to be a defensive one, even after it counter-attacked into Iraqi territory in mid-July 1982. '. . . On August the

6th and 7th, 1982, Khomeini gave public speeches stressing this point in his words: . . . we know that their troops are still holding part of our country . . . From outside too, they almost daily bomb Abadan and some other cities. As long as the situation continues like this, and as long as they do not fulfil our terms, which are logical, we will be in a state of war. We do not wish to impose ourselves on anybody, we are not oppressors . . .'[33]

For the Iraqi regime the threat was both from within, i.e. the diverse sectarian and ethnic centrifugal forces in addition to the process of development, as well as from without, i.e. the challenge of Iran. If security, as Talukder Maniruzzaman has indicated, is the '. . . protection and preservation of the minimum core values of any nation: political independence and territorial integrity . . .,'[34] then Iraq had indeed something to worry about, for the pressure from without was hoping to cause an explosion from within. Iraq, on the other hand, does not presume to pose as an ideological-value rival within the Iranian context. That is perhaps one reason why Iraq is so intent on ending the conflict through a political settlement while Iran is not.[35] President Saddam Hussein, who in the words of Helms, '. . . represents within the Iraqi context, a moderate element . . .'[36] realizes the danger posed by the prolongation of the conflict not only to himself but to the Ba'th Party's ascendency in Iraq.

It would appear that neither side is capable of achieving a decisive military victory over the other and thus be able to impose its terms and achieve its objectives. An imposition of the cessation of hostilities by an outside force or a combination of forces also seems highly unlikely at this moment. So long as the flow of oil to the western world continues, there is no need for it to interfere. The Soviet Union, though an interested party, is busy elsewhere, and prefers to stay out of the conflict while supplying arms to both parties.[37]

So long as both parties sustain the conflict and the Iranian side continues to hold on to its terms of border adjustments, vast reparations of up to US$150 billion, the return of Iranians expelled by Iraq and an '. . . international tribunal to try Saddam Hussein as a war criminal . . .',[38] the war will continue. Perhaps the best prospect to be hoped for is that neither side will win and that, eventually, the level of hostilities will decrease, turning once again to mere border skirmishes, accompanied by a change of attitude or leadership that will help pave the way for the resumption of meaningful negotiations. As of this moment no other prospect seems likely; for both nations are too charged with the heat of the battle to make a compromise, travelling through life as they are now with the wounds of the past. The sad and even tragic part of the conflict is that the two clashing sides, while neither has come close to vanquishing the other, have not been able to maintain even the positions they held at the outset of the hostilities. Both sides are now weaker, with their resentments against each other deeper and both are now more dependent on others than they ever were before. The wealth of both as well as that of the neighbouring Arab oil-producing nations has been sucked, once again, into the coffers of others, East and West. Surely, it is the clash of the irrational. The profound present ideological hostility continues to militate against the likelihood of a mediated settlement and, until some face-saving formula can be found, questions of territorial disposition, ostensibly the focus of any prospective negotiations, will remain secondary, and distinct from the underlying political objectives of the belligerents. That is why the proposal of the Egyptian National Democratic Party, alluded to earlier, is so attractive; for it can constitute a face-saving device, catering to the needs of both parties to the dispute.

Notes

1. Leonard Binder, 'Iranian Nationalism' in B. Rivlin and J. S. Szyliowicz (eds), *The Contemporary Middle East* (Random House, New York, 1965), p. 225. See also Edmund Ghareeb, 'The Forgotten War', *American Arab Affairs Journal*, no. 5, Summer (1983), p. 59.

2. Ibid.

3. Ibid., pp. 228–9, passim.

4. Leonard Binder, *The Ideological Revolution in the Middle East* (John Wiley and Sons, New York, 1964), p. 18. See also Leonard Binder in B. Rivlin and J. S. Szyliowicz, p. 227 and H. Dekmejian, 'The Anatomy of Islamic Revival: Legitimacy, Crisis, Ethnic Conflict and the Search for Islamic Alternatives', *The Middle East Journal*, Winter (1980), pp. 10–11, passim.

5. George Lenczowski, *The Middle East in World Affairs* (Cornell University Press, Ithaca, NY, 1962), p. 182.

6. Dekmejian, p. 2.

7. Binder, *The Ideological Revolution in the Middle East*, p. 274.

8. For background to this see Hussein Amin, *Shat al-Arab Wa Wad'uh al-Tarikhi* (The Historical Background of the Arabian Gulf) (Dar al-Hurriyah, Baghdad, 1981), p. 5. For further information see also Khalid al-Azzi, *al-Atma' al-Farisiyyah fi al-Mantiqah al-Arabiyyah* (Persian Crisis on Arab Lands) (Dar al-Huriyyah, Baghdad, 1981), pp. 12–14, passim.

9. Lenczowski, pp. 183–7, passim.

10. See statement of Taha Y. Ramadan, 'The World Should Prevent Iran from the Closure of the Straits of Hormuz', *al-Majallah*, 14–20 January (1984), p. 5.

11. Fuad Matar, *Sadam Hussein al-Rajul was al-Qadiyyah wa al-Mustaqbal* (Saddam Hussein, the Man, the Problem and the Future) (Mu'assasah al-Arabiyyah al-Dirasaf was al-Nashr, Beirut, 1980), pp. 138–47, passim.

12. For further details of the provisions of this treaty see al-Azzi, pp. 17–20 and 94–5 passim.

13. It was abrogated by Iran on 19 April 1969.

14. See Ibrahim al-Rawi, *Shat al-Arab Fi al-Manzur al-Qanuni Abr al-Tarikh* (Shat al-Arab in Historical Legal Perspective) (Dar al-Huriyyah, Baghdad, 1981), pp. 57–8 passim.

15. Foreign Ministry of the Republic of Iraq, *al-Niza al-Iraqi al-Irani fi al-Qanun al-Duwali* (The Iraq-Iran Dispute in International Law) (Dar al-Huriyyah, Baghdad, 1981), pp. 57–8 passim.

16. For details of the Iraqi point of view, see the speeches of the Iraq Foreign Minister before the United Nations General Assembly, 3 October 1979, and before the UN Security Council, 15 October 1979 (Foreign Ministry of Iraq, Baghdad, 1980), pp. 29 and 17 respectively.

17. See Fuad Matar, 'We Hoped that the War Would not Take Place with Iran', *al-Mustaqbal*, 25 July 1981, p. 18.

18. See the text of the Iraqi Foreign Minister's speech before the UN Security Council on 15 October 1980 (Dar al-Huriyyah, Baghdad, 1980), pp. 31–2, passim, in Arabic. In fact, Iraq agreed to the UN Security Council Resolution 279 of 28 September 1980 providing for an immediate ceasefire and the start of negotiations only one week after the commencement of hostilities.

19. The Iraqi withdrawal from Iranian territory took place in July 1982.

20. See *al-Rai*, Amman, 20 March 1984, p. 27.

21. See *al-Sha'b*, Amman, 28 March 1984, p. 10.

22. See *al-Sha'b*, Amman, 12 March 1984, p. 18.

23. Richard Cottam, 'The Iran-Iraq War', *Current History*, January (1984), p. 9. This assessment of Iranian weakness was made by Tareq Aziz in a speech in May 1980 and is reprinted in Tareq Y. Ismael, *Iraq and Iran: Roots of Conflict* (Syracuse University Press, Syracuse, 1982), pp. 89–100. See also James A. Bill, 'The Arab World and the Challenge of Iran', *Journal of Arab Affairs*, vol. 2, no. 2, Spring (1983), p. 159.

24. Ghareeb, 'The Forgotten War', pp. 59–60, passim.

25. Cottam, p. 10.

26. Idem. Fuad Ajami, however, calls Khomeini the 'great conjurer', whose attempt to lead the 'dispossessed' is 'unconvincing', in Bill, 'The Arab World'.

27. For a discussion of the statements and views of both sides on these issues, see Ghareeb, pp. 62–4, passim.

28. On this point and on Iraq's need for a political settlement, see C. M. Helms, 'The Iraqi Dilemma: Political Objectives Versus Military Strategy', *American Arab Affairs Journal*, no. 5, Summer (1983), p. 70.

29. For an additional perspective on this point, see Nameer Ali Jawdat, 'Reflections on the Gulf War', *Arab American Affairs Journal*, no. 5, Summer (1983), pp. 97–8, passim.

30. On the various types of cost, see Ghareeb, pp. 66–9, passim, and Helms, pp. 80–3, passim and Jawdat, p. 92.

31. Mohammed Ayoob, 'Regional Security in the Third World', Chapter 1.

32. See text of interview in *al-Dustur*, Amman, 12 May 1984.

33. Bill, p. 170.

34. Quoted in Ayoob, p. 5.

35. On this point see Ghareeb, p. 70.
36. Helms, pp. 83–4, passim.
37. On Soviet arms shipments to Iran, see Helms, p. 84.
38. Ibid., p. 84.

COMMENTS

Mohammed Ayoob

Kamel Abu Jaber's paper makes one thing very clear: that nobody, outside of the immediate vicinity of Iran and Iraq (and that also possibly with important exceptions), is particularly interested in bringing the Gulf war to an end. Both the superpowers are either resigned to or, in fact, may be actively interested in keeping the war going — although for different reasons. For the USSR, it is a convenient way of keeping an inconvenient neighbour, Iran, preoccupied with a war that drains its resources and attention and prevents it from either actively campaigning for the end to the Soviet occupation of Afghanistan or attempting to ideologically influence the Muslim peoples of Soviet Central Asia. At the same time, it makes Iraq heavily dependent upon Soviet arms supply thereby curbing Baghdad's newly discovered pro-western proclivities and providing Moscow with a fall-back position in the Fertile Crescent if the Soviet Union's relations with Syria turn sour at a future date.

For the US, and its Israeli ally, the war is a convenient way of keeping Arab attention divided between the Palestinian problem and the possibility of a wider conflagration in the Gulf. This obviously takes the pressure off Israel and, therefore, off the US as far as a solution to the question of the Israeli-occupied territories is concerned. Further, it also augments the view long advocated by Israel and by some in the US that the Palestinian issue is not central to the question of stability and peace in the Middle East. Again, the US is not averse to seeing revolutionary, anti-American Iran tied down diplomatically and militarily in an indefinite confrontation with Iraq, thereby unable to take full advantage of the demonstration effect of its revolution on America's Arab allies, principally Saudi Arabia and the Gulf emirates.

It is interesting to note in this connection that both the superpowers share the objective of neutralizing Iran, diplomatically and militarily, and preventing the 'Iranian infection' from spreading. This is the first time that Washington and Moscow have agreed, albeit tacitly, on such an objective since the early and mid-1960s, when they shared similar goals *vis-à-vis* Mao's China. This, by itself, is a tribute to the Iranian Revolution and its effect, potential

175

more than actual, on the international system, in particular on the strategic Middle Eastern region.

To return to the two combatants in the Gulf, the main difference between Iran and Iraq and, therefore, in their reactions as states to external stimuli lies in a fact that Abu Jaber has mentioned but not fully explored in the first part of his paper. This is the divergence in their histories of state formation. Not only was Iran a recognized political entity before the advent of Islam, what is even more important, since the establishment of the Safavid dynasty in 1502, Iran has existed as a state — a functioning political entity — within more or less its present borders. This experience gains added importance in the light of the fact that it coincided with the expansion of the Ottoman Empire which came to include within it the bulk of the territories of modern-day Iraq — the Ottoman *vilayets* of Mosul, Baghdad and Basra. The Ottoman defeat in the First World War led to a British-imposed state structure called Iraq which united the three *vilayets* under the British-imposed King Faisal, a son of the Sheriff of Mecca and a leader of the so-called Arab Revolt, more properly the Hashemite Revolt, against the Ottomans. It was essentially a consolation prize for Faisal who had lost the throne of Damascus, which he occupied for a few months, to the French when a modified version of the Sykes-Picot agreement was implemented in the Fertile Crescent. Therefore, modern Iraq is essentially an artificial creation of recent origin and suffers from the defects of the British imposed patchwork solution to the Fertile Crescent. What was known as Iraq in history is the southern and southeastern portion of modern Iraq extending as far west and north as Baghdad. This is preponderantly Shia in its demographic composition and contains within it the Shia holy places of Najaf and Karbala and has a minimal role in the power structure that exists in Baghdad today.

This brings us to the second major difference between Iraq and Iran. Iran has recently gone through a revolutionary turmoil of the order of the French or Russian Revolution. The mobilization of its population has been of a phenomenal degree, and despite the excesses of the revolutionary regime and a certain amount of in-fighting among Iran's present rulers, Tehran's capacity for popular mobilization remains high. Further, the Islamic Republican Party (IRP), aided by the personality of Ayatollah Khomeini, has been able to build a support structure among the populace, particularly amongst the *mustazafin* (the oppressed) which provides the regime with a broad political base.

On the other hand, the political base of Baghdad's present rulers has been constantly shrinking since the Baathist takeover in 1968. This has happened to such an extent that today Saddam Hussein's Takriti kinsmen occupy almost every sensitive position in Iraq. One does not have to be fond of the radical mullahs in Iran to realize that it is much easier to become a mullah or a lay member of the Islamic Republican Party (IRP) in Iran and thus have access to power than to become a Takriti member of the Baath Party related to Saddam Hussein to exercise effective power in Iraq. Therefore, the pattern of elite-recruitment in Iran is far more open than it is in Iraq and adds to the sense of identification of important strata of the population in Iran with the regime. The reverse is true of Iraq. No wonder, therefore, that Saddam's regime, in addition to its other concerns with Iran, saw the ideological and political challenge to itself from the Iranian Revolution as being of such a magnitude as to require a military response. But, as history tells us, military responses to revolutionary-ideological challenges hardly ever succeed.

Finally, no matter what catastrophe overtakes Iran, at the end of it, it is likely to emerge with its Persian core (including Azerbaijan and Khuzistan where the majority is now Persian and which has the oil) intact. This is a hardened core having been in existence since the early part of the sixteenth century. In the case of Iraq, the loss of southeastern Iraq, the former *vilayet* of Basra, would denude Iraq not only of its Shias but also its major oil terminal, like the loss of its northern Kurdish area (part of the Mosul *vilayet*) would denude it of its oil. What would be left would be only a geographic and possibly political extension of Greater Syria — because that is the Iraqi political core, if one considers the power structure in Iraq today.

It is no wonder, therefore, that the Iraqi rulers, after having realized their miscalculation in taking on the Iranian Revolution, are frantically suing for peace although the military equation in the battleground as of now is not tilted against them. It is the fragility of the Iraqi state structure, despite the sophisticated repressive measures at its command, that dictates this near-hysterical response to Iran's refusal to end the war except on its own terms. Iran's rulers, more psychologically secure — both because of their wider power base and because of the long history of the Iranian state — can, in contrast, afford to appear intransigent and wait for the

Iraqi political and psychological (rather than military) defences to crumble. This explains, at least in part, what is often described as Iran's 'irrational' attitude towards this 'futile' and long drawn-out conflict.

PART 4: GLOBAL DIMENSIONS OF REGIONAL SECURITY

8 THE SUPERPOWERS AND REGIONAL SECURITY IN SOUTHEAST ASIA

Lau Teik Soon

The strategic environment in the Asia-Pacific region is affected by several factors. These are first, the ominous power competition between the two superpowers, namely the United States and the Soviet Union; secondly, the new open-door policy of China and its search for leadership in the region; thirdly, Japan's increased defence role and its implications for other states; fourthly, Vietnam's continued occupation of Cambodia; and last but not least, the security co-operation among the ASEAN states.

The constant power competition between the superpowers extends their interaction to most parts of the globe as each seeks to achieve goals that will enhance its own national interests. Thus both the United States and the Soviet Union are concerned that neither power assumes disproportionate superiority to the extent that one is directly threatened by the other. So the two adversaries are keen to preserve parity or balance in strategic weapons, and strive for a co-operative relationship, albeit on their own terms. In this regard, both the United States and the Soviet Union maintain massive security pacts and bilateral ties with their allies. In areas of vital interests, they try to secure firm footholds and, whenever opportunities arise, they attempt to expand their power and influence as far as possible. But Washington and Moscow do have their priorities in terms of their security and national interests and consequently the locations where they deem it crucial to exert their capabilities. Presently, their priorities seem to be in Western Europe, the Middle East and Southwest Asia.

There are also their respective spheres of influence: the United States in Latin America and the Soviet Union in Eastern Europe. In these spheres of influence, the other superpower does not attempt to undermine the prevailing domination of its counterpart. Elsewhere such tacit understandings do not exist and the two often compete to advance their power and influence. Since the 1960s, however, the colossal nuclear capabilities of the superpowers have considerably restrained their competition because of the ever-present threat of Mutual Assured Destruction (MAD). So, both the United States and the Soviet Union are careful to avoid direct confrontation with each other. Instead, they employ military, economic, diplomatic and other means to achieve their interests. Such is the case in terms of their competition in the Asia-Pacific region. Here, each power, by supporting its friends and allies in the area, seeks to prevent the domination of its area by its adversary while strengthening its own influence.

In the case of the United States, the overall US policy in the area can be seen in the so-called Nixon doctrine enunciated in 1969. The Nixon doctrine, inter alia, stated that the United States would provide the nuclear umbrella for states threatened by aggression from the Soviet Union. Also, Washington would continue to abide by the treaty obligations with its allies, both the multilateral agreements and the bilateral pacts.

The United States is also obliged by the doctrine to provide assistance to those states threatened by aggression from expansionist neighbours. This doctrine makes clear the extent of American commitment and thus American interests in the Asia-Pacific. Not surprisingly the United States maintains considerable military power in the region with the US Seventh Fleet and other naval vessels plying the waters of the Asia-Pacific freely. The United States additionally has bases in Guam, in Okinawa, Japan, in South Korea, Taiwan and the Philippines, and from these bases it has considerable striking force to meet any Soviet threat in the region. Until 1976 Washington was able to assert its influence through multilateral security pacts such as the Southeast Asia Treaty Organization. But, more important are the bilateral security arrangements which allow the United States to continue to maintain its military presence in the area by extending its defence umbrella, military and economic assistance and political support to various Asia-Pacific allies. Washington has such agreements with South Korea, Taiwan, Japan, the Philippines and Thailand. For example, recently the United States has been contemplating providing Thailand with sophisticated F16A aircraft to enhance Thailand's defence capability to meet the threat from Vietnam. Thus, the United States seeks to maintain the stability and security of the Asia-Pacific region by providing viable defence systems for its allies to ward off perceived threats against them.

However, this does not imply that the Asia-Pacific area has therefore become an exclusive zone of American influence. This is because the Soviet Union and states within the region constantly try to establish a military balance vis-à-vis the United States. For example, of late, Moscow has extended its naval capability into the Asia-Pacific by securing the use of naval facilities in Vietnam, namely those at Cam Ranh Bay and Danang. From these bases, the Soviet Union is able to enhance its own defences as well as to provide assistance to its allies particularly North Korea and Vietnam. Both North Korea and Vietnam have been recipients of substantial Soviet military aid. Even though the Soviets do have access to the Asia-Pacific, they are keen to avoid any direct confrontation with the United States. Nor does Moscow encourage its allies to aggravate tensions in the area. An example is North Korean President Kim Il Sung's failure to obtain from the Soviet Union the weapons he wants in order to increase the offensive capability of the North Korean forces. This is because the Soviet Union recognizes that any increase in tension in the Korean peninsular may result in hostilities spreading beyond the two Koreas and involving the United States, China and the Soviet Union.

There is one main difference between the United States and the Soviet Union in the Asia-Pacific region today; and that is, that in this region Sino-Soviet rivalry dominates Soviet thinking regarding its military presence. In 1969 Brezhnev called for the establishment of an Asian Collective Security Arrangement which was essentially an attempt to build up a security network on bilateral bases aimed at China. Given the multifarious problems and disputes between Moscow and Beijing, the Soviet Union is anxious to avoid a two-front confrontation, that is to avoid confrontation with the United States in Western Europe and with China in the Asia-Pacific area. Thus, it is in the Soviet Union's interest to continue its détente policy with the western alliance in Western Europe. Although presently there are problems concerning the deployment of the missiles in Western Europe, nevertheless the situation in Western Europe seems to be calm compared to the situation in the Asia-Pacific area. Increasingly, Moscow has built up its military presence in the Asia-Pacific, particularly on the southern front of China. This is seen in the Soviet Union's support for Vietnam's drive into Cambodia, a move regarded as a countervailing force against the Chinese. However, the Soviet Union is careful not to encourage Vietnam to be more hostile towards the ASEAN states, particularly Thailand, despite frequent verbal attacks by ASEAN on Hanoi for its aggression in Kampuchea. The fear is that, if the Soviet Union pushes Vietnam towards any hostile action against

Thailand, then the ASEAN states may be driven to become completely dependent on the United States. This will not be in the interest of the Soviet Union.

In general, both the superpowers seem determined to support their friends and allies in the Asia-Pacific area, but not to the extent of supporting the ambitious cause of regional states intent upon aggression. Any escalation of tension will only increase the strains between them, upsetting their precarious balance. However, it should be recognized that since the 1970s the political climate has become increasingly favourable for the United States. This is because of Washington's normalization of relations with Beijing and the improved relations between Beijing and Tokyo. It is not surprising that Moscow perceives a kind of 'loose alliance' forming among the United States, China, Japan and South Korea against the Soviet Union. Should such a loose alliance be cemented, it may lead to a hostile Soviet reaction.

The most important development in the Asia-Pacific region in recent times is the emergence of China as a major regional power and its search for a leadership role in the area. There is no doubt that China seeks to exert its power and influence in what it regards as its natural sphere of influence, particularly over the Indochina states. In the Northeast Asia region, China attempts to deter the Soviet threat by supporting the American presence in South Korea and Japan. At the same time, China works to improve its relations with the United States and Japan, especially since such relationships promise benefits to China, particularly in the military and economic fields. In Northeast Asia too, China is concerned that North Korea does not increase its hostility towards South Korea thereby creating tension and the possibility of another Korean War. This will place China in a dilemma because any outbreak of conflict may involve China on Pyongyang's side to forestall North Korean dependence on the Soviet Union. Such a development will adversely affect Sino-American relations, given Washington's close ties with Seoul.

Southeast Asia is another zone which is of vital interest to China and, hence, occupies considerable importance in the foreign policy of China. This is because the region, particularly Indochina, is often regarded as China's sphere of influence. Additionally, China has long historical, cultural and economic links with the states in the area. Some of the pro-Chinese Communist parties in the Southeast Asian states can become convenient fronts for China to exert its influence. Furthermore, China has certain territorial disputes which involve Southeast Asian states including Vietnam, the Philippines and even Indonesia and Malaysia; these disputes increase the interaction between China and Southeast Asia. Finally, there is a substantial Chinese community in Southeast Asia, a sensitive issue which proves quite a thorn in the relations between China and the ASEAN states, accounting for lingering suspicions towards China in the region. Over and above all these, China is opposed to a Soviet build-up in Southeast Asia which is interpreted as a Soviet attempt at establishing hegemony. Specifically, China is opposed to the Soviet support for Vietnam and the Soviet build-up of its military capability in Indochina. To this end, China's open-door policy is aimed at enhancing its modernization policies in order to build up its defences against the Soviet Union and to allow China to have a leadership role in international politics. These Chinese efforts are not viewed with ease among Southeast Asian states which fear that China may not be a peaceful neighbour in the future. This is a destabilizing factor in the security situation of the Asia-Pacific.

Where Northeast Asia is concerned, much controversy presently surrounds the issue of Japan's defence expenditure. The United States has over the years sought to pressure Japan to take on a greater burden for its own defences. Japan is succumbing to such pressure mainly because it involves Japan's self-defence capability. However, there is apprehension that Japan's increased defence capability may lead Tokyo to take on a defence role beyond its territorial borders. Such a concern has been expressed by Japan's neighbours particularly those in Northeast and Southeast Asia, including South Korea and the ASEAN states. Japan, on its part, has reiterated that its constitution, the trauma of the Second World War and the political climate at home do not allow for any possibility of a Japanese defence role beyond its own borders. Tokyo's interest is to maintain the peace and security in the Asia-Pacific area so that Japan can continue to promote its economic interests and to play an economic role in the development of the other states in the Asia-Pacific region. To this extent, Japan supports the American security system and is a complement to the western strategic alliance in the Asia-Pacific region. It is seen as an appendix to the US defence role in this part of the world and is generally not regarded as a hostile power in the area.

For Southeast Asia, a major threat to its present security is the so-called Kampuchean problem. The Kampuchean problem is the result of the Vietnamese occupation of Kampuchea and its denial of the legitimate sovereign rights of the people of that country. In Hanoi's perspective, its occupation of Kampuchea is justified because of the security threats posed to its territorial integrity and stability by Phnom Penh in collaboration with Beijing. Such a conclusion can be explained by Vietnam's belief in the establishment of 'special relationships' among all three Indochinese states as a result of their geostrategic position and proximity to one another. For Hanoi then, this rules out the freedom of its neighbours, Laos and Kampuchea, having friendly relations with Vietnam's adversaries. In 1977 it was able to establish a special relationship with Laos through the signing of a bilateral Treaty of Friendship and Co-operation. However, the regime in Phnom Penh was opposed to such an alliance with Vietnam. Following the failure to resolve various bilateral problems between them, Vietnam took military action and replaced the Pol Pot regime with the Heng Samrin government.

Vietnam's aim is to ensure that its neighbours are supportive of its own interests. But this could mean Vietnamese colonization of the Indochina region. Hence, it is strongly opposed by China. The Sino-Vietnamese hostility constitutes the main destabilizing force for the peace and security of Southeast Asia. Both China and Vietnam have ambitions in Indochina, as both regard the area as their natural sphere of influence. For Beijing, the states on its southern front should be friendly or preferably allied to its own security interests. For Hanoi, Laos and Kampuchea form a buffer against what the Vietnamese perceive as their main security threat, namely, China. Because of the Vietnamese occupation of Kampuchea and the Vietnamese alignment with the Soviet Union, it is envisaged that Sino-Vietnamese hostilities will be aggravated. This has serious implications for the stability of Southeast Asia, especially since the animosity and misunderstanding between the two seem to be intractable and extend beyond the Kampuchean issue. These include border tensions in the north between China and Vietnam, the disputed claims over the Spratly Islands, the question of the Vietnamese treatment of the Chinese minority in Vietnam and, in general, Vietnam's dominance over Laos and Kampuchea. If these problems remain unresolved and the Sino-Vietnamese rivalry deepens, then the likelihood of a direct Sino-Soviet confrontation will become imminent. This will drastically upset the peace and stability of the region.

The most positive force for peace and security in Southeast Asia is the solidarity and cohesion among the member states of the Association of Southeast Asian Nations (ASEAN). ASEAN seeks to maintain the stability of the region through both internal development and a policy of non-alignment towards the superpowers. The priority given to internal development has been the main feature of policies within individual ASEAN states. Collectively, they have declared that they would prefer a Zone of Peace, Freedom and Neutrality (ZOPFAN) prevailing in Southeast Asia. This declaration was made in Kuala Lumpur in November 1971 and constitutes the main platform on which ASEAN's relations with the superpowers are based.

However, there is the recognition that in the prevailing security environment, the ASEAN states, individually and collectively, can play a role in contributing towards the peace and security of the Asia-Pacific area. As far as the Kuala Lumpur declaration is concerned, the concept implies the opposition of ASEAN states towards the continued military build-up of both the United States and the Soviet Union in the Asia-Pacific region. They do not support any kind of multilateral military alignment in the region. They are not inclined to form any kind of military pact among the ASEAN states themselves. Such a move would only create greater tension in the area, for a Southeast Asian military pact can only be construed as one aimed at Vietnam and the Soviet Union. For this reason, ASEAN has stayed away from any attempt to transform the organization into a security pact.

But ASEAN states have their own security ties with the United States. Both the Philippines and Thailand belonged to the Southeast Asia Treaty Organization. Both have bilateral security arrangements with Washington. In the case of the Philippines, the US-Philippine agreement allows for the continuation of the two major US bases in Southeast Asia, namely, the Subic naval base and the Clark air base. From these two bases, the United States is able to provide immediate and effective assistance to its allies and friends in Southeast Asia. In the case of Thailand, there is, aside from Thailand's adherence to the Manila Treaty, a bilateral agreement known as the Thanat Khoman agreement. By this agreement, the United States is committed to come to the assistance of Thailand in the event of any aggression against the state. So in 1980, when Thailand called for the speedy delivery of weapons to meet the Vietnamese incursion, Washington immediately responded by supplying Bangkok with the necessary equipment. The Manila Treaty and bilateral agreements between the United States and the Philippines and Thailand respectively constitute the contingency strategy which is vital for the maintenance of peace and security in Southeast Asia.

Aside from agreements with the Philippines and Thailand, the United States also has agreements with other ASEAN states by which Washington would render them military assistance in terms of the supply of military equipment and would provide them with necessary training facilities. These security ties with the United States do not imply in any way that the ASEAN states are totally committed to an alignment with the United States. In fact, the ASEAN states are clear that the organization does not form any kind of alliance with the United States. A key member, Indonesia, pursues an independent and active foreign policy and has been consistent in not becoming a partner with any superpower in the latter's competition for influence.

In general, the ASEAN states' reluctance to enter into any kind of alliance with the United States is also influenced by the US record in Southeast Asia, particularly the US role in Vietnam and the consequences of that policy. Although Washington continues to be committed to the defence of its allies and friends in the region, nevertheless, there are doubts about the credibility and even capability of the United States to come to the defence of an ASEAN state if it is attacked by a foreign aggressive power.

For this reason the ASEAN states have viewed the Soviet Union's role with a certain ambivalence. For some, like Indonesia, the Soviet military build-up can be a restraining factor, both in terms of the US domination of the area and the threat emanating from China. But other ASEAN states view the Soviet presence as destabilizing because of Moscow's support for Vietnam in the continued aggression in Cambodia. For example, Singapore sees Soviet influence in Vietnam as part of a long-term strategy to dominate the Southeast Asian region. In Singapore's view, this is an inevitable development flowing from the expansionist urge of Marxist/Leninist ideology. Malaysia and the Philippines, on the other hand, seem relaxed regarding the Soviet presence because Kuala Lumpur is primarily interested in advocating a neutralization of the area. Manila is too far away from Indochina to feel anxious about the Soviet naval build-up in Vietnam.

The differences in the perceptions of threat among ASEAN states can be seen most clearly in their conception of China's role in the region. For Thailand, China is a vital balancing force against the domination of Vietnam in the Indochina region. China provides military assistance to the Kampuchean resistance forces, particularly to the Khmer Rouge. At the same time, China has supported Thailand against the perceived threat from Hanoi, and Chinese leaders have stated that they would come to the assistance of Thailand in the event of Vietnamese aggression. Such assistance may be manifested by stronger Chinese pressure on Vietnam along the Sino-Vietnamese border. Beijing's role in Southeast Asia is thus viewed as positive by the Bangkok government.

On the other hand, Indonesia sees China as the immediate threat to the security of the ASEAN states. This perspective can be traced to some unpleasant episodes in recent Sino-Indonesian history which have affected Jakarta's attitude towards Beijing. An example is the alleged Chinese support for the abortive PKI revolt against President Sukarno. Furthermore, the involvement of China in the Partai Kommunist Indonesia (PKI) murder of Indonesian generals in 1965 has remained an obstacle in any *rapprochement* between the present Indonesian military government and Beijing. In addition, there is the concern among Indonesian leaders about the Chinese claim to leadership role in the region. Thus, Indonesian leaders have occasionally expressed their sympathy for the Vietnamese position *vis-à-vis* China. They see Vietnam as an obstacle against Chinese ambitions in the region. The Indonesian attitude towards Vietnam is a strain on ASEAN solidarity and cohesion.

As for the other states, namely Malaysia, the Philippines and Singapore, they have maintained more cordial relations with China. Malaysia and the Philippines have diplomatic relations with Beijing. Singapore has a trade liaison office in China but no diplomatic ties. This is in view of the large Chinese population in the island state which forces Singapore to be careful not to be seen to be too close to China. In fact, the official position is that Singapore will only establish diplomatic relations with Beijing after Jakarta has done so.

Another issue which affects the security and stability of Southeast Asia is the Communist problem. Presently, this problem in the ASEAN states is minimized in view of the limited manpower and military capabilities of the Communist parties in these states. The

Thai Communist Party has suffered reverses recently as a result of the defection of many of its members to the government's side. The Malayan Communist Party has limited its activities to its sanctuary in southern Thailand. The PKI has become totally immobilized because of the large scale detention and decimation of its members by the Indonesian military. In the Philippines, the Philippine Communist Party continues to be an irritant to the Marcos regime, but it does not constitute an immediate threat to the survival of the Marcos government. In Singapore, the underground Communist movement continues to try to subvert and infiltrate the trade unions and other organizations but without much success.

Thus, in ASEAN today, the major threat is the Vietnamese occupation of Kampuchea and the implications that poses for Thailand's security. Vietnam's occupation of Kampuchea is opposed by all the ASEAN states. The military intervention and occupation of Kampuchea is a violation of a basic principle of inter-state relations. The ASEAN states have over the years since 1979 made a call for a Vietnamese withdrawal from Kampuchea, the restoration of the rights of the Kampucheans to their sovereignty and independence and the establishment of an independent and non-aligned state. In the United Nations and at other international conferences, the ASEAN states have remained united in their stand on the Kampuchean issue. This, however, does not rule out bilateral contacts between the ASEAN states and Vietnam in their attempt to find a settlement of the problem. In this regard, Indonesia has been the proponent of a more friendly attitude towards Vietnam. This might be explained by the common denominators in the past experiences of the two countries which have shaped their leadership's perceptions.

Indonesia and Vietnam faced similar challenges in their struggle to achieve independence. Both had to embark on military struggles against their former colonial powers: Indonesia against the Dutch and Vietnam against the French. Both view China with suspicion. Indonesia sees China as a rival for regional leadership, while Vietnam sees Beijing as wanting to reassert its domination over Vietnam which China had before the colonial era. The Indonesian sympathy for Vietnam has been expressed to such an extent that for certain Indonesian leaders, like General Benny Murdani, the Vietnamese do not even constitute a threat to the security of Southeast Asia. Such a view is refuted strongly by Thailand which takes a far less conciliatory approach towards Hanoi. Thailand's stand is generally supported by Singapore, Malaysia and the Philippines.

The differences among the ASEAN states are also reflected in their support for the coalition government of Democratic Kampuchea. The parties to this coalition are the Khmer Peoples' National Liberation Front led by Son Sann, the coalition forces called FUNCIPEC led by Prince Sihanouk and the Khmer Rouge led by the Pol Pot-Khieu Samphan group. Although it is recognized that the Khmer Rouge controlled the genocidal regime which suppressed its people during its rule and is an ally of China, nevertheless, in general, the ASEAN states find it expedient to support the coalition government for diplomatic and political reasons. However, all the ASEAN states have expressed reservations about the Khmer Rouge's participation in the coalition government. Some ASEAN states have provided military assistance besides diplomatic support to the non-Communist coalition partners, particularly the KPNLF and Prince Sihanouk's faction.

Because of Indonesian sympathy for Vietnam, Jakarta has been less vocal in its support for the coalition government of Democratic Kampuchea. This is reflected in the Indonesian role in the United Nations. The relative Indonesian reticence might also be explained by Jakarta's involvement in the East Timor issue. Jakarta does not want to be criticized too strongly for its incorporation of East Timor into Indonesia. Additionally, the East Timor issue is still on the United Nations' agenda and excessive attention to the Kampuchean problem could direct attention to East Timor also — a situation Jakarta wants to avoid.

In the long run, the ASEAN states seek to restore the legitimate government of Democratic Kampuchea without the participation of the Khmer Rouge. This, however, may prove to be a difficult task because the Khmer Rouge constitutes the major fighting force in the coalition government and has the strong backing of China. But ASEAN does not want a weak coalition government in Phnom Penh, for a weak coalition government can either be dominated by China or Vietnam or, worse, by the Khmer Rouge. Presently, the continued restraint in superpower relations in the Asia-Pacific region and the stalemate between China and Vietnam over the Kampuchean problem are seen as favourable circumstances for continued peace and security in Southeast Asia. What is feared is that, in the event of a Sino-Soviet rapprochement, the Chinese may be able to exert influence over the Indochina region. That is to say, that the Soviet Union may put pressure on Vietnam to accommodate Chinese interests. The prospect of a strong China in the region is not viewed favourably by the ASEAN states, especially, as mentioned earlier, by Indonesia.

Within the ASEAN states various efforts have been made to maintain internal security and contribute towards regional security. The ASEAN states have built up their defence forces and modernized their military equipment. There may be a move towards the standardization of equipment among ASEAN states. Among themselves there is constant co-operation on a bilateral basis. Such co-operation is reflected mainly in joint exercises, consultations and discussions. Specifically, Malaysia and Thailand have an agreement concerning their border security, the same is the case with Malaysia and Indonesia. Both Malaysia and Singapore are members of the Five Power Defence Arrangement, the other three being Australia, New Zealand and the United Kingdom. The Five Power Defence Arrangement is most effective in terms of the air defence of the area, namely the establishment of the integrated air defence system. Australia takes the lead in these joint exercises involving the air forces of Australia, Malaysia and Singapore. Of late there have been exchanges of officers among the ASEAN states, for example, a few Indonesian officers train at the Staff and Command College in Singapore and a few Singaporean officers train at the Guerrilla Warfare School in Kota Tinggi in Malaysia. It would seem that among the ASEAN states co-operation on a bilateral basis may lead to general security co-operation within ASEAN. But this cannot be taken to mean that ASEAN is a military organization.

Despite the presence of foreign powers' influence and even ambitions in the region, the prospects for peace and security in the Asia-Pacific area seem good. First, the superpower relationship is expected to continue to maintain a balance thereby providing restraint against any escalation of conflict in the region. At the moment, both the United States and the Soviet Union are interested in reducing tensions in both the Korean peninsula and in Indochina. Secondly, China and Vietnam appear to be deadlocked in their rivalry over Indochina. With their attention focused on Kampuchea, it is unlikely that either China or Vietnam will entertain hegemonistic ambitions towards Southeast Asia in the immediate future. Thirdly, ASEAN is the main force in terms of stability and security because of its peaceful and diplomatic role. It advocates regional co-operation, particularly efforts towards internal development including economic growth, social stability and peace. However, this optimistic outlook for the Asia-Pacific region can undergo change and take a turn for the worse if the superpower relationship deteriorates and the Sino-Soviet conflict escalates.

Some basic problems remain. In the long run, the ASEAN states must come to terms with the fundamental issues which affect the region's peace and security. These include: first, how does ASEAN accommodate China's role in the region? Secondly, how does ASEAN ensure Vietnam's security interests while seeking a restoration of Kampuchean independence and sovereignty? The key to peace and security in Southeast Asia seems to be ASEAN's role in the normalization of relations with China and Vietnam. If the ASEAN states, individually and collectively, are able to normalize their relations with China and Vietnam, while ensuring that the latter two do not constitute threats to the ASEAN states, then the future of the region seems bright. Specifically, the following developments should occur if peace and security are to be assured. One, that there be a resolution of the Kampuchean problem. Such a resolution should involve Vietnam's withdrawal from Kampuchea, the restoration of Kampuchea's sovereignty and the membership of Kampuchea and other Indochina states in ASEAN. Two, that the ASEAN states normalize relations with both China and Vietnam. Here the major obstacle may be Indonesia's opposition to China. However, if Vietnam and the other Indochina states are accommodated within ASEAN, then the regional grouping can act as an obstacle to any Chinese ill-intention towards Southeast Asia. Three, that a possible rapprochement among the ASEAN states, China and Vietnam should not be seen to be opposed to the interests of either the Soviet Union or the United States. In fact, the legitimate interests of the superpowers in the region must be acknowledged and accommodated. Whether these developments can come about will depend very much on the nature of the strategic environment and the policies of the major states, principally the superpowers, in the 1980s and the 1990s.

COMMENTS

Juwono Sudarsono

Lau Teik Soon has provided a comprehensive overview of the nature and scope of superpower involvement in Southeast Asia. I have two criticisms to make and two additional comments on this particular problem area.

The first criticism is that Lau has not put enough emphasis on the natural advantage that the United States has over the Soviet Union in the *overall indices* of regional presence. United States government interests in Southeast Asia, particularly in the ASEAN group of states, are virtually unmatched by the Soviet Union for obvious ideological reasons. All of the ASEAN states, as Lau has pointed out, have chosen essentially non-Communist paths of national development. As such they are all favourably disposed towards conventional types of western economic policy-making: trade and investments, banking and services, petroleum and engineering enterprises — all of these are viewed as favourable assets in the development process. The Soviet Union possesses none of these 'value added' advantages.

In the field of 'software' presence, there is no Soviet equivalent to the dominance of western newspaper, journal and broadcasting media. Almost 65 per cent of the ASEAN business and governmental elite absorb and are shaped in their initial psychological attitudes by the business (and, therefore, political) predispositions of the western cosmopolitan super culture. From these are derived much of the key decision-making in foreign policy, economic and business strategy as well as cultural dispositions at various layers of important social strategic groups. Again the United States wins hands down in this respect.

The second criticism is that, viewed in historical perspective, the American-Japanese presence in Southeast Asia has not been basically challenged by the emergence of Soviet naval activity in the South China Sea through its access to facilities in Da Nang and Cam Ranh. What has changed is the nature of United States preponderance in the Western Pacific. American leaders must get used to the fact that, since its recognition as a military superpower in the early 1970s, the Soviet Union should be taken into account as a

194

legitimate participant and must be encouraged to co-operate in finding means of establishing regional order based on the accept-ance of a new 'correlation of forces', one which in its thrust works against previous American notions of order based on the power of the US Seventh Fleet alone. There is no way that Soviet power can be rolled back or isolated from efforts to establish a durable frame-work of consensus supported by all interested parties in this par-ticular region of the world. (It is interesting to note that the deliberate policy of successive American administrations to isolate the Soviet Union from the peace process in the Middle East has only served to increase its support for Syrian 'intransigence' and 'steadfastness' against virtually every American-initiated peace plan for the Middle East.)

In this light, I take issue with Lau's view that the Soviet Union is bound to be a continuously destabilizing and interventionist force in Southeast Asia. As has been noted above, the growing Soviet role in Southeast Asia is only 'new' in the sense that it has altered the previous preponderance of United States' military and economic presence. Soviet presence in Vietnam, Laos and Kampuchea is still fragile, not least because the presence of Soviet advisors in Indo-China may serve to provoke undue Chinese inter-vention in the internal affairs of each of these states. One might even suggest that Soviet gains so far have been restricted and the Soviet logistic as well as supply lines to and from its port accesses in Vietnam and Kampuchea are vulnerable to interdiction.

Finally, there cannot be mathematical even-handedness in regard to an optimum level of interest of each of the superpowers. I must re-emphasize the clear advantages that the United States possesses in the ASEAN grouping, particularly if viewed from the broader perspective of business, cultural as well as technological presence. The only cause for concern among American embassies in the region is that the varying degrees of problems of political succes-sion in each of the ASEAN states be consummated in the smoothest possible manner, without undue violence leading to internal insta-bility; or worst of all, leading to possible Soviet support to dissident groups within ASEAN countries.

9 THE SUPERPOWERS AND REGIONAL SECURITY IN THE MIDDLE EAST

Abdel Monem Said Aly Abdel Aal

Introduction: Conceptual Problems

Any study which addresses itself to the dimensions of regional security will have to deal with the identification of the geographic area which might be the subject of external threat, and the political authority which is entitled to define and calculate the proper responses to that threat. Traditionally, the concept of security is related to a well-identified territory: a state ruled by a government which is entitled to define and identify what is to be a threat to 'national security'. After the Second World War, regional security was linked to the establishment of regional organizations which have specified in their respective charters the territories and the 'core values' to be defended against external attack. Some, such as NATO in the North Atlantic region and the Warsaw Pact in Eastern Europe, have made their primary purpose the protection of their regional security. Others, such as the Arab League, included, in addition, various social and economic integrative functions.

With regard to the Middle East region, one of the main problems at issue is the absence of well-defined boundaries; a problem that it shares with many regional sub-systems in the world.[1] This region also shares with others the characteristic of being in itself both 'tenuous and dynamic'.[2] Historically, the term Middle East evolved in European usage. (The areas far from Europe, i.e. from India eastward, were called the Far East. The lands of the Eastern Mediterranean were called the Near East. It seemed logical, then, that the region between the Far East and the Near East should be simply designated the Middle East.) During the Second World War, United States and British military activities in Turkey, Iran and the countries of the Arabian peninsula were placed under the British Middle East Command.[3] Thus, the habit of designating these territories as the Middle East continued since then, and the region has been gradually enlarged to include an area that extended from Pakistan to Morocco and from Turkey to the Horn of Africa reflecting the superpowers' changing interactions and conflicts.

196

The studies on the Middle East region have faced this problem of territorial identification and failed to reach an agreement on what constitutes it. In one of the earlier studies about the Middle East as a regional 'subordinate system', Leonard Binder defined it as the area from Libya to Iran, with fringe areas including Afghanistan, Pakistan and the Maghrib, and a core area including the Arab states and Israel.[4] Cantori and Spiegel divide the Middle East into three different parts: a core (Egypt, Iraq, Lebanon, Sudan, Jordan, Syria and the states of the Arabian peninsula); a periphery (Israel, Turkey, Iran and Afghanistan); and an intrusive system (US, USSR, France, UK, West Germany and PRC).[5] Michael Brecher defines the Middle East as three interrelated areas: a core (Egypt, Israel, Syria, Iraq, Jordan and Lebanon); a periphery (Algeria, Kuwait, Saudi Arabia, Iran, Turkey, Cyprus and Ethiopia); and an outer ring (Somalia, South Yemen, Sudan, Yemen, Libya, Tunisia, and Morocco).[6] Armajani, Evron, Thompson and Pearcy offered different criteria for the states that should be included in the Middle East regional system.[7]

Reflecting on the above mentioned literature, Dessouki and Mattar argue that: (1) the term Middle East does not refer to a geographical area but rather it represents a political term in its creation and usage; (2) the term is not derived from the nature of the area or its political, cultural, civilizational and demographic characteristics; for when we use the term 'Middle' we have to ask a 'Middle' in reference to what?; and (3) the term tears up the Arab homeland as a distinct unit since it has always included non-Arab states. Indeed, the western portrayal of the Middle East concept is based on the assumption that the area is an ethnic mosaic, composed of a mixture of cultural and national groups.[8] Dessouki and Mattar continue to argue that the goals of this western image are basically to reject the concept of Arab nationalism, the call for Arab unity and to justify the Zionist existence in the area.[9]

If the Middle East concept appears to be vague and western-oriented, Dessouki and Mattar and other Arab scholars offer, instead, the concept of 'the Arab regional system' as a key for the analysis of interactions among Arab states, with their neighbours, and with the international system at large. In their view, the Arab states, in addition to geographic proximity, exhibit a striking homogeneity which qualifies them to be a region. They share a common culture, history, language, institutional forms (the Arab League and an extensive network of governmental and non-governmental organizations) and a religious tradition. They also share, along with the new states of the Third World, the goals of economic development and a viable political order. They have a common experience of foreign domination, including a common response to certain global issues, notably colonialism. They are also deeply attached to nationalism and the symbols of independence. As a result of these important intangibles, they are psychologically knit together as a community. Indeed, 'the common assumption among the mass of politically conscious Arabs has been that they constitute a single nation which ought to be integrated if not united'.[10]

In terms of regional security, the Arab regional system's perspective has the advantage over the Middle Eastern one of being generated from within the region itself and not 'as a euphemism for secure spheres of influence'[11] for either Moscow or Washington. The Arab region, however, did not represent by any means what Karl Deutsch calls a security community.[12] The region lacks, in Deutsch's terms, the formal or informal institutions or practices, sufficiently strong and widespread to assure peaceful change among Arab states with 'reasonable' certainty over a 'long' period of time. Intra-Arab conflicts have become so widespread through the past four decades that they cast serious doubt upon the above mentioned ties among Arab states.

However, these conflicts reflect the deformations of a newly regional order which suffers from the lack of completion of 'the state formation' stage in the region and the pressures from the international system. Indeed, as Third World states still lack the degree of internal cohesion and nationhood which were achieved in the northern industrial states during a long historical period, Third World regions are still far behind in consolidating their regional identities as compared with Europe, for example.

This lack of a mature crystallization of regionalism in the Arab region, and certainly more so in the Middle East, creates serious problems for those who would like to examine the security issues of these regions. One can, however, investigate these issues by looking at the Middle East as a system of interactions[13] which includes a network of co-operative and conflictual interactions which are partially self-generated from within the system and partially generated from without. From an Arab vantage point, the Arab system will constitute the core of the Middle East region, broadly and generally defined, and non-Arab states will form its periphery.

In that sense regional security in the Middle East as related to the superpowers' behaviour can be understood as the sum total of three types of threats to the physical well-being and core values of the countries which constitute this region (from Pakistan to Morocco and from Turkey to the Horn of Africa): (1) intra-regional feuds and conflicts which might be manipulated by the superpowers; (2) threats which emanate from a globally bipolarized international system; and (3) superpower competition in the area and the way regional states manage the insecurities that evolve out of it. In the following pages an attempt will be made to elaborate on those three types of threats. And, finally, in the concluding section of this paper another attempt will be made to integrate them in terms of the past, present and future.

A Region of Vulnerabilities

The problems of state and regional formations in the Middle East are reflected in intra-regional conflicts and disputes which have been subjected to superpower manipulation and direct or indirect interference. One can identify two types of contextual regional ruptures in the area: (a) inter-Arab conflicts; and (b) Arab-non-Arab conflicts.

Inter-Arab Conflicts

The post-colonial era witnessed continuous and persistent feuds, disputes and conflicts within and among the Arab states which reached in a few cases the point of military confrontation. The Yemeni Civil War (1962–7) and the Lebanese one (1975–present) are vivid examples of how ethnic, religious and socio-economic dimensions could bring the legitimacy of the state into question from within and from without. The Egyptian-Sudanese border dispute (1958), the Kuwaiti-Iraqi border conflict (1961), the Algerian-Moroccan War (1963) and the Egyptian-Libyan Mini-war (1977) are other examples of the inability of the Arab system to manage, far less to settle, disputes without resorting to force and dependence on external powers to interfere on behalf of the parties involved. Although these conflicts reflected geopolitical as well as national contradictions, they have been usually expressed in the Arab world as questions of national destiny: progressive republican regimes versus traditional monarchies, feudal or reactionary versus revolutionary socialism; Muslim fundamentalism versus secular trends; and independent Arab states versus the puppet or dependent regimes which are subservient to western imperialism.[14] Outside the Arab world, these conflicts are recognized more often than not as conflicts between moderate and radical regimes and/or between pro-Soviet and pro-American states.

Arab–non-Arab Conflicts

Because of historical, colonial, geopolitical and ethnic factors, Arab relations with non-Arab states in the Middle East have not been characterized by harmony and co-operation. Indeed the very recent history of the area has witnessed conflicts between one or more Arab state(s) with Israel, Iran and Ethiopia. And, as has been mentioned earlier, Turkey was in direct confrontation with Arab nationalist forces from the time of the Ottomans to the 1950s.

Most dominant among Middle East regional conflicts is the Arab-Israeli one. On several occasions (1948, 1956, 1967, 1969–70, 1973 and 1982), this conflict turned into full-scale war. Perhaps these wars should be thought of as episodes in one longer war; more than battles, of course, but periodic campaigns of brief duration in a bigger war that has no end in sight.

One prominent feature of this conflict is that Israel has succeeded not merely in consolidating its existence, but in expanding far beyond the territories assigned to the Zionist state under the UN partition plan of 1947. The post-Camp David era witnessed significant developments within and between the Arab states and Israel:

(a) the Egyptian-Israeli peace treaty and the Iran-Iraq War, in addition to several other factors, contributed to the fragmentation of the Arab world to a degree unknown since the October 1973 War;

(b) the Arabs' power position was further weakened by the glut in the oil market which, in turn, deprived the Arab states of a major bargaining asset;

(c) in marked contrast to the Arab world, Israel's power has been increasing substantially. The military balance between Israel and the Arab world continues to be drastically in Israel's favour in both conventional and nuclear fields;[15]

(d) as a result of this imbalance of power, Israel began to put its 'historical' expansionist orientation into action. In addition to the direct annexation of Jerusalem and the Syrian Golan Heights, Israel continued its creeping annexation of the West Bank by intensifying its efforts to build new settlements. Israel, moreover, declared that it would claim its 'sovereign rights' over the West Bank and Gaza;[16]

(e) further, Israel extended its 'security' concept to include the rest of the Middle East. Indeed, the Israeli attack upon the Iraqi nuclear reactor marked a new era in which Israel's political and military domination of the area has become synonymous with its proclaimed security.

The Arab-Israeli conflict is not, however, the only conflict in the Middle East area. The Arab-Iranian contradictions could be traced back to ancient history. Recently, Iran has presented a challenge to Arab security in general and to the security of the Arab Gulf states in particular, under both the Shah and the Khomeini regimes. The fall of the Shah and the installation of an ideologically aggressive Islamic revolutionary regime set in motion the forces that led to Iraq's ill-fated invasion of Iran in September 1980. Since then another prolonged war was added to the open wounds of the Middle East.

Finally, the Horn of Africa represents another area of tension which adds to the vulnerabilities of the Middle East in a way that invites superpower intervention. The protracted conflict in Eritrea, the Ethiopian-Somali War, the revolutionary socialist regime in Ethiopia and the potential for spillover of tensions that might involve Egypt, Sudan, Libya, South Yemen and Saudi Arabia are examples of this point. In sum, intra-regional conflicts, tensions and disputes are the endogenous threats to the Middle East regional security which invite superpower intervention with the latter attempting to utilize them for their global as well as local objectives.

The Superpowers: The Threat is also Real

While the previous section emphasized the threats from within to regional security in the Middle East, this section will be concerned with the impact of the broad contextual characteristics of the international system on the Third World regional sub-systems in general and the Middle East in particular. The proposition that will be presented in this section is that the more there are tensions or relaxation of tensions in the international system the more this will be reflected in the regional sub-systemic level.

After the Second World War international politics were characterized by a pattern of interactions dominated by a political and ideological conflict between the United States and the Soviet Union in Europe. These two superpowers organized their power through collective alliances in which they were preponderant both politically and militarily. Ultimately, the conflict spread from Europe to Asia, the Middle East, Africa, the Caribbean and Latin America. The superpowers adapted their competition to the heterogeneous and fluid regional and local patterns of politics emerging out of the destruction of the colonial system.

The structure of power distribution in the post-war era reflected a largely bipolar world divided into two major blocs. Not only was the world divided among territorial, military and strategic lines, but also along politico-socio-economic frontiers. Each bloc's perception of the other reflected such divisions. In the cold war period, such dichotomous phrases as imperialistic and democratic or socialist and capitalist, on the Soviet side, and free world and Communist or totalitarian and democratic, on the American side, were condensed symbols of that bipolar world. In practice, the cold war was essentially a zero-sum contest between the two superpowers who surmised that an aggression by any small state, or a change in its political system, would shift the world balance of power toward one of the two blocs.[17]

In the Middle East, regional politics corresponded to the cold war climate of the 1950s and 1960s. 'The Arab Cold War', as Malcolm H. Kerr called it, was in fact a regional reflection of the international system. The battle over the Baghdad Pact of 1955, the Lebanese Civil War of 1958 and the Yemeni Civil War of 1962, were examples of regional tensions and conflict which were partially an extension of worldwide tensions and conflict.

The détente period witnessed another correlation between international and regional politics. Détente had been a pattern of interactions between the superpowers with the purpose of avoiding nuclear war and establishing a modus vivendi based on a network of agreements (particularly in arms control) and understandings held together by a process of bargaining and the linkage of mutual accommodations.[18] In that sense détente was a strategy of managing adversary relationships in the international system.

In the Middle East, a corresponding management of adversary relationships took place between 1970 and 1977. Inter-Arab conflicts were at their minimum. Their disagreements over the Palestinian question were reduced and when the civil war erupted in Lebanon in 1975, the Arab states legitimized the Syrian intervention in that country by forming an Arab Deterrent Force to de-escalate the conflict among the Lebanese warring factions. The Arab-Israeli conflict was brought to the bargaining table and three disengagement agreements were concluded in 1974 and 1975. Military means in this conflict were not used any more in a 'life or death struggle' but they were used to improve bargaining positions, for example the October 1973 War. Furthermore, Iran and Iraq were able in 1975 to reach a settlement in Algeria over their long-standing border dispute.

By the late 1970s, once again the adversary relationship between the superpowers put serious pressures upon the politics of détente. East-West tensions escalated and dominated the international situation. Gone were the days of the North-South dialogue, the new international economic order and the politics of world inter-dependence that some thought might obscure the 'high politics' of global power interactions.[19] The international system once again entered another period of intense cold war characterized by a higher level of armaments. The doctrine of mutual assured destruction, which some thought could prevent the unthinkable nuclear holocaust, was replaced by the doctrine of flexible response made possible by the creation of intermediate nuclear missiles (e.g. SS-20 and Pershing and Cruise missiles) which could achieve military and political advantages. Strategic parity between the US and the USSR, which some thought would ensure, with the help of arms control agreements, world peace, was finally replaced with policies aimed at achieving strategic superiority on earth and in outer space.

The new cold war, like the old one, has been contagious. Its infection plagued the already vulnerable Middle East. The Arab coalition was fragmented between those who supported the Camp David Accords and those who steadfastly stood against them, and between those who supported Iraq and those who chose to stand by Iran in the Gulf War. Israel took advantage of Egypt's isolation after the Camp David agreements and destroyed the Iraqi nuclear reactor in June 1981, invaded Lebanon in June 1982 and strengthened its hold upon Arab territories occupied since June 1967. The Gulf War continued from September 1980 without abating with a strong potentiality to spread beyond Iraq and Iran. And finally, the tensions in the Horn of Africa escalated dramatically involving Ethiopia, Somalia and Sudan.

The international system has posed a real threat to the security of the Middle East region. Next to Europe, the Middle East has been the major area of potential superpower confrontation. On three occasions (1956, 1967 and 1973), this potential case was very close to becoming a reality. The bipolarity of the system more often than not fed local and regional conflicts. In many instances direct interference in the area by one of the superpowers was justified on the basis of 'denying' it to the other superpower. The American intervention in Lebanon in 1958 and the Soviet invasion of Afghanistan in 1979 are two examples. Their military presence in many Middle Eastern countries by obtaining military bases and facilities makes these countries the objects of military attack by the rival superpower.

In fact, each of the superpowers has assigned a significant military force to the area in order to deny one or more Middle Eastern country to the other power. Soviet and American fleets in the Mediterranean Sea, the Red Sea, the Indian Ocean and the Gulf are capable of posing a significant threat to the physical well-being of the countries of the Middle East.

The Superpowers: Taking Sides

Historically, students of inter-state relations between Middle Eastern states have ascribed a high degree of political and military influence to a variety of external parties, from the ancient Greeks and Romans to the contemporary superpowers. There is a sizeable body of literature devoted to the policies of both Washington and Moscow in the Middle East since 1945. However, there is no consensus on the degree of influence those policies have had upon the conflicts in the area.

One line of argument holds that the Middle East, as Brecher argues, is a highly penetrated region, due primarily to the reliance of its member states upon external sources for military and economic aid.[20] According to this line of reasoning, the persistence of the Arab-Israeli conflict might be an expression of superpower rivalry. Eugene V. Rostow wrote that until a dialogue between Israel and the Arab states occurs 'the Middle East will remain what it has been throughout history, an arena where great powers exploit local passions for their own ends'.[21]

A contending interpretation maintains that aid does not necessarily produce influence and, therefore, the Middle East remains an autonomous sub-system whose members' interactions are not significantly affected by external parties. Some writers even go so far as to describe this relationship as an example of 'the tyranny of the weak'.[22] Egypt and Israel have been cited often as obvious examples of this type of relationship with the superpowers. Martin Indyk contends that Egypt traditionally has been regarded as a successful exploiter of the rivalry between the United States and the Soviet Union, by playing one of them against the other. Israel has also benefited from the cold war competition by holding itself up as the standard bearer of American interests and its bastion against the spread of Soviet influence in the Middle East.[23] Also, in their study of the role of third parties in the Middle East, Gregory A. Raymond and Richard A. Skinner concluded that the superpowers' direct impact on the sub-system has been 'slight, episodic, and after the fact'.[24]

However, both lines of argument do not give enough attention to the variations in the amount of influence each side has over the other at different time periods. Nor do they give enough attention to the differences in attitudes, capabilities, tactics and strategies and interests of each power. Therefore, it is extremely dangerous to analyse system-sub-system interactions in the Middle East on the bases of either the suggestion that the interests of weak states will be sacrificed on the altar of a world order established by the superpowers, or that small states in the Middle East act autonomously as their interests dictate. In security terms, superpower relevance to the Middle East should be viewed in the context of four interrelated variables: (1) the western powers' retreat from their colonial holdings in the area; (2) the rise and fall of pan-Arabism; (3) the Arab-Israeli conflict; and (4) the superpowers' global rivalry.

At the beginning of the cold war, superpower competition was on the periphery of the region. Due to the events in Greece (1947), the Truman doctrine was issued 'to support free people who are resisting attempted subjugations by armed minorities or by outside pressure'.[25] The Truman doctrine contained provisions offering military and economic aid to Greece on a bilateral basis. But, in a protocol of 17 October 1951, NATO extended mutual security guarantees to Greece, Turkey and the Eastern Mediterranean sea.[26]

The Truman doctrine was the beginning of a series of western policies which equated the regional security of the Middle East with the security of the West. The Tripartite Declaration in May 1950, the Baghdad Pact in February 1955, the Eisenhower doctrine in January 1957, the US agreements with the members of CENTO in March 1959 and the Carter doctrine in January 1980 were manifestations of this vision. The essence of these declarations has always been the preservation of the status quo in the Middle East *vis-à-vis* not only Soviet threats but also against any domestic or regional challenges that might affect negatively the West's advantageous position in the area.

On the other hand, the Soviet Union, which developed its own concept of security in Europe and in Asia, did not formulate one for the Middle East. Indeed, Soviet posture in the area has been a reaction to western and particularly American behaviour. Soviet 'defence' arrangements in the area were established on bilateral bases, and never once did the Soviet Union link the security of any Middle East country with its own security — the sole exception being Afghanistan after the Marxist coup of April 1978.

It was the Arab-Israeli conflict and the rising force of Arab nationalism in the 1950s that allowed the Soviet Union to interfere in this area and sometimes, particularly in the 1960s, compete with the United States in the Middle East. Ironically, during the early stages of the Arab-Israeli conflict, there was no polarization in the superpowers' attitudes towards the parties in the Middle East. In November 1947 the US and the USSR voted with the majority in the UN to partition Palestine into Arab and Jewish states. Both superpowers were among the first countries to extend diplomatic recognition to Israel when it declared independence on 14 May 1948.

However, the initial agreement on the establishment of Israel was not to last long. As early as 1952 the fear of a superpower confrontation in the Middle East started to take shape. In a document declassified in 1975 by the US State Department, the chief problems facing the US in the Middle East were outlined as follows:

(1) a large residue of bitterness over US support of Israel . . .;
(2) suspicion of US intentions as a result of US support of the UK and France; (3) *fear that a US–USSR clash is inevitable*; and
(4) *the suspicion that present US interest in the area will have the*

result of making the Near East a theatre of war.[27] (emphasis added)

By 1955, the Arab-Israeli conflict became one of the major issues in the cold war agenda. Within the framework of the American containment strategy against the Soviet Union, the American-promoted Baghdad Pact was signed on 24 February 1955. Four days later Israel massively raided the Egyptian army in Gaza. Both events, in addition to the Egyptian nationalist stand against the Baghdad Pact, led to the Czech-Egyptian arms agreement in September 1955 according to which the Soviet bloc agreed to furnish Egypt with arms. The Czech arms deal gave the Soviet Union the opportunity to establish its presence in the Middle East for decades to come, and it forced the Arab-Israeli conflict into superpower competition.

The regional security of the Middle East henceforth has been formulated into two distinct concepts. The first has been endogenous as formulated by Nasser and other Arab nationalist leaders. The second has been exogenous as formulated by the US. In the former the threat to regional stability and well-being came from US imperialism and Israel which acts as a western extension in the heart of the area. Security policies emphasized building regional capability by achieving Arab unity and the pursuit of a policy of non-alignment which flirts with Soviet power in order to counter-balance American power in the area. In the latter, the source of threat is the Soviet Union. Security policies, in this concept, emphasized building regional alliances by-passing the Israeli-Palestinian issue to contain what is perceived as Soviet expansionism. Indeed, Israel is considered to be a major asset in facing this threat.

The first concept of security prevailed in the area in the late 1950s and 1960s. The June 1967 Israeli victory struck a serious blow to the concept's credibility and it was finally replaced with the second concept, particularly after the October 1973 War. The transformation was not abrupt or sudden. Initially, the Soviet Union seemed to benefit globally from the Arab defeat through its presence in Egypt and Syria. An expression of the impact of the Soviet presence on its strategic position in the Middle East was published in *Pravda* on 23 July 1968:

Soviet-U.A.R. (Egypt) relations put an end to imperialist

monopoly over influence in this important region . . . The Egyptians sincerely want to pay back the Soviet people for all they have done for them. And if the U.S.S.R.'s prestige in the Eastern Mediterranean is now higher than ever before, the UAR and other Arab countries have been and are instrumental in this process.[28]

However, the decade of the 1970s witnessed the decline of Soviet influence and presence in the Middle East partially because of détente and partially because of regional developments, such as the de-Nasserization of Egypt and the oil boom. The 1973 War ended with an American show of power and monopoly of the management of the Arab-Israeli conflict, leaving the Soviets waiting in Geneva for the reconvening of the Middle East Conference. Sadat's initiative to settle the Arab-Israeli conflict with American involvement ended any possible Soviet participation in the process.

Finally, by late 1970s the western concept of security in the Middle East prevailed. Not only did the pan-Arab idea fade away, but also the division among Arab states made them easy prey for Israeli actions. Islamic fundamentalism of the Iranian Revolution and elsewhere questioned the legacy of the status quo and hence invited American security arrangements in the area. The Carter doctrine vowed to resist external aggression by military force and the US was ready to create the Rapid Deployment Force (RDF) in order to defend the Gulf oil states. The Reagan administration tried to establish a 'consensus of strategic concerns' to counter 'the Soviet threat' and upgrade the RDF to enable the US to fight protracted conventional wars in more than one theatre in the Middle East simultaneously.[29] Finally, the US formalized in September 1981 the unique Israeli-American de facto alliance in an agreement for 'strategic co-operation' against the Soviet Union. The Israeli invasion of Lebanon and the subsequent American involvement in that country indicated the supremacy of the American-oriented concept of security in the Middle East.

The Soviet response to this American dominance in the area has been reactive, reluctant and mostly defensive. Having lost the force of Arab nationalism as a potent variable to rely on in the Middle East equation, the Soviet Union opted for a strategy of minimizing losses in the area. The Soviet invasion of Afghanistan was partially a result of the American dominance over the Middle East core and partially a result of the rise of Islamic fundamentalism in Iran:

Afghanistan gave the Soviets the advantage, at a heavy price, of disturbing American calculations in the Gulf area.

Other than Afghanistan, the Soviets consolidated the Syrian defences after the Lebanese débâcle and pledged to defend the Syrian territory proper. The Soviets opted for building a coalition of South Yemen, Ethiopia and Libya to disturb the American position in Egypt, Sudan and Somalia. However, Soviet activities did not achieve much success in countering American intrusion in the area. The invasion of Afghanistan has damaged the Soviet image as a supporter of national liberation movements. It further complicated Soviet relations with Iran. Soviet military support to Syria has not tipped the balance in Syria's favour although it helped in halting possible further advances by Israel. Finally, the coalition of South Yemen, Ethiopia and Libya suffers from the poor capabilities of its members, in addition to the contradictions among them.

Soviet eclipse[30] in the Middle East is a result of several factors. It was partially related to the domestic environment and the rapid change in Soviet leadership. However, the fear of direct confrontation with the US in the area has always been an important factor. Finally, and probably the most important factor, was that while Soviet capability to project military forces in the Middle East was growing it remained inferior to those of the United States.[31]

Conclusions: Regional Security in the Middle East: Past, Present and Future

Throughout this paper an attempt has been made to macro-analyze the relationship between the superpowers and regional security in the Middle East. This relationship has been conceived systematically as containing three related sources of threats: the international system, the Middle East sub-system and system-sub-system interactions. In that sense, this paper rejects the view that instability and conflict in the Middle East is largely generated from within the region. Although it suffers from serious vulnerabilities, the Middle East has been a subject of real threat deriving from the insecure nature of the international system and superpower rivalry in the area.

Preserving the territorial integrity and core values of the states in the Middle East has been subject to two types of security arrangement. The first was generated from within the region and emphasized regional integration to consolidate regional defences against outside intervention directly or indirectly through Israel. The second was generated outside the region by western powers and particularly the US.

During the 1950s and 1960s both conceptions of regional security struggled with each other with the former achieving considerable successes. However, in the 1970s and 1980s, the latter dominated the area. An externally-oriented concept of security carried with it certain insecurities to the region itself since it defines the sources of regional threats according to perceptions and interests not necessarily of importance to the region.

The future of regional security seems bleak. Regional instabilities, conflicts, chaos and turmoil will be the order of the day during the coming years. The reasons behind this gloomy forecasting can be summarized as follows:

1. Any regional security arrangement not only has to preserve the status quo but also to allow for peaceful development and the adjustment of national interests of the countries in the region. In the Middle East such an arrangement does not exist at present and is not likely to develop in the foreseeable future. In the meantime there are fundamental socio-economic and ideological changes taking place in the Middle East. Most potent of all, the rise of Islamic fundamentalism in Iran with its transnational nature will constitute a considerable pressure on the stability of every Middle Eastern state and of the region as a whole.

2. The post-Israeli invasion of Lebanon era has witnessed the increasing weight of the American-Israeli alliance in the overall western security concept of the Middle East. The agreement of strategic co-operation between the US and Israel contains a higher American commitment to Israel's conception of what constitutes its security which, in turn, causes insecurities to the Arab states. The upgrading of the American-Israeli alliance is taking place at a time when the balance of power in the area is decisively in Israel's favour.

3. With the Soviet Union realizing that détente is dead, the new cold war will intensify in the international system in general and in the Middle East in particular. The introduction of more potent intermediate nuclear missiles in Europe by both sides will enmesh the security of Europe and of the Middle East more than at any

time earlier. Thus, any increase in the level of tension in the European continent will have a spillover effect in the Middle East. 4. The third industrial revolution is making a corresponding revolution in the sophistication of armaments particularly in the fields of information and space-situated early warning systems. So far, the superpowers monopolize these types of systems. Hence, regional powers will increase their reliance on them to achieve more favourable military positions thus adding to the polarization in the area.

Notes

1. The literature on regional systems is sparse. See, for example, Richard A. Falk and Saul H. Mendlovitz (eds), *Regional Politics and World Order* (W. H. Freeman, San Francisco, 1973); Oran R. Young, 'Political Discontinuities in the International System', *World Politics*, vol. 20, April (1968), pp. 369–92; Larry W. Bowman, 'The Subordinate State System of Southern Africa', *International Studies Quarterly*, vol. 13, June (1968), pp. 232–62; Michael Brecher, 'International Relations and Asian Studies: The Subordinate State System of Asia', *World Politics*, vol. 15, January (1963); George Modelski, 'International Relations and Area Studies', *International Relations*, vol. 2, April (1961), pp. 143–55.
2. Louis J. Cantori and Steven L. Spiegel, 'The International Relations of Regions', in Falk and Mendlovitz (eds), p. 341.
3. Don Peretz, *The Middle East Today* (Holt, Rinehart and Winston, New York, 1963), p. 3.
4. Leonard Binder, 'The Middle East as a Subordinate International System', *World Politics*, vol. 10, April (1958), p. 417.
5. Cantori and Spiegel, p. 337.
6. Michael Brecher, 'The Middle East Subordinate System and Its Impact on Israel's Foreign Policy', *International Studies Quarterly*, vol. 13, June (1968), p. 118.
7. See Yahya Armajani, *Middle East: Past and Present* (Prentice-Hall, Englewood Cliffs, New Jersey, 1970); Nair Evron, *The Middle East: Nations, Superpowers and Wars* (Elek, London, 1973); William Thompson, 'The Regional Subsystem: A Conceptual Explication and a Propositional Inventory', *International Studies Quarterly*, vol. 17, March (1973), pp. 84–119; Etzel Pearcy, 'The Middle East, an Indefinable Region', *The Department of State Bulletin*, 23 March 1959.
8. A. E. H. Dessouki and G. Mattar, *The Arab Regional System* (Centre for Arab Unity Studies, 1979), pp. 24–6, in Arabic.
9. Ibid., pp. 27–8.
10. Malcom H. Kerr, 'Regional Arab Politics and the Conflict with Israel' in Paul Y. Hammond and Sidney S. Alexander (eds), *Political Dynamics in the Middle East* (American Elsevier, New York, 1972), p. 31.
11. Mohammed Ayoob (ed.), *Regional Security in the Third World*, Chapter 1, p. 19.
12. Karl W. Deutsch, *Political Community at the International Level* (Random House, New York, 1954).
13. Charles A. McClelland and Anne A. Gilber considered the Middle East to be the strongest among four world sub-systems (the Middle East, Southeast Asia, USSR and Eastern Europe, the USA and Atlantic allies), in terms of interactions. In their comparison which utilized the World Event/Interaction Survey (WEIS) data,

the Middle East, in the period between 1966 and 1971, had a level of inter-group action almost double that of the US and its allies and that of the Southeast Asian nations, and four times as much as the USSR and Eastern Europe inter-group action. In terms of interaction with other sub-systems, the Middle East directed and received action at about the same rate as the other sub-systems studied. See Charles A. McClelland and Anne A. Gilber, 'An Interaction Survey of the Middle East' in William Beling (ed.), *The Middle East: Quest for an American Policy* (State University of New York Press, Albany, NY, 1973), pp. 157–8.

14. A very useful discussion of inter-Arab cleavages can be found in Malcom H. Kerr, *The Arab Cold War: Gamal Abdel Nassir and His Rivals, 1958–1970* (Oxford University Press, New York, 1971).

15. According to a military analyst, Anthony Cordesman, the Israel defence force can mobilize a 500,000-man army in 24 hours. Against this is ranged a Syrian army of perhaps 220,000, a Jordanian army of 73,000 and less than 10,000 PLO irregulars. If Egypt could be counted, its current estimated manpower of 452,000 would not suffice to tilt the balance in favour of the Arabs. The Arab forces combined would still remain inferior quantitatively and, most assuredly, qualitatively in terms of effective combat units and combat equipment. The key to Israel's military superiority lies in its training, high technology and organizational support. Cordesman estimates that Israel spends $27,000–$36,000 per man, per year, while Syria can only spend $7,000 per man, per year. Cited in Michael C. Hudson, 'The Ineffectiveness of the Arab States' Diplomacy on the Palestine-Israel Issue: An Inventory of Explanations', a paper presented to the Seminar on Alternative Approaches to the Arab-Israeli Conflict, The Centre for Political and Strategic Studies, Al-Ahram, Cairo, 28–30 March (1983), p. 23. Regarding the nuclear balance, it has been estimated that, under present conditions, the nuclear balance will continue to be in Israel's favour up to the end of this century. See Abdel Monem Said, 'Israel's Nuclear Strategy' in *Sh'oun Arabiyya* (forthcoming), in Arabic.

16. Shlomo Avineri, 'The Continuing Peace Process in the Middle East', *Working Papers*, no. 33 (The Wilson Centre, Washington DC, 1981), pp. 6–7.

17. For a discussion of the cold war, see William A. Gameson and Andre Modigliani, *Untangling the Cold War* (Little, Brown & Co., Boston, 1971); John L. Gaddis, *The United States and the Origins of the Cold War 1941–1947* (Columbia University Press, New York, 1972) and Robert E. Osgood, 'Introduction: Reappraisal of American Policy' in Robert E. Osgood, *et. al.*, *America and the World: From the Truman Doctrine to Vietnam* (The Johns Hopkins Press, Baltimore, Ma., 1973), p. 4.

18. Robert E. Osgood, *et. al.*, *Retreat From Empire: The First Nixon Administration* (The Johns Hopkins Press, Baltimore, Ma., 1973), p. 4.

19. See Robert O. Keohane and Joseph S. Nye, *Power and Interdependence: World Politics in Transition* (Little, Brown & Co., Boston, 1977).

20. Michael Brecher, 'The Middle East Subordinate System'.

21. Eugene V. Rostown, 'America, Europe and the Middle East', *Commentary*, February (1974), p. 41.

22. For the term see, Astri Suhrke, 'Gratuity or Tyranny: The Korean Alliances', *World Politics*, July (1973). For empirical support of this view see Jeffrey S. Milstein, 'Soviet and American Influence on the Arab-Israeli Arms Race: A Quantitative Analysis' in Walter Isard and Julian Wolpert (eds), *The Middle East: Some Basic Issues and Alternatives* (Schenkman, Cambridge, Mass., 1972); James M. McMoric, 'Evaluating Models of Crisis: Some Evidence from the Middle East', *International Studies Quarterly*, vol. 19, March (1975).

23. Martin Indyk, 'Détente and the Politics of Patronage: How the October Middle East War Started', *Australian Outlook*, vol. 30, April (1976), p. 171.

24. Gregory A. Raymond and Richard A. Skinner, 'An Extension and Republication of Findings on the Role of Third Parties in the Middle East', *International Interactions*, vol. 4, no. 2 (1978), p. 171.

25. *New York Times*, 13 March 1947.

26. 'The Middle East: US Policy, Israel, Oil and the Arabs', *Congressional Quarterly Inc.*, 4th edition (1979), p. 36.

27. 'Problems and Attitudes in the Arab World: Their Implication for US Psychological Strategy', *Intelligence Report*, no. 5914, Department of State, 19 May 1952, p. 7.

28. Quoted by Ilana Kass, *Soviet Involvement in the Middle East: Policy Formulation 1966–1973* (Westview Pres, Boulder, Colorado, 1978), p. 111.

29. Robert E. Osgood, 'The Revitalization of Containment', *Foreign Affairs*, America and the World 1981, vol. 60 (1982), p. 475.

30. See Karen Dawisha, 'The USSR in the Middle East: Superpower in Eclipse', *Foreign Affairs*, vol. 61, Winter (1982/83), pp. 438–52.

31. *The Middle East*, Congressional Quarterly, 5th edition (1981), p. 80.

COMMENTS

Muhammed Amien Rais

What I do not quite agree with in this paper is the statement that basically we have two concepts of security in the Middle East, the first is now gone and the second is taking hold. The first is endogenous as formulated by Nasser and other Arab nationalist leaders and this concept was very much influenced by the Soviet view. The second concept of regional security is exogenous as formulated by the US. The first concept prevailed in the late 1950s and 1960s, while the second one is now prevailing. I believe this is true as far as Egypt is concerned. The problem is that the Middle East is far larger than Egypt, although I agree that Egypt has been the most important country in the Arab Middle East.

The Soviets have disappeared from Egypt, but, as we know, they have found new clients in Syria, Libya, Iraq and South Yemen and also Ethiopia. Therefore, I suspect that the first security concept is still there and strong and what we are witnessing today is the result of this clash between two different concepts of regional security in the Middle East. The question, therefore, arises: what are the objectives of the US and USSR in the Middle East respectively?

With the risk of oversimplification I would say that the US objectives are:

1. denial of control over Middle East resources to hostile powers, especially the Soviet Union;
2. preservation of the assured destruction capability of the regional element of US strategic forces;
3. assured supply of Middle East natural resources to American industry and military and also to American allies;
4. continuation of the benefits resulting from US commercial investment and operations in the Middle East; and maintenance of US credibility by meeting American commitments.

Support for Israel which later on became support for Israeli expansion and aggression is not, strictly speaking, an objective or an interest of the US. Support for Israel is a national duty for the Americans, or at least a moral obligation stemming from the

214

Holocaust, as argued by American Jewish leaders, or as a means to achieve the American objectives I have mentioned. That is why we see that the Israeli national interests have become an integral part of American national interests.

Soviet Middle East regional objectives, on the other hand, continue to centre on avoiding conflict with the US, minimizing western influence in the Middle East, increasing Soviet security to its south, and also increasing Soviet regional influence. Changes in Soviet objectives since Egypt expelled the Soviets in 1972 have been subtle; in most areas the changes have been of degree rather than of substance.

Both the US and the USSR place a high priority on avoiding superpower military confrontation in the Middle East. Of course, this does not rule out the possibility of such conflict in a very special, crucial and vital case, but both superpowers, at least up to now, are heavily inclined to avoid an open confrontation.

The parameters within which decisions on confrontation are made seem to be reciprocal perceptions of the importance of the issues which arise. Namely, each superpower seems understandably more willing to take a strong stand and an uncompromising stance when it is certain that the other will back down. Therefore, positions that indicate new firmness in taking sides are particularly important. In this context I would like to emphasize that as long as both superpowers feel that their interests in the Middle East can only be fulfilled largely in zero-sum-game terms, the future of regional security in the Middle East will be gloomy.

We notice that US policy in the Middle East, especially in the aftermath of the Camp David agreement, has been pursuing a zero-sum game. The US probably has an illusion that the Arab-Israeli conflict can be solved without giving the Soviet Union any role in it.

I agree with the four conclusions drawn in the paper indicating that the future of regional security in the Middle East seems bleak, or at least uncertain. But let me highlight one of its conclusions, i.e. that we have witnessed the increasing weight of the American-Israeli alliance after the Israeli invasion of Lebanon. I would like to remind the author that American commitment or overcommitment to Israel is not a 1980s phenomenon. In the early 1970s the blind and total commitment of the US could already be observed very clearly. Joseph Sisco, the then Assistant Secretary of State, the best-known proponent of American total commitment to Israel, stated:

Superior Israeli military strength, backed by American support, could enforce the status quo on a long-term basis; . . . the Arabs, recognizing their military helplessness . . . would do nothing to shake the status quo and would either resign themselves to it . . . or eventually undergo fundamental change of attitude and sue for peace; . . . the United States could turn this (new) partnership (with Israel) into a positive asset, with Israel as its policeman in the Middle East; and . . . the Soviet-American detente . . . could be counted on to confirm the continued freezing of the Middle Eastern status quo.

As has been indicated by the author there are three other factors which can aggravate the situation in the Middle East: the rise of Islamic fundamentalism, the Soviet-American new cold war and the sophistication of armaments. However, I am of the opinion that real and durable peace and security in the Middle East will depend to a very great extent on the American attitude towards Israel.

Until the US adopts more or less a policy of even-handedness towards Israel and the Arab countries, the situation in the Middle East will most probably go from bad to worse. Needless to say that the policy of even-handedness also implies the necessity of giving back their inalienable and human rights to the Palestinians.

Any peace proposal could be made, but as long as the US does not change its blind commitment to Israel I can definitely say that these proposals will remain inapplicable. I think this is a very crucial matter we must not overlook. But unfortunately the American support for Israel has been more and more 'irrational'.

Israel is a country with an annual inflation rate of 1000 per cent at the end of 1984 and with a stagnant GNP. On per capita basis it is by far the most indebted nation on earth, owing about US$25 billion. However, Israelis have a relatively comfortable standard of living only because of American aid. In fact, the Israelis are consuming vastly more than their own national income.

Americans are, therefore, like wealthy parents indulging their stubborn and adolescent son. Whatever is asked and whatever mistakes, even crimes, committed by the beloved son, will naturally be given and forgiven by their parents. Here I think lies the miscalculation of Sadat and, for that matter, of the Saudi leaders. They tried to compete with Israel for American favour, forgetting completely that the best they could achieve is only to be the stepchildren who will be unjustly discriminated against.

There is no question that the US has been time and again by-passed or even dictated to by Israel in the Middle East. For example, Washington did nothing when Israel committed flagrant violations of international law, such as the bombing raid that annihilated Iraq's nuclear reactor, annexation of the Golan Heights, the bombing raid on PLO headquarters in Beirut in July 1981 and the extensive expansion of illegal Jewish settlements on the West Bank. Can we imagine that another country allied with the US which undertook such flagrant violations would not be faced with serious hostile reaction on Washington's part? But, in the case of Israel all these violations lead only to increased US assistance. It is not an exaggeration to say that not only does the US treat Israel as if Israel were the fifty-first state of the US but as if Israel were the most important state as well.

So in concluding my remarks I would say that the main business for the Arabs to deal with is to make every effort to convince the US that it has made a fatal strategic mistake which is against its national interest by supporting Israeli expansion and aggression.

PART 5: REGIONAL ORGANIZATION AND REGIONAL SECURITY

10 ASEAN AND REGIONAL SECURITY

Noordin Sopiee

The ASEAN experience has been one filled with paradox. Intended by its founding fathers to be an organization for primarily economic and cultural co-operation, it has developed only in the field of politics. Judged from the perspective of 'economic intergration' EEC-style, it has been a substantial disappointment and arguably an abysmal failure. In overall organization terms, its level of integration is extremely low — it still decides on the basis of the lowest common denominator (euphemistically called a system of 'consensus'); there has been little in the way of sacrifice of sovereignty on the part of its members; its institutional structure is more rudimentary than modest. The machine works because it is not asked to do too much work; because not too much is demanded of it or of its members; because it is not pushed to the limit or overloaded. It might be interesting to note also that in the entire 17 years of its existence, there has possibly never been one instant when integration has been seriously elevated to the status of being an end in itself as opposed to being a means to other ends. It may be unfair to judge ASEAN on the basis of criteria borrowed from some other geographical area and on the basis of yardsticks that are inapplicable in the context of ASEAN's ambitions and intentions. Most certainly, when it comes to producing security, stability and sub-regional order, it has been a resounding success, whose record is possibly unmatched in the contemporary experience of the Third World.

This paper is an attempt to look at the ASEAN contribution to the security of the ASEAN community and to regional security in Southeast Asia. It has no polemical purpose and no theoretical pretensions. It will not suggest that regionalism is a panacea (a clearly preposterous idea), or that it is easy to make it work or that if it works it will at all times and in all contexts make a major contribution to peace and security. It merely contends that one regional organization, an association of five (now six) Southeast Asian nations founded in August 1967, has made a substantial difference not only to the ASEAN sub-region but also to Southeast Asia as a whole.

One way to demonstrate this is to imagine what it would have been like if the beast had not been born. If ASEAN had not existed it is possible that there would have been substantial turbulence in the relationship between Malysia and the Philippines with regard to the Sabah territorial claim, with regard to the southern Philippines Muslim problem and possibly the mutual interventions and verbal altercations which would have been *de rigueur* in the tense relations between countries that are adversaries. Without the psychological cushion that was provided by ASEAN and if Thailand had felt alone and isolated, might it not have panicked — not once but twice in the last dozen years? Would it have been pushed into finding solace in the dragon's den in order to ensure its security from the ancient enemies of the East, even before they themselves went into the warm embrace of the northern bear? If in the mid-1970s, Thailand did not succeed in making an alliance with Beijing, would it not have been intimidated by Vietnam? Would the whirl-wind events of ten years ago not have hurled it from pillar to post? If it had succeeded in making a military alliance with the only available and functionable partner, China, what would have been the repercussions on Thai-Malaysian relations, indeed on Indonesia, Malaysia and even Singapore? Assume bad Malaysian-Thai relations and one can imagine the southern Thai Muslim problem and the problem of Thai refuge for the remnants of the Malayan Communist Party blowing up into something more than peripheral irritations.

If Indonesian foreign policy had not been conceived within the ASEAN parameter, would it be what it is today? Indeed, what would have been the shape and substance of the foreign policies of each of the ASEAN states had they been evolved separately instead of in a context of co-operation and full consultation? Not an academic question given that there have been and there are different strategic perspectives, ambitions, emotions and historical experiences. Indonesia is a large far-flung country of islands twice removed from Indochina. Thailand is in Southeast Asian terms a medium land power at the very doorstep of confrontation. It is clear beyond any doubt that the existence of the ASEAN system has worked for the harmonization, moderation and accommodation of interests and policies among the ASEAN states.

If ASEAN had not been there, would Singapore have become an armed citadel, surrounded by an antagonistic Malay world, living in dread of the 'Brown Peril' and arming itself to the teeth in order to fend off its real or imagined enemies? Could Singapore have become an 'Israel'? What would have been the consequences to the region? Would the ASEAN community have become a cockpit for the big powers in the same way that the Indochinese states have been and continue to be?

What would have been the consequences of general panic in 1975? What would Southeast Asia be like today if the nations of ASEAN, instead of finding solidarity and confidence and generating dynamic and developing societies, had instead been living in fear, in isolation, with a sense of immense insecurity and vulnerability, quarrelling among themselves and tempting all sorts of intervention from powers, big and not so big, Communist and non-Communist? Would the ASEAN states have been able (in the end) to dismiss the domino theory with such aplomb and arrogance? What would have been the effect of diverting precious resources to economically unproductive military tasks? What would have been the political and security consequences (never mind the economic and social repercussions) if the ASEAN community had failed to attract foreign expertise, technology, investments and markets, if the ASEAN states (without exception) had not been able to chalk up impressive growth rates which have made the community as a whole one of the most dynamic areas of the world? Throughout the ASEAN community, the political and security consequences would have been serious, whilst in a country like Malaysia the ramifications would have been grave. Would the community (save the Philippines) be facing the future as it does now, with so much confidence, hope and expectation?

It is absolutely true that if the overall configuration of ambitions and correlation of forces had been substantially different, if other crucial cards had fallen in other ways, the ASEAN community today might be in different shape. But this only means that ASEAN has not been the sole determinant. There is no gainsaying that as a variable it has had a crucial impact as a producer of security for each and all of the member states, for the ASEAN community and for the Southeast Asian region.

First, the Association has played a critical role in banishing that psychological sense of isolation which can often lead to panic or ill-advised action. ASEAN has given its member states that psychological sense of confidence and security without which mature responses and policies would have been less likely. Over the years, the psychological shield that ASEAN was seen to provide and the confidence in dealing with the external environment that it engendered, allowed the ASEAN states to concentrate their primary attention on domestic, not external, concerns, as important a factor as any in explaining the security success of the community, given that the greatest threats to each of the ASEAN states lay within rather than without.

Second, it has succeeded over the years in preventing a sense of powerlessness on the part of the member states. If power corrupts, so too does weakness and powerlessness. Over the years, ASEAN has given its member nations a sense of power and capability which has allowed them to behave not as objects but as subjects of the international political system. It has allowed the ASEAN states to adopt active foreign policies, to seek solutions rather than to have them imposed, to attempt to shape their environment and their future. ASEAN has worked for the realization that one's destiny is not to be decided by others and that the helping hand one needs is at the end of one's right arm. In the ASEAN community, there is little of the psychology of dependence that is found in many other parts of the world; there is much of the psychology of self-help, assertive self-help. When the Americans left, the political vacuum in the ASEAN sub-region was filled by the constituent states themselves, acting nationally and through the ASEAN concert. The process has made the entire community the stronger for it.

Third, ASEAN has provided the community with a sturdy policy 'meat grinder'. What has often been referred to as the ASEAN process has resulted in continuous and repeated discussions and deliberation — talk, talk and more talk — and multilateral decision-making. The process subjects the most persuasive arguments, ideas, and proposals to the test of open debate and criticism; it subjects the strongest of personalities to peer pressure. By the time proposals, ideas and initiatives come out of the meat grinder they will have been given the works. Some important foreign policies do not go through the meat grinder of course. And there must have been many great ideas that have been reduced to sausage. But in the main, the principal strands of ASEAN foreign policy have been unusually sophisticated and mature. To give just two examples: immediately after the fall of South Vietnam, the general line was conciliatory but not weak; again, despite the fact that the ASEAN states generally felt that they had been taken in by the Hanoi peace offensive of mid-1978, whether there had been a deliberate intention to do so or not, there was no immature emotional response following the Vietnamese Christmas Day invasion which led to the conquest of Kampuchea.

It is suggested here that the confidence and security, the assertiveness and feeling that one does not have to play the role of spectator or victim and the process of consultation and deliberation that are the rotating blades of the meat grinder (that are there because ASEAN is there) have contributed most substantially to a broad range of common policies which have in turn contributed most substantially to the security of the ASEAN community and, at least indirectly, to the peace and security of Southeast Asia.

Historically, without the confidence and psychological crutch that ASEAN provided to Thailand especially and to the others in general it is possible to perceive of response fluctuating from crass defiance to cringing appeasement. Without the confidence that ASEAN helped so substantially to generate there would have been a rush either to arms, which would have meant arming oneself to the point of bankruptcy or economic disaster; the alternative would have been a clutching at the straw of military alliance with some big power guarantor, which would have been provocative and which would have intensified their rivalry. Because there was good sense and confidence, the ASEAN states adopted a policy of big power equidistance, a policy and a process that was dynamic, differential but never deferential.

Meat grinder wisdom and confidence lay behind the common position that the main guarantee of national security lay in national resilience, making sure that one has the capacity to deal with one's internal problems, that one provides no strategic opportunity or cause for external intervention and that one has the capacity to bounce back after the most serious setbacks. These factors lay behind the recognition that the legitimate interests of all the big powers, even of Vietnam, ought to be accommodated by the ASEAN states and within the ASEAN community. They also underpinned the common stand that one must act in such a way as to maximize non-provocation, that the ASEAN states should be above involvement in the Soviet Collective Security System, above involvement in China's anti-hegemonism drives, and not as far as is possible involved in the Sino-Soviet conflict. Meat grinder wisdom and confidence have also played a major part in ensuring the enduring common stand that for the long-term peace, security and stability of the region as a whole it is necessary to prevent the permanent division of Southeast Asia into two confrontationist blocs, one determinedly anti-ASEAN and the other determinedly anti-Communist.

Fourth, the ASEAN process, less productive in the first ten years, much more productive in the last seven, has created an ASEAN sense of community. Anyone who underrates what has been achieved on this score should go back to the situation of the ASEAN area before the advent of ASEAN. Before the birth of the Association, the sub-region had no sense whatever of unity, solidarity, oneness of any sort. There was a pan-Malay feeling which to Jakarta and Kuala Lumpur embraced Indonesia and Malaysia, but not the Philippines. There was, at times, a paraded pan-Malay feeling on the part of the Filipinos that generally meant little beyond the dictates, attractions and exigencies of the moment. Certainly, in the pan-Malayism, Singapore merited a footnote and Thailand was not in the book at all. As Arnfinn Jorgensen-Dahl notes in his study on *Regional Organisation and Order in Southeast Asia*, 'there existed in Southeast Asia no indigenous tradition of thinking which conceived of the . . . states that came to form . . . ASEAN . . . as a political, economic and cultural entity which could serve as an ideal alternative to traditional interstate politics and to which appeal could be made and from which inspiration could be received'.[1] Outside the handful of diplomatic technocrats, Thailand and Indonesia, Thailand and the Philippines, Malaysia and the Philippines, the Philippines *vis-à-vis* all the others, were as strangers. Worse than strangers, many of the relationships were relationships of enmity. Malaysia, the only country sharing a common border with all its ASEAN partners, had endured a period of undeclared war with Indonesia call *Konfrontasi*. Relations between Kuala Lumpur and Singapore were tense in the aftermath of separation in 1965. Diplomatic ties had been broken with the Philippines as a result of the Sabah claim. There were tensions between Singapore and Indonesia as a result of the execution of Indonesian marines. The ASEAN states are strangers no more (except perhaps in the case of the newest ASEAN member, Brunei) and, more important, they are enemies no more.

It might well be asked how an ASEAN sense of community contributes to the security of the ASEAN community. It does so in a myriad of ways. Members of the same family are more open to give and take, are not so fast in flying off the handle with each other. Without ASEAN, there would not today be the level and intimacy of bilateral intelligence and military co-operation. There would be less probability of joint naval patrols. There would be less co-operation with regard to sea lanes. There would be more problems arising out of the delineation of territorial seas, the division of economic zones. There would be more conflict in quantitative as well as qualitative terms. There would not be quite the same motivational impetus to bury hatchets, to resolve conflicts, to work for consensus and agreement.

There is a fifth way in which ASEAN has contributed most substantially to the security of the ASEAN community. There can be no doubt that as a result of reasoning together, talking together, quarrelling together, the ASEAN process has created a sturdy structure of trust, confidence and goodwill between the member states. Most international organizations are generally preceded by such a structure. In the case of ASEAN, trust, confidence and goodwill have been the result rather than the cause.

The contribution that confidence in each other, the reduction of unpredictability on the part of member states, trust and goodwill make to the structure of peace, security and stability requires little elucidation. How the ASEAN states have been able to put these things in the place of suspicion and animosity over the years is of more than academic interest.

There have been four basic methods used to strengthen trust, confidence and goodwill. There has, first, been the most liberal use of loosely structured, non-crisis ridden, non-problem-solving summitry at the topmost level. Taking the Philippines out of the reckoning, it has become a convention for every new ASEAN head of government to touch base with his counterparts at the earliest opportunity. Secondly, there has been a seemingly endless number of meetings between ministers and between officials at the less elevated plane. The number of non-governmental, basically ASEAN-wide meetings on matters ranging from body-building to librarianship is legion. In 1982, the Thai Foreign Ministry is said to have counted more than 400 such meetings.

The third method of strengthening the structure of confidence, goodwill and trust has been intense problem- and issue-oriented diplomatic consultation with all partners with regard to new initiatives or new responses to external events. Thus, Malaysia, which for domestic election reasons felt it had to pioneer the opening of diplomatic relations with the PRC, briefed every ASEAN capital fully before it proceeded. Since 1971, all ASEAN countries have adopted the practice of exchanging notes on their individual dialogues with China, Vietnam, the Soviet Union, Kampuchea, the EEC, Japan and the United States. It is not rare to find several ASEAN states issuing similar if not identical communiqués at the end of a visit by a common visitor.

The fourth activity which has contributed to the building of a substantial structure of goodwill, trust and confidence in the ASEAN community has been joint diplomatic-political action and co-operation in pursuit of goals that are of salience to one or two member states but not to all. As examples it is possible to point to the joint action against Japanese synthetic rubber production, the joint confrontation of Australia over its airline policy.

The sixth contribution that ASEAN has made to the security of the ASEAN community has been in the area of actual conflict resolution, the most serious of which, the conflict between Malaysia and the Philippines over Sabah destroyed ASA (the Association of Southeast Asia) and virtually put ASEAN in cold storage in the first two years of its existence. The second Sabah crisis broke out when the Manila press reported in March 1968 the Philippine government's training of Filipino soldiers for possible use in Sabah. In August of that year diplomatic relations were once again severed between Manila and Kuala Lumpur. A Thai initiative in December to resolve the crisis failed. The process of political and diplomatic de-escalation only started as a result of the Indonesian initiative of May 1969. And it took another seven months to re-establish diplomatic relations between the two member states. Interestingly, it was not until the Kuala Lumpur ASEAN Summit of 1977 that President Marcos announced that 'the Government of the Republic to the Philippines . . . is taking definite steps to eliminate one of the burdens of ASEAN, the claim of the Philippine Republic to Sabah'. As, interestingly, these definitive steps (repeal of the Bill passed by the Philippine Congress on 20 August 1968) have not yet been taken although the claim has not since been resurrected, the conflict has been completely de-escalated and the issue swept under the carpet (a technique for dealing with conflicts that has all too often been underrated).

There have been cases of other less serious conflicts being resolved, which might not have been so easily or quickly resolved had the ASEAN process and the pressures and the intangible but real 'spirit' of ASEAN not existed. It might be argued that as important a role has been played by ASEAN in sublimating and defusing conflicts as in actually resolving them.

If that counts as ASEAN's seventh major contribution to security in the ASEAN community, number eight is the role that ASEAN has played in laying down the rules of the peace game within the sub-region and in getting system-wide acceptance of these rules. Through a combination of the process of deliberate 'legislative' action (laid out in such documents as the 1976 Treaty of Amity and Co-operation in Southeast Asia signed in Bali) and implicit acceptance and espousal over the years, the ASEAN process has established at least four ground rules of inter-state relations within the ASEAN community with regard to conflict and its termination. The first rule of the game is system-wide acceptance of the principle of the pacific settlement of disputes. The second is non-interference and non-intervention in the domestic affairs of member states. The third is respect for each others' territorial integrity and independence. The fourth is the principle of not inviting external intervention on one's behalf in the pursuit of disputes.

The sum total of all these contributions has been to bring the ASEAN area to the brink of what Karl Deutsch has called a pluralistic security community. Such a system is one at peace, where no nation continues to accept war or violence as an instrument of policy against another community member and where no actor seriously prepares for war or violence against another. There is no guarantee that such a situation will be sustained in the future. Peace is always a constant struggle. But to come close to being a security community from a starting point so distant within a time span so comparatively short is no mean achievement. Admittedly the ASEAN security community has in part been the result of other factors, not the least of which was the perception of extra-ASEAN threats. But without the existence of ASEAN there would today be no such quasi-security community. And history tells us that common external threats can lead to division as well as unity.

Given that the ASEAN contributions noted above have almost exclusively been to the ASEAN community, might it not be argued that whilst ASEAN has played a central role with regard to the sub-region, it has not played a significant role in the context of the wider region? Though it is patently clear that the Association's contribution outside the ASEAN community has been of a different order, there are two reasons why that proposition is incorrect.

First, the ASEAN community is the core of the Southeast Asian region and the Indochina states and Burma are its periphery. Such is the attention that war attracts, such has been the perceptual neglect of those parts where the guns are silent that it will be a surprise even to scholars of Southeast Asia that the ASEAN area constitutes five-sixths of the region's land area, and more than 90 per cent of its total GNP. Just about four out of every five Southeast Asians are residents of the ASEAN community. An organization that contributes so substantially to the security of so much Southeast Asian real estate cannot be said to contribute insignificantly.

Secondly, the existence of ASEAN and the activities of ASEAN have contributed significantly also to the periphery of Southeast Asia and to the entire region. In the same way that a peaceful, stable and unaggressive Indochina would contribute to the security of the ASEAN sub-region and the region as a whole, a peaceful, stable and unaggressive ASEAN community has contributed to Indochina and to Southeast Asian security. By denying to the big powers any vacuum in the ASEAN community and giving them no opportunity to propel themselves into any void and by sanitizing the sub-region from high-profile big power rivalry too a contribution is made. It is also arguable that the existence, solidarity and strength of ASEAN provides a balance of political power to Hanoi and imposes a psychological check and counter to Vietnam, thus contributing to the security of the entire region (including that of Kampuchea and Laos in the future).

History may yet prove the ASEAN states right in their belief that Vietnamese aggression in Kampuchea has to be punished and not rewarded — because it is aggression, and the punishment of aggression perpetrated by any state in the region must be part of the rules of the game in Southeast Asia. ASEAN's posture, policies and actions with regard to the Kampuchean question cannot be divorced from the endeavour of every ASEAN state to seek to impose upon the region as a whole the rules which they have legislated for the ASEAN community: the pacific resolution of conflict, non-interference and non-intervention in the domestic affairs of other states, respect for each state's territorial integrity and independence, commitment to the principle of non-invitation of external big power intervention on one's behalf. They are unlikely to succeed in the foreseeable future in their endeavour. But it is perhaps not wrong for them to try.

Notes

1. Arnfinn Jorgensen-Dahl, *Regional Organization and Order in South-East Asia* (Macmillan, London, 1982), p. 70.

COMMENTS

Arnfinn Jorgensen-Dahl

The record of regional organizations in the Third World is on the whole a poor one, including that in the field of regional security broadly defined. It is, therefore, all the more noteworthy to come across an organization about which it may be said that it has contributed substantially to regional security. In the case of ASEAN the task is to determine the nature and the extent of its contributions.

In his paper Noordin Sopiee rightly emphasizes the transformation which the political climate among the five (now six) members of ASEAN has undergone over the last eighteen years or so. The political relations in the ASEAN region have indeed travelled a long distance since the troubled days of the mid-1960s. He is also right in pointing to the enhanced standing of the members in the international system at large. These and many other developments which Sopiee regards as important to regional security are by and large attributed to ASEAN which receives uniformly high marks and little short of enthusiastic praise for its contributions.

Admittedly there is much to be said in favour of ASEAN's role even by those who are less enthused than Sopiee. It must nevertheless be asked to what extent the developments Sopiee mentions in his paper are the result of the existence of ASEAN as such? Can it not be argued that a good deal of that to which Sopiee points would have come about in any case, that too much is attributed to ASEAN?

In arriving at his conclusions about ASEAN's role Sopiee's chosen method is to imagine what the nature of the relations between the five would have been like had it not been for the existence of ASEAN. His view is that relations by and large would have continued to follow, perhaps even in an augmented form, the unsavoury paths they had before the advent of ASEAN. This is possible but not very likely. As with that of all other states, the interaction between the ASEAN five takes place within a wider and always changing international environment. This is a crucial factor which, in Sopiee's scheme of things, figures as a peripheral matter of no particular consequence.

During the years in question, that is the time since the mid-1960s,

232

international events and changes with a bearing on Southeast Asia have been many and followed each other rapidly. Let me mention a few which in my view have had a particularly strong impact on relations among the ASEAN states. In the mid- and late 1960s we had the Vietnam War, the Cultural Revolution in China, the British withdrawal from east of Suez, and Nixon's Guam doctrine. In the early and mid-1970s came the Sino-American rapprochement, the US withdrawal from Vietnam and the Communist victories in Indochina accompanied by the US military withdrawal from mainland Southeast Asia altogether. Then came the Vietnamese invasion and occupation of Cambodia which put the final seal on the evolving polarization process which Southeast Asia has undergone since the end of the Second World War. It is the perceptions and assessments of what these changes implied, and the question of how to cope with them which more than anything else (but not exclusively) brought the five states together.

In other words, it seems to me quite impossible to explain not only the much improved political climate but also the formation of ASEAN itself without reference to this chain of external events, something which Sopiee has not done. Once formed, ASEAN no doubt facilitated the process of conciliation the beginnings of which nevertheless not only predate but also contributed to the very formation of the organization. In short, without ASEAN the improvement in relations between the five would have met with many more difficulties, stops, starts and even reversals but nevertheless would have moved in much the same overall direction as they have done with ASEAN present on the scene.

In arguing in favour of the predominant influence of external factors, as I have done, it is well worth remembering that Southeast Asia is one of a string of regions through which runs the dominant fault line of the international system in the post-Second World War period — the Communist-non-Communist cleavage. What in the eyes of ASEAN leaders lends particular weight and importance to the external events referred to above was that they were either a part of, or had a strong bearing on, the development and the state of this cleavage. Hence their impact on relations among the five states.

When one turns to ASEAN's contributions to regional security in Southeast Asia at large, Sopiee has little to say. It is especially regrettable that he has almost nothing to say about the Kampuchean conflict which is after all the most immediate and important regional security issue in Southeast Asia today. It is also an issue in which the ASEAN states have involved themselves consistently and strongly, and one to whose resolution ASEAN's contributions may not attract the same level of approval as have those contributions to regional security that Sopiee concentrates on in his paper.

11 THE GULF CO-OPERATION COUNCIL AND REGIONAL SECURITY IN THE GULF

Osama Al Ghazaly Harb

This paper deals with the Gulf Co-operation Council as a regional organization in relation to the issue of security in the Gulf, the Middle East and the international system. It is not the purpose of this paper, however, to discuss the theoretical contents of the concepts of security and regional security either generally or in connection with the Third World in particular. Taking the description and analysis offered by Mohammed Ayoob of the concept of security and regional security in the Third World as points of departure,[1] this paper would try to polish these concepts and attempt to discover their meaning in the Third World by studying the concrete facts and understanding them as they are.

The Gulf Co-operation Council is regarded by many scholars as an organizational experiment that reflects the needs of regional security. This paper will tackle the GCC directly without a predetermination of its character or identity. Such qualifications will be made during the process of analysis.

The security of Third World countries should be tackled from the methodological point of view from several angles: there is first the need for a comprehensive and not a partial view of the study of these societies. Secondly, there is a need to adopt several approaches and not a single one. Thirdly, there is the need to speak in particular terms rather than in general ones. Over-generalization is a great methodological mistake in the study of the Third World, which is formed of societies and regions that have different historical experiences, geographical determinants, as well as diverse cultural and psychological characteristics.

In the light of these conceptual and methodological considerations, the paper will proceed to handle the GCC, which was established formally on 25 May 1981, as an existing security organization on the local (internal) level as well as on the sub-regional and international levels.

It is not difficult for a person who studies the GCC to notice that the main issue which motivated the establishment of the Council was co-operation and co-ordination between member states (i.e.

Saudi Arabia, Kuwait, Qatar, Bahrain, the United Arab Emirates and Oman) to preserve security within their territorial borders. In other words, this meant the maintenance of public order as defined by the regimes in these countries. This is a fact that cannot be deduced only from official documents of the GCC or its declared objectives. It is rather a logical conclusion from the understanding of the nature of those states, their political systems and their priorities within the framework of their current political circumstances.

The Gulf states share with several of the Third World countries the characteristic that they are 'new' states. The political systems in these countries thus still suffer from the 'crisis' of political development — if we are to use the terminology of political development literature.[2] Yet, in these countries, such a crisis has features and characteristics that are extremely particular in nature and are derived from their historical and cultural heritage, their economic and social conditions and the international environment. Indeed, these countries suffer a severe contradiction between the inherited traditional and tribal style of their political systems on the one hand, and the processes of development and modernization, to which they have been exposed in a short period of time, on the other hand.

The Gulf regimes became concerned with the preservation and consolidation of their authority specially after the great economic and cultural changes that have occurred lately in their societies. Such changes became a source of danger that jeopardized their legitimacy and influence. Although the Gulf states had always been prey to the big powers due to their unique strategic situation on the trade routes, the discovery of oil at the beginning of the century has had a more profound impact on these states' societies. In fact, oil has been responsible for the continuous change in the lifestyles of the Gulf states. This has taken place through the penetration of the Gulf countries by the giant western oil companies which erected in the Gulf desert oil exploration posts and refineries as well as ports for their exports. It was also a result of the huge oil rvenues which kept flowing into the Gulf countries or, to put it more accurately, into the hands of the ruling families and tribes. While the social, economic and cultural changes and the opening up to the outside world which accompanied the oil discovery and export gave rise to great challenges to the existing regimes, the flow of oil revenues enabled those regimes to resist the challenges.

The regimes of the GCC member states did not witness the violent political shake-ups or attempts at military *coups d'état* that took place in most of the other Third World countries. This is not a proof of the ability of these regimes to 'respond' to the 'crisis of political development', nor is it an example of the model formulated by Huntington[3] on the attainability of 'stability' and 'public order' through effective political institutions. Rather, it is the huge and exceptionally great oil revenues that have enabled these regimes to continue to exist till the present time. The policies of public welfare, the wide-scale technical and material modernization processes and the policies of immediate suppression of any rising opposition, also contributed to this reality.[4]

However, this does not mean the non-existence of internal threats to these regimes, not only because of the impossibility of the continuation of the traditional mode of authority and government amid the modernizing changes in society and the lack of integration between the social forces, but also due to the nature of the model of development itself. Inherent in this model are new threats and perils.

Putting aside the changes adopted by some Gulf countries, particularly Kuwait, the regimes in the GCC member states are still patriarchal in nature and are founded on tribal bases. The ruler in each of these states is a member of a family or a tribe that has imposed its power and control by force. The ruler assumes his authority and tasks in the manner practised by the tribal chieftain. His power is absolute and he selects his advisers from among prominent figures, experts and notables, and is not committed to their opinion. With the exception of Kuwait, none of the GCC member states experiences any genuine kind of political participation. They do not recognize election or nomination rights nor do they have any kind of elected parliamentary institutions. Accordingly, it is important to point out that the GCC itself was a product of governmental decisions in which there was no trace of popular participation.

At the same time, the population structure of the six Gulf states entails several threats to their 'internal security' that are no less important than the threats which result from the practices of the regimes. For many decades prior to the discovery of oil, and due to its limited population, the Arab littoral of the Gulf had been a centre of attraction for a large number of immigrants from neighbouring Asian countries. Both the permanent and temporary migration movements were intensified after the discovery of oil. A large, non-indigenous population has grown up in the six Gulf states. In three of these countries the non-indigenous population exceeds half their total population (more than half in Kuwait, around two-thirds or more in the United Arab Emirates and Qatar) and this is expected to continue in the future.

Whether or not these foreign elements formed settled foreign communities or acted as temporary immigrants who sought work in the Gulf countries but intended to return to their home states, the issue of the non-indigenous population in general has a direct impact on the social, economic and cultural conditions in the Gulf states. What is important here is the striking contrast in the living standards between this large sector of foreigners and the indigenous population. The hard living conditions in which most of the first group lives renders them an imminent source of unrest that could jeopardize internal security. Moreover, the situation becomes even more critical when the minorities or immigrant manpower are nationals of strong countries that seek to exercise influence over the area. A prominent example is the Iranian presence in the Gulf area and Iran's attempt to use Iranian and Shiite inhabitants as a basis for its continued presence in these countries.

In other cases, countries like India and Pakistan have sometimes interfered to protect the interests of their nationals. In fact, some researchers in the Gulf warned against the para-military character of the manpower coming into the Gulf countries from some of the East Asian states, particularly South Korea.

Thus, a comprehensive security agreement was proposed to face up to sources of internal threats. It was, however, one of the most controversial issues put before the GCC and is still resisted by Kuwait, one of the most contributing and open member states, which has hindered the completion of the project.

The review of the security agreement draft indicates the nature of Gulf security for which the GCC aspires. According to its preamble, the agreement seeks to preserve security and stability, and protect Islamic Shari'a and supreme values from atheist and destructive ideas and military activities. The general principles of the draft also 'stipulate the abandoning of out-laws from among citizens of the GCC member-states or others and combating their activities that harm the security of the member-states' (article 1), and 'banning the entrance, dealing in or exporting of all kinds of publications that are in opposition to the Islamic beliefs, can breach public ethics or are directed against the regimes of the member-states' (article 2). The draft also stipulates that 'each of the member-states should adopt the necessary measures to guarantee the non-interference of its citizens in the internal affairs of other member-states' (article 3). Moreover, according to article 16, names of suspects should be exchanged, their movements notified and they should be prevented from leaving the country. The draft also regulates the process of extradition of criminals. While article 24 stipulates at its beginning that no extradition would be permitted if the crime is political in nature, yet it considers 'sabotage and terrorism' an exception to political crimes. This exception also applies to assaults against the heads of state of the member countries, their parents, descendants and wives as well as crown princes, members of the royal families, ministers and persons of their standing in the member states and those who commit 'military crimes'.

Even though the signing of the agreement has been held up, the GCC has succeeded in adopting several measures in the sphere of 'internal security'. The GCC imposed strict rules on the entrance of persons who are not citizens of the Gulf states into these countries and used computers in checking names of persons on blacklists. On the other hand, other measures were adopted to facilitate the free movement of Gulf citizens between the member states. In this regard, however, the Sultanate of Oman refused to cancel visa requirements except for members of the ruling families, prominent figures and official delegations of the GCC member states. A statement issued after the meeting of the interior ministers of the GCC in February 1982 also added prominent businessmen to the list of persons who did not need entrance visa.

The focus on internal security reflects in a substantive and direct manner the Saudi viewpoint regarding the role of the GCC and the priorities of its activities. Saudi Arabia conceives the GCC as primarily an instrument that assists the Gulf regimes to tighten their grip over their nationals against any prospective internal perils. It also regards the security agreement as a means to prevent other GCC member states, particularly those that enjoy some freedoms, from becoming a 'haven' for elements that oppose the Saudi regime or those of which the latter does not approve.

In the studies of international politics, the Gulf states are regarded as constituting a sub-regional system. From this perspective, the six GCC states comprise a distinct block inside that sub-regional system of the Gulf *vis-à-vis* other countries in the same system namely, Iran and Iraq (some also like to add North and South Yemen).

On that level, and from the perspective of sub-regional security, the GCC reflects: (1) the long-stading Saudi ambition to control the Arabian peninsula; and (2) the rivalry between Saudi Arabia and the two other big powers inside the sub-regional system, Iraq and Iran.

A good part of the history of the Arabian peninsula since the mid-eighteenth century is characterized by attempts by the 'Saudi family' to extend its control over it. The alliance that was formed at that time between the founders of the Wahabi movement, Sheikh Mohamed Bin Abdel Wahab and Prince Mohamed Bin Saud, was the beginning of the Saudi sweeping control over most of the Arabian peninsula which was part of the Ottoman Empire. Fifty years after the alliance, the Saudis extended their control over Najd, the Hijaz, Hadramout, Assir and Bahrain, as well as other parts of the Arabian peninsula. In confronting that expansion, the Governor of Egypt, Mohamed Ali Pasha, launched, upon the request of the Ottoman Sultan, a large military land and naval expedition in order to stem the expansion of the Wahabi movement and Saudi influence. In the years between 1811 and 1843 the Egyptian army was involved in fierce battles with the Wahabis and the Saudis and the Egyptian expeditions succeeded in weakening the Al Qawassem tribes, the allies of Saudis in the Gulf.

The Egyptian expedition which came to an end in 1843 did not eliminate the influence of the Saudis and their allies, but it weakened it. This development was in the interest of Britain which was concerned at that time with the occupation one after another of the emirates that lie on the Gulf coast. Although the Wahabis succeeded in restoring their position after the withdrawal of the Egyptian forces from the peninsula, the British were the main force that prevented Abdel Aziz Al Saud (1880–1953) the founder of the Saudi state, from extending his control to the eastern parts of the Arabian peninsula. In exchange for British recognition of his state during the First World War, King Abdel Aziz pledged not to encroach upon the Gulf emirates. The British played the same role to the west of the Arabian peninsula when they convinced the Saudis, through their support for the Hashemite family in the Hijaz, for his role against the Ottoman Empire during the First World War.

The British interest in the area in the aftermath of the First World War and the defeat of the Turkish Empire made Britain abandon Sherif Hussein, and this subsequently enabled the Saudis to launch their attack on him and annex Assir and the Hijaz. The same British interests in the Gulf area necessitated the preservation of British control over the Gulf emirates. In 1932 King Abdel Aziz Al Saud declared the unity of all the areas that fell under his control or which he was permitted to control under the name of the 'Arab Saudi Kingdom' with its present borders.

Thirty years later, i.e. in the early 1960s, the Gulf emirates, in turn, began to obtain their independence from Britain amid different international and regional circumstances. However, Saudi Arabia continued to play the role of the dominating country in the peninsula.

The salient role of Saudi Arabia is not accounted for by its eventful historic heritage only, but also by the fact that it is the largest and the most populous state on the Arab littoral of the Gulf. It is the first ranking oil-exporting country, and consequently carries great weight in OPEC and OAPEC. Saudi Arabia is also the only country that shares its borders with all the Arabian peninsula states but has no borders with Iran. Moreover, the existence of the Islamic holy places in Saudi Arabia (Mecca and Medina) gives it great weight in the Arab and Islamic world.

In the light of these facts, Saudi Arabia regarded the security of the Arabian peninsula as synonymous with Saudi security or, to put it more accurately, the security of the Saudi regime. Many years before the establishment of the GCC, Saudi Arabia played an important role in maintaining the security of the Arabian peninsula, based on its own understanding of this security. It settled conflicts over its borders with other countries in the peninsula and among the Gulf states.

On the other hand, Saudi Arabia has considered any radical development that took place in the other Arabian peninsula states as entailing a direct threat to its security. It has linked the preservation of its conservative political system to the sustenance of other conservative systems. That is why, when Bahrain and Kuwait closed down their Parliaments in 1975 and 1976 respectively, following the rise of strong domestic opposition, Saudi Arabia reacted positively to these developments and Saudi officials began to speak about the importance of the Islamic Shari'a, the values of society and the establishment of a system of government based on the conditions of the country.

More important in this respect is the stand of the Saudi regime towards the revolution in Dhofar in Oman and in North and South Yemen. These developments were not only feared because of the regional threats they presented on the Saudi borders, they were also regarded as revolutionary ideological dangers that were directed against the essence of the Saudi regime. Thus, Saudi Arabia offered Sultan Qaboos of Oman large military and financial assistance (mainly in co-ordination with the USA) against the revolutionary movement. It supported with all its power the royalists in the civil war in North Yemen (1962–70) against the republicans and the Egyptian forces that supported them. Saudi Arabia also adopted all possible measures to weaken the leftist regime in South Yemen by backing anti-regime tribes, forming a bloc under its leadership that comprised all the Arabian peninsula states in order to impose a political and economic blockade of South Yemen, and led the propaganda to describe it as a Communist and Soviet-satellite regime.

Finally, Saudi Arabia encouraged mergers between the regimes of the Arabian peninsula states, as long as they took place under its guidance. It supported the establishment of the United Arab Emirates and, at different times, sought to push Kuwait and Bahrain to join it. Moreover, the attempts by Saudi Arabia to settle the border disagreements among the seven emirates were part of its continuous efforts to solve the intra-mural problems of these states.

Within this context we can understand the Saudi stance towards the GCC and the predominance of the Saudi notion of security in the councils of that organization. However, the aforementioned events cannot alone account for the formation of the GCC in 1981. Other factors related to the rivalry between the Saudi regime and other states within the sub-regional Gulf system are also of great significance.

As pointed out, the expansion of the Saudi regime in the Arabian peninsula was historically restricted by the existence of an outside force capable of curbing and competing with it (Egypt and later Britain). In the Gulf sub-regional system, such forces were represented by Iraq and Iran. As attempts in the mid-1970s to establish a sub-regional system for Gulf security comprising Saudi Arabia, Iraq and Iran in addition to the smaller Gulf states failed, endeavours to form the GCC were met by quick success. In fact, the establishment of the GCC after the eruption of the Iraqi-Iranian War was not a coincidence. Each of the two regimes of Iran and Iraq has a notion and understanding of regional security in the Gulf that stems from its own nature and that is, consequently, different from the Saudi understanding. The engagement of the two countries in the ferocious war gave the Saudi regime a golden opportunity to impose its own understanding of regional security within its traditional sphere of influence, namely the Arabian peninsula.

The question of Gulf security as a joint venture that involves the three big Gulf powers, Saudi Arabia, Iraq and Iran, was raised following Britain's declaration of intent to withdraw from east of Suez in 1968. Britain made efforts to guarantee stability in the area by encouraging the establishment of the United Arab Emirates as well as by attempting to solve the perennial problems between the states of the region, particularly by bringing closer Saudi Arabia and Iran, the two powers on which it could rely to guarantee the required stability. For about a decade, from the withdrawal of the British forces in 1971 up to the outbreak of the Iraqi-Iranian War in 1980, the three countries did not agree on the nature of Gulf security and the means to realize it. The gap in viewpoints appeared in particular at the conference which was held in Muscat in November 1976 among the six states that formed the GCC later on as well as Iran and Iraq.

Yet, the victory of the Islamic Revolution in Iran and the monopoly of Shiite clergymen over its leadership, posed new challenges to Saudi Arabia and Iraq. The new regime in Iran, which shares with the Saudi regime its Islamic ideology, denounced the Saudi system as well as all other 'Islamic' Gulf systems as anti-Islam, thus directing a blow against the very basis of Saudi legitimacy. The Iranian regime also condemned Saudi Arabia's subordinate, close relations with western, anti-Islam countries, particularly the US. Moreover, the Iranian Revolution contributed to transforming the Iranian communities in the Gulf states as well as followers of the Shiite creed within them into a reserve dormant power, to serve not only the interests of 'Iran as a state', but also of 'Iran as a revolution'. This last element was undoubtedly the main reason why the Iraqi regime feared the Iranian Revolution, particularly with the existence of a large Shiite majority under its non-democratic system of government. In brief, the Iranian Revolution constituted a challenge to the claims of 'revolutionary' legitimacy of the Iraqi regime just as it constituted a challenge to the claims of 'religious' legitimacy of the Saudi regime. This was all of course in addition to the long history of antagonism and rivalry between Iraq and Iran which goes back scores of years and was basically over the demarcation of borders between them, especially in the Shatt-Al-Arab area.

In the light of these contradictions between the three ruling systems in Iraq, Iran and Saudi Arabia, and the antagonism among the three powers which took different forms and shapes, the GCC was born, at the right moment, as a bloc inside the sub-regional system that embodies the highest actual capabilities of the Saudi regime. It is a capability that is characterized by *dominance* and *supremacy* within the framework of the Arabian peninsula, but which is also faced with challenge and competition from other powers in the Gulf. This means that regional security in its agreed-upon 'model' has no existence in the Gulf area. The GCC is so limited in its extent and objectives that it cannot be considered a sub-regional security system in the Gulf area. It is rather a regional bloc (alliance) led by Saudi Arabia that seeks to preserve the Saudi regime through the preservation of the existing regimes in the other Gulf mini states and to consolidate its capabilities *vis-à-vis* the other two powers in the Gulf, Iran and Iraq.

Based on these points, we can interpret the stand of Saudi Arabia and its allies in the GCC towards the Iraq-Iran War. One of the advantages of this war for them is that it has drained the two powers and reduced their relative power *vis-à-vis* Saudi Arabia and the Gulf mini states, because of the huge human and material losses incurred by the combatants. On the other hand, what Saudi Arabia and its allies fear most from the Iraq-Iran War is its possible out-comes: either one of the two countries achieves a complete victory over the other, which qualifies it immediately to assume the position of the unrivalled supreme regional state and enables it to impose its policies on the area (within the limits of the international balance in the area), or for the war to continue 'more than it should', with neither of the two parties achieving a decisive victory. This would push the two warring parties, out of despondency or boredom, to expand the war at least regionally in the hope of exercising pressure on the other side. The danger of the prolonga-tion of the war 'more than it should' forces Saudi Arabia and its allies to determine their stands more clearly and definitely and certainly places them at a disadvantage.

Speaking about the Gulf states as forming a sub-regional system means, implicitly, that they belong to a large regional system, namely that of the Middle East. It is not our concern here to discuss the numerous, intertwined and sometimes vague definitions of the Middle East area. However, it is important to point out that the term Middle East is not widely accepted by many Arab scholars and academics. They see in this term an attempt to undermine another regional system, namely the Arab regional system. The Arab regional system does not only display the features of a regional system in its conventional sense, but, above all, it is characterized by being a national system, i.e. it combines states that share the same nationality, embodied in its concept of Arab nationalism, and which aim at achieving integration among themselves.[5] The Arab states of the Gulf are considered part of this Arab system.

The Arab-Israeli conflict is the main source of threat to regional security (both of the Middle East and the Arab systems) within the limits of the concept of security and regional security in the Third World as pointed out by Ayoob.[6] Therefore, it is possible to tackle the issue of the link between the GCC and regional security through the examination of the relationship between the GCC member states and their role in the developments related to the Arab-Israeli conflict.

From the point of view of Arab nationalism, the Arab Gulf states must be 'an effective party to the Arab-Israeli confrontation'. That is why any consolidation of the power of these countries is a consolidation of Arab power against Israel and vice versa. In fact, the Gulf participation in the war against Israel took place, and still takes place, mainly through financial assistance to the Arab front-line states, i.e. to Egypt (before the Camp David agreements), Syria, Jordan and Lebanon, in addition to the PLO. However, the maximum support which the Gulf states could offer in the war against Israel was the oil embargo which was imposed during the October War in 1973 on the countries that supported Israel, or what was known as the use of the oil weapon. To confront this measure, Israel and the countries that support it, particularly the USA, resisted the attempts of the Arabs to establish a link between Gulf security and Arab security and this was clear from the US reaction to the oil embargo in October 1973. The Americans strongly refused to give in to Gulf pressures. They also did not exert any effective pressure on Israel, but rather threatened to adopt direct measures against sources of oil pressure. In fact, the oil embargo was the main reason behind the crystallization of ideas for direct US military intervention in the Gulf, which culminated in the establishment of the Rapid Deployment Force, now the US Central Command (Centcom).

At the same time, Israel continuously sought to abort any attempt that could jeopardize it and which emanated from the Arab Gulf states. Israel's relations with the Iranian regime under the Shah constituted one of the most diverse, and at the same time mysterious, modes of relations between countries. Even after the fall of the Shah and the new Iranian regime's hard-line measures against it, Israel appeared amongst the countries that exported arms to Iran in its war against Iraq. In fact, Israel is among the main countries that benefit from the Iraq-Iran War both by weakening the revolutionary regime in Iran and complicating its relations with the Arab states, and through draining Iraq's economic and military power. The most flagrant act of Israeli aggression in this context was the strike against the Iraqi nuclear reactor on 7 June 1981.

Practically, it is difficult to imagine that the GCC could be an addition to Arab power against Israel. Even though the resolutions of the first Gulf summit held in May 1981 said that 'The gauarantee of stability in the Gulf is linked to the establishment of peace in the Middle East', this statement was not repeated. The GCC member states only asserted their position of supporting the rights of the Palestinian people and condemning Israeli actions, within the framework of the Arab League resolutions. This, however, does not mean that the GCC states have no interest in putting an end to the conflict with Israel. According to a 'secret working paper' submitted by Saudi Arabia to the meeting of the foreign ministers of the GCC states on 13 August 1981, which was published in one of the banned papers in Oman, the security fears of the GCC states with regard to the Arab-Israeli conflict stem from: (a) the eruption of a destructive war whose direct impact would reach the Gulf area; (b) the spread of a situation of political turmoil and chaos in the Arab world as a whole; and (c) the possibility that the delay in the settlement of the Palestinian issue would lead to a situation of despondency among the Palestinian people wherever they are, which can be manipulated by the Soviets or extremist local elements in fomenting disturbances inside the GCC member states.[7] In short, what the GCC states fear most is the possibility that developments in the Arab-Israeli conflict could lead to internal turmoil in these states, involving the Palestinian minority within them. Once more, the main security functions of the GCC are highlighted but they are functions that help isolate and not merge the peoples of the GCC states with the peoples of the Arab nation.

Unlike the vagueness that characterizes the issues of regional security in the Gulf, the question of international security in the area is indisputable. The Gulf area derives its importance with regard to international security from the existence of interests vital to the western world. This is represented in the continuous flow of oil from the Gulf states and the freedom of transport and movement through the area. Moreover, the fact that the Gulf area lies close to Soviet territories creates an additional interest of preventing Soviet control over it. When politicians and mass media in the West speak about the security of the Gulf, they mean specifically the preservation of the western interests in the Gulf and their protection from any threats.

The importance of the Gulf area for international security is reflected in any regional organization in the Gulf, in a manner that is different from other Third World regions. That is why questions are raised regarding the relationship between the GCC and the issue of international security in the area.

If we once more underline the fact that the primary objective of the GCC is to preserve the regimes of the member states and consolidate them, the main issue under discussion here would be the relationship between the preservation of the conservative Gulf states which are members of the GCC and the maintenance of the vital interests of the West in the Gulf.

The fact is that the Gulf regimes have been linked since their establishment to western interests in the area. The relationship between the two parties can be considered one of mutual support, meaning that the existence of the conservative Gulf regimes reinforces western interests and the latter, in turn, help consolidate the Gulf regimes. This link has been challenged with the overthrow of the Shah in Iran and the victory of the Iranian Revolution. These developments faced the Gulf states with a new fact, namely that the West is primarily concerned with the preservation of its vital interests more than with the preservation of 'friendly regimes', as long as the new regimes that take over 'have an understanding' of western interests and have no desire to destroy them. No doubt it was due to these developments that feelings of concern were one of the main motives behind the establishment of the GCC as a means by which these regimes reinforce each other through their joint co-operation on the one hand, and, on the other, by convincing the western world that the preservation of its interests is linked to the sustenance of these regimes.

From the practical point of view, it can be said that the responsibility of protecting western interests in the Gulf is primarily shouldered by the western countries themselves. The participation of the Gulf states in this protection is seen within the context of the western strategy in the Gulf. The protection of western interests in the Gulf is primarily achieved through direct military presence (particularly American) in the Gulf area and the Indian Ocean. More than one member state of the GCC has offered bases or facilities for this military presence.

The October War and the oil embargo which accompanied it are the two main factors which contributed to the crystallization of plans for direct military intervention and the formation of the US Rapid Deployment Force. The task of the Force, as outlined from the outset, was to use force against oil-producing countries. But the developments that took place after the fall of the Shah made one of the purposes of this force the protection of the Gulf states against domestic and external aggression, i.e. the protection of the regimes of the Gulf states.

Other means of protecting western interests in the Gulf were exemplified in particular by Iran under the Shah. At that time Iran occupied a special position in the US strategy in the Middle East. Even though the fall of the Shah opened the way for Saudi Arabia to play the role of the regional power, there was no confidence in the actual ability of the Saudi regime to do so. This made the Americans look for another regional power outside the Gulf to play that role. This power was mainly Israel, and secondarily Egypt (particularly under Sadat). Some plans for co-operation with Jordan in this regard were also made.

These facts brought into question the huge arms deals which Saudi Arabia and the other Gulf states have concluded with the US and its West European allies. It is of course not a secret that the main goal which these deals serve is the consolidation of the arms industry in the US and Europe. The deals also involve the payment of high commissions for officials in the purchasing countries and are surrounded by propaganda that seek to present a deceitful image of potency to the peoples of these countries, but the real ability to use these arms is questioned.

This means that the role of the GCC is basically one of offering bases and facilities as well as finance for the western military forces to protect their interests in the Gulf and consequently the regimes in power.

This study of the GCC leads us to some conclusions with regard to regional security in the Third World in general:

1. It asserts the idea that national security means, in the first place, the security of the regimes in the sense that they continue in power and consolidate themselves in the face of domestic and external threats.

2. It asserts the possibility of forming a successful regional bloc as long as it comprises systems that are similar in their social and class structures and their external relations and as long as they seek co-operation to consolidate each other.

3. The possibility of success of such a bloc increases with the presence of a dominating power inside it that is feared and respected by others.

4. The preservation and continuation of such a security alliance is linked to its compliance with the security of either of the two world camps within the context of international security in general, and the ability of these regimes to suppress internal opposition. Consequently, the idea of regime security has become much stronger in its essence in the Gulf than in any other region in the Third World.

5. The oil wealth has also opened Gulf societies to the flow of labour from the Third World and to the invasion of the giant companies and institutions from the advanced world in a manner that has ultimately led to the intertwining of the sources of domestic and external threats to its security. It has consequently resulted in increasing sensitivity towards the external world whether at the regional or international levels.

6. For all these reasons, Gulf security has become in its core meaning something that has no existence. There are blocs and conflicts and there are also regimes that are conscious of their security and seek to preserve it. There is an international security which the big powers are in charge of controlling and preserving. But regional security is still a chimera.

Notes

1. Mohammed Ayoob (ed.), *Regional Security in the Third World*, Chapter 1.

2. This terminology is with reference to the works of the Committee of Comparative Politics, affiliated to the Centre of Sociology Research in the USA. For a good review of the Committee's work, se Binder, *et. al.*, *Crisis and Sequences in Political Development* (Princeton University Press, Princeton, NJ, 1974).

3. See Samuel P. Huntington, *Political Order in Changing Societies* (Yale University Press, New Haven, Conn., 1968).

4. See Gabriel Almond and Bingham Powell, *Comparative Politics: System, Process and Policy* (Little, Brown & Co., Boston, 1979), p. 387.

5. Gamil Matar and Alieddin Hilal Dessoukr, *The Arab Regional System* (Centre for Arab Unity Studies, Beirut, 1983), pp. 24–32.

6. Ayoob.

7. *Sawt Al Thawra*, Oman, 21 March 1982.

COMMENTS

Obaid-Ul-Haq

Over the last decade or so an interesting trend has manifested itself in the politics of regional organizations: there is a marked mood of disillusionment and disenchantment with large, geographically diffused and thematically loose concourses of nations such as the Organization of African Unity (OAU), the Organization of American States (OAS) and the Arab League. The move is away from such continental associations towards geographically compact and small organisations focusing on a few key objectives of common interest. The Association of Southeast Asian Nations (ASEAN), the Contadora group in Central America and the Organization of Front-line States in Southern Africa are cases in point.

The formation in May 1981 of the Gulf Co-operation Council (GCC) is illustrative of this general trend. Osama Al Ghazaly Harb's paper seeks to analyze the genesis of the GCC, the motivations of its members and the role it can play in the maintenance of security in an area of vital importance. The paper is rich in detail, careful with facts and thoughtful and balanced in analysis and I am in basic agreement with it.

The idea of some kind of Gulf organization had been mooted since the British withdrawal from the region in 1971. The small states of the Gulf, however, were ambivalent about joining an organization which, they feared, would be dominated by Saudi Arabia. What spurred them into action with a great sense of urgency was the series of events since 1979 which had turned the backwaters of the Gulf into a very volatile and dangerous area of conflict. First, was the fall of the Shah of Iran and the advent of the Ayatollah and his revolutionary brand of politics. This was enough to cause extreme anxiety to traditional tribal regimes of the Gulf states. The outbreak of war between Iraq and Iran heightened their fears and forced them to look for some confidence-building measures and ways to ensure co-operation in meeting threats and dangers emanating from the Gulf War.

The Gulf states have a unique combination of qualities. First, with increased oil revenues they are extremely rich; second, in

251

demographic terms they are extremely weak — both quantitatively and qualitatively. This combination of sudden wealth and endemic weakness makes them vulnerable to both internal dangers and external threats.

It is no secret that the GCC consolidates and reinforces the Saudi predominance in the Gulf region. The Saudis were clearly the prime movers in the establishment of this sub-regional organization for they regard the preservation of traditional regimes in the mini states of the Gulf absolutely essential to their own stability in the Arabian peninsula. What made Saudi protection and predominance acceptable to the Gulf sheikhs and ruling families was their greater fear of the Ba'athist revolutionaries of Iraq as well as the Shi'i fundamentalists of Iran.

The Gulf Co-operation Council has acquired a great deal of salience in the calculation of member states in the last three years. There have been regular consultations among rulers and increased military co-operation and periodic joint military exercises. In view of the uncertain military situation in this sensitive area these co-operative efforts are likely to continue and increase in importance.

The Gulf states are beset with many dangers, but of these two are crucial:

(a) The danger of domestic instability and that of internal radicalism of Islamic, leftist or Palestinian provenance;
(b) The Iraq-Iran War is a nest of troubles. The war of attrition as well as a clear victory of either of the two can pose serious threats to the viability and stability of small Gulf states.

The attitude of the Gulf states toward the United States is shaped by two contradictory impulses. The GCC has the tacit approval of the United States and the Gulf states would not like to deny themselves American protection should the situation go beyond their limited capabilities; but, at present, they aim to minimize the American connection. Too open a presence on the part of the US would be provocative to political forces in the Gulf and beyond. The GCC — if it can acquire some credibility and demonstrate some capacity for effective action — may yet obviate the possibility of great power intervention in this turbulent area.

Harb does not seem too sanguine about the present role and the future prospects of the GCC. I find this judgement pessimistic. If stability and peace (or at least avoidance of a wider war) in the

Gulf region is a desirable objective — as it must be for the peoples of the region — then there is a distinct possibility that the GCC can make a valuable contribution to that goal.

12 THE ARAB LEAGUE: BETWEEN REGIME SECURITY AND NATIONAL LIBERATION

Mohammed El Sayed Said

Introduction

The social sciences are still handicapped by semantic chaos. This problem is compounded in the Third World by valid doubts about the relevance of many concepts which have evolved historically from the particular experience of the West. Some Third World social scientists have responded to this double crisis by adjusting, or more accurately 'fitting', such concepts to the conditions of their societies. This response has failed to furnish adequate basis for an authentic social scientific tradition in the non-western world.

The concepts of national and regional security illustrate this point. It goes without saying that security is a universal problem. But what we see in western literature is not a genuine attempt to tackle this problem, but a certain ideology or perspective which takes the concept of security as a launching pad. This perspective carries the hegemonic heritage of western imperialism.[1] It is also notorious for having been deliberately used to justify colonial wars and internal repression and deprivation of human and civil rights.

In its original, unadulterated sense, security refers to a principle implying the right of individuals and groups to protection against arbitrary encroachment on their integral mode of existence, including their ethos and culture.

As a historically-specific problem, a proper perspective to security in the Third World should satisfy the three main following conditions:

(a) It must be contextual; not only that its specific social content must be determined, but also the connection of the security problem in the Third World to the dominant practices in the global system should be uncovered.

(b) It must be objective; in the sense that it provides an adequate basis for the interrogation of every claim to security by references to material conditions and practices.

(c) It must be critical; this refers to the need for reconstructing the problematique of security on a conceptually higher plane, so that light is thrown on the most profound contradictions of change in Third World.

Functions of the Arab League between Security and Liberation

The basic function of all regional organizations in the post-colonial era is the consolidation of the state system. This seems to be the essential proposal of the security perspective to that early generation of order-builders in the Third World. But judged from the vantage point of a liberation perspective, this function does not necessarily reflect the social realities and desires of Third World societies.

Security, in the liberation perspective, is contextually identical with the right to 'collective self-determination'. In this sense, this perspective refuses to grant an equal status to security of colonizer and colonized, or oppressor and oppressed. In other words, the liberation perspective insists on giving a critical appraisal of the social content of all security schemes.

Security schemes in Third World regions were installed in the context of what may broadly be called the inheritance situation.[2] *Elites indigenous to decolonized societies took over political power and used it to assign themselves the privileges previously enjoyed by the colonizers.* Not only the system of rule built by colonialism was conserved in essence, but also mechanisms of privilege-giving were entrenched in the newly decolonized society. *The state system, i.e. the division of regions into fixed areas of authority competence,* represented an important mechanism of privilege maintenance.

On the Arab regional level, the social realities of the new state system included complex patterns of identity formation, the struggle against cultural and economic hegemony and in certain areas the struggle against peculiar forms of colonialism and oppression.

On the other hand, the political context in which the League of Arab States was established was characterized by three basic factors. These were as follows:

(a) The quest for Arab unity, especially in the Arab East. In response to the frustrating developments in the region since the mid-nineteenth century, Arab political movements have moved to a position of universal consensus on the supremacy of Arab identity and Arab nationalism. The differences between these movements related to the extent to which this identity is compromised with the Islamic character of the region and the local circumstances of each society.[3]

(b) The search of western imperialism for a post-war Arab order based on collective cliency to the West. The desire of British colonialism and later American imperialism for a security regime in the Arab world tied as an appendage to the western security system motivated them to encourage the establishment of a regional organization.[4]

(c) Growth of the Zionist project in Palestine. By the time the Arab League was inaugurated, the Zionist scheme in Palestine had advanced into a qualitatively higher stage. Legal and illegal Jewish migration increased substantially during the Second World War and thereafter.

These factors reflected some elements conducive to the inheritance situation and others hostile to it. The establishment and character of the Arab League came much closer to the former than to the latter. While these factors were manifested more clearly in the overall ideology which nurtured the League, they were also inherent in the various components of its security system. Below is a brief review of this system.

Scope of Membership

The charter of the Arab League is decisive on the question of membership. The most important qualification of membership in the League is being an Arab state. While Arabism was not defined, it conserved the collective Arab identity of the League (article 2).[5]

Peaceful Settlement of Disputes

The main function of the League is, in fact, the legitimation of the status quo and the consolidation of the state system. It is evident from the debates and deliberations which led to the establishment of the League that representatives of all Arab states rejected the idea of a central government and the idea of a federation or confederation with an executive authority and a constituent assembly, or entrusting any supra-state authority in whatever form with substantive security functions not mediated by the member states.[6] Accordingly, the charter repeatedly emphasized the sovereignty and independence of member states within their colonially-drawn boundaries.

These principles were crystallized in the voting system in the League. This system works according to three rules: the equality of states in voting rights (nothing parallel to the UN Security Council was established), the rule of consensus on all important issues and the principle that decisions are binding only on those members who vote affirmatively in respect of a decision.

Moreover, the Arab League system of voting is not tied to effective means of control over the implementation of decisions. The League lacks compulsive and punitive means or judicial authority to ensure the implementation of its decisions.[7]

But the legal structure of the Arab League went much beyond the mere consolidation of the state system in the Arab world. Existing regimes, in view of the charter, are legitimate regardless of the harm they may cause to the rights of their citizenry. Article 8 of the charter asserts that 'every member state in the League must respect the existing system of rule in other states, and considers it one of the rights of those states and commits itself not to undertake any action with the aim of changing the system in them'. The legitimation of existing regimes, according to the charter, is not conditioned by respect of any general principles, either on the regional level or in the domestic affairs of every state.

Given all these features, the Arab League had to face the problem of disputes between member states and regimes. The general principle which the League has adopted is peaceful resolution of disputes. However, the charter has granted the League only a limited role in the peaceful resolution of conflicts between Arab states. The charter was influenced by principles laid down by the League of Nations. It confined the League's role to mediation and (political) arbitration, and ignored the other means which the UN charter has included. The Council of the League cannot undertake the function of mediation and arbitration of disputes without the explicit consent of the states directly involved (article 5). Only in the case of actual armed aggression did the charter allow the Council to take 'the necessary measures' to repulse aggression on request of the states subject to aggression or other member states (article 6). The primitive system of peaceful resolution of conflict in the Arab League caused increasing discontent amongst Arab intellectuals as well as in the League's secretariat.[8]

External Security Function

The striking feature of the Arab League is its lack of a comprehensive conception of security in the Arab world. The League has not developed a consistent threat analysis for the region nor did it articulate a security strategy. Even the Israeli threat was not explicitly recognized as a matter of concern for the whole Arab world, and consequently it failed to commit all member states to some role in the security tasks of the whole region.

The second feature of the League's scheme is its almost exclusive emphasis on the overt military aspect of threat and insecurity. Economic, cultural and political threats were not recognized except lately and sporadically.

The third feature of the League's scheme of security is its uneven character. In the overall political sphere, the charter did not oblige member states to follow a common line on foreign policy. The absence in the charter of a binding commitment on matters of foreign policy was by-passed by an agreement on the least common denominator based on the negative inhibition against foreign commitments by any member state which constitute a violation of a common stand on certain issues. So, article 8 of the Treaty for Joint Defence and Economic Co-operation between the States of the Arab League which was adopted by the League Council in April 1950 reads as follows: 'Every one of the contracting states commits itself not to engage in any international agreement which contradicts this treaty and not to act in its international relations with other states in a way which denies the aims of this treaty.' This general commitment, which obliges only those states which signed the treaty (on joint defence), the membership in which was left optional, was detailed and made compulsory by a decision of the League's Council issued in the same year (1950) in regard to Israel.[9] This decision forbids any state from negotiating or signing a separate agreement with Israel. Such states are liable to dismissal and the imposition of penalties. Ironically, this resolution, which was proposed by Egypt in 1950, was implemented only once and in regard to Egypt in 1979 after the signing of the Egyptian-Israeli Treaty. Hence, while the League is hesitant in demanding even the most elementary basis of unity on foreign policy issues, it was keen to prevent cracks and fissures in it, especially in regard to individual Arab policies towards Israel.

In the military field the security endeavour of the Arab League is crystallized in the Treaty for Joint Defence and Economic

Co-operation. According to the treaty: 'The contracting states consider armed aggression against any one or more of them or against its forces an aggression against all of them . . . [They are] bound to run to the aid of the states or states aggressed upon, and to take, individually and collectively, all necessary measures and to utilize all means available to them including the use of armed forces to repulse the aggression' (article 2). The participant states will also 'consult' on the request of any one state when its territorial integrity, independence or security are threatened, and 'start at once' co-ordinating their plans and efforts to take precautionary and defensive measures in case 'of an immediate danger of war or the emergence of a potentially dangerous international situation'. The treaty created a military committee and a council on joint defence to propose and supervise measures conducive to its goals.

In spite of the theoretical significance of this treaty, it amounts in practice to very little. First, the treaty is not considered a part of the charter, and membership of it was left optional. Second, it failed to grant the League an independent armed force under its command. In fact, the goals of the treaty were thus aborted even at the moment of its signing since it shared with all the League's decisions the lack of effective means of implementation, other than the free will of the member states. The same fate afflicted a series of decisions made by the summit conferences since 1964 which established a joint command of Arab armed forces. While this command exists in theory it does not possess any independent power.

Lastly, in the economic field, a consistent comprehension of economic security has been lacking until very lately when efforts on the modification of the League's charter have picked up the issue. Nevertheless, the most effective measure on Arab security taken by the League lies in the domain of economic warfare in regard to Israel. Most Arab scholars agree that 'The Council on Economic Blockade of Israel is the only part of the League's political apparatus which acted with increasing efficiency since its inception, without faltering or collapsing under the effect of continued crises in inter-Arab political relations.'[10]

A systematic assessment of the League's security system must take as a starting point its basic function, namely, consolidating the state system, and judge this function according to changing needs. In this perspective one can assert with confidence that the Arab League did not promote the idea of Arab liberation from internal and external oppression and constraints. In fact, the League's charter did not mention independence as one of its goals at a time when the majority of Arab societies were effectively under occupation. This explains the judgement of independent Arab thinkers that 'The Arab League was not in reality a step towards a specific unification goal',[11] and that it was established 'to diffuse increasing Arab national consciousness which threatened the interests of neocolonialism'.[12]

However, an appropriate analysis of the League's role in Arab security or liberation should not stop at the conditions at its birth. A dynamic view of organizations is necessary to comprehend the changing character of such organizations.

Dimensions of Arab Regional Security

In a dynamic perspective, four dimensions are pertinent to the security competence of regional organizations. They are pertinence, cohesion, autonomy and efficacy.

Pertinence: Order of Security Concerns

Some security arrangements on the regional level seem to be directed against perceived sources of threat that are internal to the region, in the sense that they represent an integral part of the regionally-specific cultural and economic pattern. Other regional security arrangements seem to be directed against external sources of threat. Externality refers to either extra-regional powers, or, when geographically located in the region, to powers which make a rupture with the regionally-specific cultural and economic pattern. We can distinguish, therefore, between external and internal security concerns and, in terms of the arrangements based on them, between externally-oriented and internally-oriented security schemes.

When these concerns are reflected on the regional level, it is central to make the distinction, within internal security concerns, between regime security concerns and institutional security concerns. The former pertains to the maintenance of existing regimes in their domestic relationship as well as in their relationships to other regimes in a given region. The latter, on the other hand, pertains to dissatisfaction that is socially rooted with the institutional set-up which characterizes the region; whether this is derived from the state system itself, for example non-correspondence with social identity configurations, or from social contradictions between the nations involved over cultural and economic interactions.

External security concerns could be differentiated, according to their forms and degrees of immediacy, into military and ideological. Military threats are those which seek to shift a given balance of power and undermine territorial integrity, national independence or welfare of one or more states. Ideological threats are determined by cultural, ideological or psychological influence over a certain society by an alien power.

The pertinence of national or regional security schemes is demonstrated by the degree to which the specific order of security concerns on which they are based coincides with the matrix of socially manifested needs and rights for security.

The possibility of divergence between the societal right for security on the one hand, and the specific order of security concerns in a given regional scheme on the other, springs from many sources. For example, regime security is likely to be maximized at the expense of societal security. The quest of certain regimes for greater security may push them to compromise or undermine national security. And regimes may contract one superpower's support and invoke the hostility of the other even when the former constitutes the real danger to national security.

The pertinence of the security scheme of a regional organization is high when:

(a) external concerns precede internal concerns;
(b) issues of institutional security precede issues of regime security; and
(c) military threats are given primacy over ideological challenges.

The application of these ideas to the Arab League security scheme yields mixed conclusions.

In the first place, the most important fact in the Arab security system is that the member states of the Arab League rely only very marginally, in drawing and implementing their security policies, on the principle of collective security as embodied in the Arab League (especially in the treaty on joint defence). Therefore, we are confronted in the Arab regional system with an agglomeration of individual security policies for which the Arab League's security system represents the least common denominator and basically just a propaganda plane.

Secondly, in terms of its legal structure the League's measure of pertinence of the security of the Arab system is somewhere in the middle. This is demonstrated by several factors:

(a) External security concerns take clear precedence over internal security concerns. Evidence of this fact can be found in certain important decisions related to cases of disputes or opposition between the two fields of security. Two such cases are highly demonstrative. The first case is the West Bank crisis in 1950. The League dismissed as illegal the Jordanian claim that annexation of the West Bank was vital for Jordan's security. The collective Arab interest in maintaining the independence and integrity of Palestine took primacy over individual regimes' claims for security.[13] A second case arose when the Arab League rejected, in the Baghdad Conference of 1979, Egypt's peace treaty with Israel, and implemented the decision taken in 1950 that any member state which pursues or actually contracts a separate peace should be expelled from the Arab League. The supremacy of external over internal security concerns is further shown by the fact that the most positive and legally binding act of the League is represented by the treaty on joint defence. This must, however, be balanced by the fact that the treaty has scarcely moved from a mere legal commitment to reality.

(b) Within internal security, regime security concerns take clear precedence over institutional concerns. The League has not initiated any positive plan of action to mitigate or solve contradictions between Arab societies arising from territorial injustices or mischiefs in economic and cultural exchanges. Meanwhile, a good portion of the League's activity was spent on mediation in inter-regime disputes.

(c) Within external security concerns, military security takes a clear precedence over ideological security issues. The League did not yield to the pressures of certain Arab regimes which aimed at making Communism and the Soviet Union the chief threat to Arab security. Accordingly, most security proposals which were built on this assumption (the Baghdad Pact and the Islamic alliance) had to be institutionalized outside the League framework, in fact as alternatives to that framework.

However, a great deal of this pertinence is lost between

theoretical omissions and ineffective implementation of legally binding commitments. Many essential components of Arab external security were omitted both in theory and in practice. And in many instances other basic components of Arab security were lost due to failure in action.

Cohesiveness

When regional organizations lack the power to legislate and implement security policies independently of its member states, the cohesiveness of individual states' security policies acquires the greatest importance. Cultural homogeneity and continuity of economic pattern throughout the region furnish the basis for a certain level of cohesiveness. In certain regions of the Third World cultural and economic homogeneity is ruptured by artificial implantation of colonial settlement societies which draw on the aggressive aspects of western cultural patterns. Those societies tend to be over-militarized and to play the role of sub-imperialism, especially in the military-political sphere.

Within the Arab world Israel represents a model case of violent intrusion which shatters the overall homogeneity of the area. But what is important is not the break which Israel represents with the surrounding cultural and economic pattern, but the fact that this break serves as the milestone of imperialist practices in the region.

Negative spillover effects of Israeli colonialist practices might not have had profound consequences on Arab unity if the Arab League had managed to serve as the catalyst for a real process of creative reconstruction of Arab culture. Symbolic assertiveness might have transcended idle homogeneity to a positive cohesiveness as a great asset for a strategy of resistance. But the League was too embattled, by inter-regime disputes, to undertake this task.

In other regional state systems incohesiveness is manifested in an ideological polarization which has to be resolved in the context of intensive historical interactions. One model is the case of a revolutionary state which, through its messianic role, seeks to revitalize the cultural and political patterns of its respective region. It is possible that the struggle which ensues with the surrounding regimes will eventually lead to reconstruction of the regional system on new lines. In many other cases, especially when the conservative environment has a greater strategic depth, the struggle ends up with the defeat of the revolutionary regime. The Concert of Europe (1815–71), for example, was installed as a counter-revolutionary hegemonic system against revolutionary France and later against the 1848 Revolution.

Another extreme case is the reverse of the previous one. It takes place when a counter-revolutionary regime holds power in one major state in the regional system and seeks to upset a revolutionary tide in the whole region. The Nazi experience was one such case.

The Arab world represents no such extreme cases. The ideological struggle between Arab regimes expressed the contradictions between different modalities of an inheritance situation, but in so doing it also manifested a more profound conflict between the striving for liberation, on the one hand, and the deep-seated legacy of backwardness and colonialism on the other.

The striving for liberation in the Arab world revealed itself in various shades of petty bourgeois radicalism at various points in time. Radical ideologies were generally composed of certain elements: anti-imperialist inclination, call for pan-Arabism, quest for distributive justice, an economic system of state ownership and control and a modernized image of political Islam. These ideologies, however, were eclectic, built on a technocratic-authoritarian model, and armed with such thematic elements that are prone to lapse into the advocacy of a renewed system of privileges. Their performance in reality was generally regulated by implacable misorientation between radical outrage and readiness for disorganized retreat. All these elements were further reinforced by managerial incompetence.

The fundamental similarity of radical ideologies did not lead to greater unity between radical regimes. In fact, ideological similarity was strangely associated with petty frictions between regimes. This may be accounted for, on the ideological plane, by a mix of factors: organizational autocentrism (Ba'athists v. Nasserites), a tendency towards statism and exclusivist control and the pull of historically peculiar debates and controversies.

The legacy of backwardness and colonialism, on the other hand, was manifested in certain Arab regimes which advocated a mix of ideologies. Other than the case of Tunisia, the general ideological pattern of these regimes was composed of several elements: inflated obsession with Communist danger, emphasis on an archaic image of political Islam, justifications based on norms and history of sultanic authoritarianism, economic liberalism and an instrumentally justified alliance with western powers.

In turn, the fundamental similarity of these conservative ideologies could have led the regimes which adopted them into orchestrated actions. This has been minimal because of the isolationist policies pursued by these regimes in the Arab arena, and because of competing claims for the historical representation of the religious ideal.

The outcome of the struggle between these ideological trends was a great magnitude of ideological incohesiveness, mixed with mobile alliance formation and propensity to hold to the minimum degree of unity.

Ideological incohesiveness within the Arab regional system fluctuated over time according to changes in regimes. These fluctuations reflected upon individual security policies of various regimes. The ideological impact on these policies could be traced in the differences within the Arab system on three major aspects of security: philosophy, approaches to security and its functional support fields.

In the Arab world the concept of security is implicated in the same general duality of nation (or state) and religion. Radical regimes view security more from a statist and national angle. For these regimes security means a condition which helps the nation (the Arab nation) to transcend its state of fragmentation through struggle against its enemies. The proper approach to this security relies on manipulating the environment (the international system) in such a way as to promote the chances of overcoming colonialism and economic backwardness. In fact, basically nationalist (pan-Arabist) movements have passed through a process of political and economic radicalization as a result of experiments with this concept of security. When installed in power these movements resorted to the Soviet Union as their major global ally and the major source for armaments and economic aid. This coincided with the high points of internal radicalism.[14]

Conservative regimes, on the other hand, view security more from a passive religious angle. To them security means a system which insulates society from external influences which lead to cultural restructuring.[15] But since these regimes are highly liberal in the field of economic exchange, their major preoccupation has become the improvement of censorship whose aim is to separate economic exchange and organizational innovations from their cultural content. Hostility towards sources of political and cultural change push these regimes to an extreme anti-Communist stand.

By implication, approaches to security reflect both anti-Communism and fetishism of power and commodity. The cornerstone of their security is almost complete reliance on the West, and the US in particular, for protection. This reliance is contracted by a bargain. In return for organically linking the economy and military of these societies to the West, the latter provides a system of protection that is culturally filtered to ensure correspondence with regime needs and images.

These two images of security are variously mixed with the classic statist conception of security in accord with degrees of complexity and sophistication of Arab societies. They have come into conflict in the arena of Arab politics. But in so far as the League is concerned, the balances between those two images, for most of the time, made the League hold fast to the statist image of security appropriately flavoured with slogans of Arabism.

Mode of Power Derivation: Autonomy versus Cliency

Regional systems have been conceptualized as being subordinate to the global system. This implies not only that regional systems are less important determinants of political change, but also that they are themselves, at least partially, determined by the global system.[16] This is shown by modes of power derivation in regional systems.

However, regional systems are subordinate neither equally nor in the same way. Regions located in the inner circles of both superpowers' security systems tend to be dominated by one or the other superpower. Regional organizations built in those regions are literally underwritten by one of the superpowers. In other words, these organizations derive their power to a great measure from the superpowers, and they are doomed to function as forums based on collective cliency.

Regions collected in the outer fringes of the superpowers' security system have a more complex status. By virtue of strategic distance from the first order of global balance they can maintain a certain level of autonomy from both superpowers. Regional organizations established in these regions have to derive a good deal of their power from their constituent states. Nevertheless, while the regional system is autonomous in this case from each of the superpowers individually, its real autonomy from the global system, or more specifically from the balance of power between the two great world alliances, is only relative and partial.

Looking at power in a functional sense, i.e. from the vantage point of uses to which it can be put, we can conclude that the greater the magnitude of change or tasks to be accomplished in a given regional system the less real autonomy is this system likely to possess. This also corresponds to the proposition that the greater strategic significance a region has the less real autonomy it is likely to demonstrate in relation to the global balance of power. On the other hand, individual regimes in regional systems vary in the extent to which they derive their power from sources external to their respective states and regions.

There is no question that the Arab world possesses intrinsic strategic significance, and that it has been passing through a process of substantial change in both its internal socio-economic character and in its political regional structure. The existence of the state of Israel as a violent and expansive intruder has added a great burden and source of conflict. Accordingly, the connection between the Arab regional system on the one hand and the global system on the other has been very strong since the inception of the former.

The Arab world was subject to the colonial western system. By the end of the Second World War its quest for a formally independent regional structure was underwritten by Britain, the greatest power in the area at the time. The rise of the Soviet Union and the US had given the region a greater opportunity for real autonomy in its relationship with each of the two global alliances. Radical Arab regimes tried to take advantage of the situation by pushing for greater autonomy for the region as a whole. In this period the Arab League moved rapidly out of the British umbrella and adopted a balanced position with regard to both the superpowers.

With the passing of time the Arab system saw the relative autonomy it had achieved being increasingly eroded. The major reason for this erosion was the substantial increase in the magnitude of insecurity in the system due to both a faster rate of socio-economic change and the failure of the system to meet the challenge of Israeli expansionism.

The increasing loss of autonomy on the part of the Arab system revealed itself in a process of marginalization of the Arab League in overall Arab politics, especially after the isolation of Egypt since 1979. What underlay this process was the proliferation and deepening of the individual regimes' reliance on cliency to one of the two superpowers, especially to the United States.

This situation of erosion of autonomy could have been avoided if Arab regimes agreed to undermine the state-centric model of their regional organization in the direction of greater unity. Contrarywise, the reinforcement of properties of sovereignty in the context of increasing insecurity eventually leads to a greater distrust in the capacity of the regional system to provide adequate support for the constituent states. And this distrust pushes these states to greater reliance on superpower protection.

Efficacy

Arab thought which tends to condemn the Arab League for its ineffectiveness ignores the fact that effectiveness can only be measured relative to the tasks which it addresses itself to accomplish. It is also true, however, that a regional organization could, in the course of evolution, pursue tasks which lay beyond its formal assignments. In fact, the vitality of such organizations is shown by the expansion of such tasks. Such vitality is contingent on objective factors that are germane to the system's characteristics.

The security competence of a regional organization hinges on three major objective factors: scope of threat, availability of extra-regional sources of support and the power structure within the system.

(a) The broader the scope of threat, i.e. the more the number of states facing the threat, the greater the incentive for solidarity in security fields and the wider the base for potential regional security schemes. In the Arab world, where the greatest source of threat is represented by the state of Israel, geographical distance from this source makes for illusions of natural immunity from aggression in a majority of Arab states. Consequently, the level of real participation of these states in the League's security arrangement is very low.

(b) The level of commitment to a regional organization's security arrangement also hinges on the availability of extra-regional protection or support. When other conditions are equal, a state tends to prefer extra-regional protection over a commitment to a regional security arrangement when the former does not imply a direct colonial relationship and when trust in the latter is minimal. Several Arab states, especially the weak ones which are economically tied to the West, have traditionally relied on western guarantees for their security and territorial integrity. This may last as long as oil exports and oil wealth continue to be vital considerations for the western security system. Consequently, the participation of these states (e.g. Saudi Arabia, the Gulf states) in the League's security arrangement could be expected to remain minimal and hesitant.

(c) The structure of regional power has much to do with the security competence of regional organizations. The presence of strong regional leadership, for example, is a function of the given configuration of power. This leadership promotes the chances for greater security competence on the part of a regional organization. But it may also stimulate fears in other states to the point of considering it as another source of security threats.

The structure of power relations could be examined, in form, on two dimensions: the degree of concentration of power among the region's units, and the degree of polarization and mobility of alliance formation among these units. A highly diffuse power structure presents little chance for the emergence of strong regional leadership, and tends accordingly to lack a unified orientation to security issues. This lack could be compensated for by a moderate level of polarization so that a core set of states undertakes the functions of leadership without substantial opposition. A high level of polarization in the context of diffused power splits the region with potentially contradictory images of security.

A highly concentrated power structure produces effective leadership. The greatest power acts to underwrite the whole regional security or orchestrate security policies of individual states after its own image of security. When polarization is very low this hegemonic security system is taken for granted and becomes almost unchallengeable. The outcome is different when polarization is very high. In this case, the greatest power itself is perceived as the major source of threat by the antagonistic bloc of states.

The Arab world is characterized by a structure of power that is neither highly concentrated nor highly diffuse. Polarization tends to be high in various issue-areas, but alliance formation is closer to fluidity rather than fixity because of rapidity of regime change and multiplicity of sources of threat for different Arab states. Under these conditions the Arab system tends to be formed into sets of states which group and degroup at various points in time and over varying issues of concern. This prevents the system from constructing stable security institutions and deprives it of the advantages from accumulated experience and mutual trust.

To the previous characteristic of the system we must add another important feature. The Arab system has moved over time to a more

diffuse power structure. This is attributed to the unique phenomenon of oil wealth in the last decade. The concentration of certain
sources of power in certain states, e.g. population and military
capabilities in Egypt, is balanced by the concentration of other
sources of power in other states, e.g. oil wealth in Saudi Arabia and
the Gulf mini states.[17] The effect of this factor is that Egypt's traditional leadership role in the Arab world has been persistently
undermined in the last two decades.

Conclusion

Back to the State-centric Model or a New Initiative?

At this moment, the Arab world stands in complete disarray. The
scope of internal instability, e.g. inter-regime conflicts and civil
wars, is enormous. Arab states are pulled away from the central
concern of Arab societies by involving themselves in marginal but
destructive conflicts with other oppressed nations, e.g. the Iraq-
Iran War, the Sudan-Ethiopia conflict. Moreover, Arab states, one
after the other, are slipping away from an Arab to an American
security umbrella. While all this cannot be attributed to the failure
of the Arab League, this failure has certainly played a major role in
making this outcome possible.

Under these stresses, Arab thinkers have been assiduously
searching for a way out of the crisis. A good number of Arab intellectuals moved in the direction of reforming the Arab League.
Their efforts culminated in the new draft charter, work on which
was completed by March 1980. The new charter included many
innovations. The goals of this new charter were to institutionally
modernize the League and to eliminate some of the old charter's
shortcomings. All these attempts at innovation went unheeded. The
draft charter was not formally adopted by the summit or the
council. In fact, it would have been a surprise to everyone if this
draft was adopted at this point in time when the Arab world is
disintegrating.

But even if the new draft was adopted, it is doubtful that it would
have made a substantial difference to the present Arab situation,
for several reasons. In the first place, the draft charter has not
transcended the same basic model on which the charter of 1945 was
based, i.e. the state-centric model. Properties of sovereignty are re-
emphasized on more than one occasion. Arab unity is not

considered a direct goal. The draft charter committed the League only to 'lead the Arab nation towards conditions conducive to realization of unity'. All other principles and mechanisms initiated by the draft charter were either formulated vaguely or made contingent upon the consent of the member states. In brief, the draft charter was an attempt to manipulate the will of the member states without significantly adapting the political structure of the League to the new challenges and circumstances of the Arab world by subtracting from the sovereignty of member states. If the aim is to hold the centrifugal forces, which have disassembled Arab societies, in check, we are forced to conclude that the draft charter falls far short of the necessary minimum.

Notes

1. Mohammed Ayoob (ed.), *Regional Securty in the Third World*, Chapter 1.
2. This term was coined by Nettl. See J. P. Nettl and R. Robinson, *The International System and the Modernization of Societies* (Basic Books, New York, 1968), pp. 79–86.
3. Arab societies have never ceased to feel the strains of identity crisis. Conflicts between identities and fluctuations in patterns of identification characterize political evolution over the last century; lines of Arab identification are religion, regionalism, localism and culture. This means that various institutions built on one or more of these lines have been proposed as alternatives to the Arab League. See Ghassan Salama, 'The League and Arab Blocs' in Centre for Arab Unity Studies, *The League of Arab States: The Reality and Ambition* (Centre for Arab Unity Studies, Beirut, 1983), pp. 771–884, in Arabic.
4. See Ahmad Goma'a, *The Foundation of the League of Arab States: Wartime Diplomacy and Inter-Arab Politics, 1941–45* (Longman, London, 1977), pp. 105–12.
5. Article II, *The Charter of the League of Arab States*.
6. The League of Arab States, *Proceedings of the General Arab Conference's Preparatory Committee* (Official Press of Bolak, Cairo, 1946).
7. Al Azhar Bo'oni, 'Systems of Decisions in the League of Arab States' in *The Question of Modifying the Charter of the League of Arab States* (Faculty of Law and Political and Economic Sciences, University of Tunisia, Tunis, 1981), p. 171.
8. See the debates on this point in Centre for Arab Unity Studies, pp. 93–9.
9. A. B. Auda, 'Arab League and the Palestinian Question', *Egyptian Journal of Political Science*, no. 67, July (1970), p. 146.
10. Hassan Nafa'a, 'The Political Role of the Arab League in the Independence of Some Arab Countries and in the Palestinian Question' in Centre for Arab Unity Studies, p. 149.
11. Ali Mohafaza, 'Historical Genesis of the Arab League' in Centre for Arab Unity Studies, p. 66.
12. See K. S. Hossary in Centre for Arab Unity Studies, p. 100.
13. See B. B. Ghali, *The Arab League and the Settlement of Local Disputes* (Arab Research and Studies Institute, Cairo, 1977), pp. 43–56, in Arabic.
14. Michael Hudson, *Arab Politics: The Search for Legitimacy* (Yale University

Press, New Haven and London, 1977), pp. 231–4.

15. In this point lies the fault of several analysts who were overwhelmed by Huntington's 'king' dilemma. In fact, traditional monarchies in the Arab world have managed to articulate modernity of ways with conventional modes of thinking and acting. For an illustration of this dilemma, see John Waterbury, *The Commander of the Faithful* (Columbia University Press, New York, 1970), especially Chapter 7.

16. L. Binder, 'The Middle East as a Subordinate International System' in Falk and Mendlovitz (eds), *Regional Politics and World Order* (W. H. Freeman and Company, San Francisco, 1973), pp. 328–34 and pp. 355–66.

17. Gamil Mattar, 'The Arab League, the Arab Regional System and Challenges of the Eighties' in Centre for Arab Unity Studies, pp. 887–907.

COMMENTS

Obaid-Ul-Haq

Since 1945 international relations have been marked by two seemingly contradictory trends. First, there has been an unprecedented increase in the number of sovereign states as a result of decolonization and the break-up of existing political units. Secondly, independent states have sought to create supra-national organizations to further their national interest.

A rapid increase in recent decades in the number of regional organizations in different parts of the globe is a testimony to, and a recognition of, two fundamental trends in the modern world. First, states today face many problems that do not yield to unilateral national solutions but respond only to joint or co-ordinated multinational efforts. Secondly, modern technology and expanding economy are making countries interdependent and inducing their political and economic elites to take a broader view of their interests.

A regional framework, in this context, besides promoting mutually beneficial co-operation in diverse fields of activity, can also provide institutional mechanisms for peaceful resolution of contentious issues that inevitably arise as the by-product of this very interdependence. Moreover, a regional approach to their common international concerns is likely to enhance their bargaining position *vis-à-vis* great powers, adversaries and other regional groups.

The League of Arab States — better known as the Arab League — was one of the earliest of regional organizations. Founded in 1945, the Arab League is a voluntary association of Arab states designed to strengthen the close ties linking them and to co-ordinate their policies and activities in areas of common interest. The Arab League is at present composed of 21 states including Somalia and Djibouti (which are not Arab states, strictly speaking) and the Palestine Liberation Organization (which is not a state). Egypt's membership has been suspended since March 1979 because of its treaty with Israel and the headquarters of the League have been moved from Cairo to Tunis.

It is worth emphasizing that states form or enter into regional organizations with a view to strengthening their individual security and separate viability. The purpose of regional groups is not to undermine state organization or to seek unification in a larger political entity: they are exercises in the consolidation of the state system. This is the inherent impulse of the state and Arab states are not immune to it.

This is precisely the focus of Mohammed El Sayed Said's paper. Written from a radical perspective it launches a vigorous and sustained attack on the institution of the state and the notion of security. Said argues that the major flaw of regional organizations — the Arab League in particular — is that they are conceived as instruments fashioned to promote the security of the territorial sovereign state. His premise is that the idea of 'state security' is unsuitable and inapplicable to the newly independent post-colonial Third World countries.

Said has several objections to the use of the security perspective in the analysis of the needs and problems of Third World states. Of these three seem to be important:

1. The idea of security is deeply enmeshed in the status-quo oriented mentality. By its very nature it is conservative in function. It serves the interests of dominant elites who inherited power from the colonialists and justifies their perception of national needs.
2. It fails to maintain the distinction between regime security and national security. The slogan of national security becomes a ploy to underwrite the security and hegemony of ruling groups.
3. In Third World states there is a need to strike a balance between order and change. Change is called for to promote social justice but insistence on state security prevents desirable social change.

In view of these biases implicit in the concept of security and paying greater attention to the urgent needs of the people in Third World states, Said postulates the idea of 'liberation' as contextually relevant, objective and a critical focus for a better view of Third World problems and its needs.

Nowhere in the paper does Said spell out what he means by liberation. It is, however, clear that he advocates that the Arab people transcend the state system and seek new political forms. He argues that the subservience of the Arab League to its component states is its major flaw. This is quite clear in his conclusion where he says, '. . . the efforts made for reforming the Arab League are misplaced, because what the Arab world needs is precisely a new initiative which transcends the state system'. He is not forthcoming and candid about what can replace the Arab states but one can assume that he is arguing for a pan-Arab state.

Said evaluates the performance of the Arab League on the basis of four criteria: pertinence, efficacy, cohesion and autonomy. The League's role and fortunes have fluctuated in response to the volatility of Arab politics and the endemic disunity of the Arabs. While there were periods of substantial unity of purpose and action — such as between 1967 and 1975 — there can be no two opinions about the fact that the Arab world now stands in complete disarray, exposed to both internal and external dangers.

I have several difficulties with Said's basic approach. In the first place, I believe his attack on the state is misconceived and misplaced. The institution of the state, whether we approve of it or not, is here to stay. I see no sign of its diminishing powers. On the contrary, the state's role in politics — both internal and external — is growing dramatically. The mystique of the state has conquered the world and people who do not have a state of their own are engaged in the struggle to establish one. Given the realities of the modern world the goal of transcending the state is an illusion. Like people everywhere the Arabs will have to seek their destiny within the confines of existing nation-states. The Arab League can help forge closer links among member states, provide a modality for their collective action, but it is hopeless to conceive of it as the harbinger of a pan-Arab political order.

It is a valid argument that more often than not the notion of state security has been a ploy and a mask to consolidate and further the interests of ruling groups and, therefore, one must make a distinction between regime security and state security. But the cognizance of this possibility does not in any way negate the fact that in operational terms the security of the state is linked to the security of the regime. The threat to the security of a regime invariably has profound implications for the integrity of the state. For this reason the question of the overthrow of a particular regime should never be considered in isolation from an equally weighty concern about what could replace it. Where no viable or preferable political alternative exists — as, I venture to suggest, is the case in many Middle East states and particularly in the Gulf region — the overthrow of the traditional order holds no clear prospect other than that of chaos, anarchy or, at best, a repressive dictatorship — military or Marxist. This is a matter of life and death for the people who live in these lands and it must be considered in the context of political realities, with a sense of responsibility and an awareness of possibilities and *not* in accordance with some fashionable political stance.

The present plight of the Arabs cannot be attributed to the institution of the territorial state or the shortcomings of the Arab League. The nation-states are here to stay and the Arabs will have to work with them and through them. The Arab League can provide a framework for the co-ordination of their national efforts and can become a useful forum for consultation about their common problems. Said has dismissed rather lightly the constructive role which the League played in the past such as in the peaceful resolution of conflicts between Arab states. The League has not lost its potential to become an active agent in inter-Arab affairs.

Said's paper is interesting and provocative and his logic is seemingly sound but it proceeds from questionable assumptions to conclusions which are unquestionably wrong.

LIST OF CONTRIBUTORS

Abdel Monem Said Aly Abdel Aal is at the Center for Political and Strategic Studies in Cairo.

Mohammed Ayoob is in the Department of International Relations at the Australian National University, Canberra.

Leszek Buszynski is in the Department of Political Science at the National University of Singapore.

Osama Al Ghazaly Harb is at the Center for Political and Strategic Studies in Cairo.

Obaid-Ul-Haq is in the Department of Political Science at the National University of Singapore.

Kamel S. Abu Jaber is at the Center of Strategic Studies at the University of Jordan in Amman.

Chandran Jeshurun is in the Department of History at the University of Malaya, Kuala Lumpur.

Arthur Lim Joo-Jock is at the Institute of Southeast Asian Studies in Singapore.

Arnfinn Jorfensen-Dahl is in the Department of Political Science at the National University of Singapore.

Sami Mansour Ahmed is at the Center for Political and Strategic Studies in Cairo.

Abdul Monem Al-Mashat is in the Faculty of Economics and Political Science at Cairo University.

Felipe B. Miranda is in the Department of Political Science at the University of the Philippines.

Sukh Deo Muni is in the School of International Studies at Jawaharlal Nehru University, New Delhi.

Robert O'Neill is Director of the International Institute of Strategic Studies in London.

Sukhumbhand Paribatra is at the Institute of Security and International Studies in the Faculty of Political Science at Chulalongkorn University, Bangkok.

Richard Pennell is in the Department of History at the National University of Singapore.

Muhammed Amien Rais is at Gajah Mada University in Indonesia.

Mohammed El Sayed Said is at the Center for Political and Strategic Studies in Cairo.

Chai-Anan Samudavanija is in the Faculty of Political Science at Chulalongkorn University, Bangkok.

Lau Teik Soon is in the Department of Political Science at the National University of Singapore.

Noordin Sopiee is at the Institute of Strategic and International Studies in Kuala Lumpur.

Juwono Sudarsono is in the Faculty of Social and Political Science at the University of Indonesia in Jakarta.

INDEX